Repertoires and Cycles of Collective Action

EDITED BY MARK TRAUGOTT

Duke University Press
Durham and London 1995

CW00504512

9
9

Except for "Recurrent patterns of collective action," by Mark Traugott,
" 'Initiator' and 'spin-off' movements: Diffusion processes in protest
cycles," by Doug McAdam, and "The roar of the crowd: Repertoires
of discourse and collective action among the Spitalfields silk weavers
in nineteenth-century London," by Marc W. Steinberg, the essays in
this book appeared originally in volume 17, numbers 2 and 3 of *Social
Science History*.

Library of Congress Cataloging-in-Publication Data

Repertoires and cycles of collective action / edited by Mark Traugott.
p.   cm.
Includes bibliographical references and index.
ISBN 0-8223-1527-0 (alk. paper) : $28.95. — ISBN 0-8223-1546-7
(pbk. : alk. paper) : $13.95
1. Protest movements.   2. Revolutions.   3. Government, Resistance
to.   I. Traugott, Mark.
HM281.R455   1994
303.6'4—dc20   94-37271

Contents

Recurrent Patterns of
Collective Action

MARK TRAUGOTT

THIS VOLUME is the outgrowth of two sessions that appeared on the schedule of the 1991 meetings of the Social Science History Association. Their respective themes were the concepts of repertoires and cycles of collective action. While most of the original papers gave primary emphasis to one or the other of these topics, all authors were urged to explore and comment upon the possible interrelations between the two. The resulting essays and the discussions that they provoked proved so promising that additional contributors were sought, in an effort to round out the range of theoretical perspectives and empirical case materials.

The result is an unusually varied array of geographical and historical points of reference. The reader will discover arguments framed within the context of eighteenth- and nineteenth-century Britain (Tilly and Steinberg), nineteenth-century France (Traugott), and twentieth-century Italy (Tarrow). But Europe, that ever-fertile testing ground for novel historical ideas, is by no means the exclusive focus of this collection. The New World is also well represented by the case of the early nineteenth- and late twentieth-century United States (Calhoun), by the Civil Rights movement

I would like to acknowledge the role of Ron Aminzade who, as co-chair of the 1991 program committee, helped instigate those sessions and, as an editor of *Social Science History*, helped arrange to publish several of these papers in the summer and fall 1993 issues of that journal. My collaborators and I have benefited enormously from his wise counsel at every stage of this collective project. I would also like to thank Michael Hanagan, who served as commentator for one of the Social Science History Association panels.

of the 1960s (McAdam), and by Guatemala and El Salvador in the 1980s (Brockett). A long-term perspective that draws upon a remarkable data set covering the history of contention in Japan from 1590 to 1877 (White) completes the roster. Readers may recognize in this list of authors not only the two innovators whose names are most closely associated with the concepts of repertoires and cycles of protest, but also several highly regarded analysts of collective action and a couple of younger scholars whose work points in provocative new directions for social movement theory.

The logic that determined the order in which the contributions appear is easier to explain than to defend. The first three chapters are primarily oriented to the discussion and analysis of repertoires of collective action. The second three, conversely, bear mainly on cycles of protest. The last two essays constitute wide-ranging applications or extensions of social movements theory which fit neither of the preceding categories perfectly, but demonstrate the heuristic value of these concepts for the understanding of historical and contemporary collective action. Since every author considers both focal concepts in some measure, this organizational device has a somewhat arbitrary character. I have nonetheless adopted it as a convenient way of framing the following comments on specific chapters.

REPERTOIRES OF COLLECTIVE ACTION

Charles Tilly, the creator of the repertoire concept, provides a rapid overview of its origin and evolution as well as an illustration of how it can be applied. Many readers will be intrigued to learn that it developed as an alternative to his own typology of competitive, reactive, and proactive collective action. Though the distinction, especially between reactive and proactive styles of protest, continues to be used by many social movement analysts, Tilly himself had concluded by 1977 that the categories were not mutually exclusive and that the continuum they implied more than hinted at modernization theory, the last remnants of which he had long struggled to purge from his conceptual scheme. The metaphor of the repertoire allowed him to stress, without unnecessary teleological implications, both the great continuity that collective action exhibits over many generations and the sweeping changes in the accepted form of protest that occur only at long intervals.

Tilly demonstrates the utility of the concept with reference to contention in Great Britain from 1758 to 1834. This period witnessed a shift from an eighteenth-century repertoire that he terms *parochial* (i.e., confined to a single community), *particular* (i.e., situationally specific), and *bifurcated* (i.e., involving direct action on local issues but working through patrons or other intermediaries where national issues were concerned) to a nineteenth-century repertoire that was *national*, *modular*, and *autonomous*.

This represents a significant specification of the differences between the two modern European repertoires when compared with Tilly's earlier formulations. He had previously emphasized that the collective action of the past century and a half was distinctive for its national orientation, but this chapter explicitly links the autonomy participants exercise as well as their increased access to public actors to the decline of direct (and, in particular, violent) collective action.

Tilly's discussion of the modularity of routines of collective action is also new to this description of the nineteenth-century repertoire. This notion, which refers to the ready transferability of recognizable forms through time and space, creates a bridge to the writings of Tarrow, who first pointed to the role that modular transmission plays in cyclical peaks of protest. But by designating modularity as a distinguishing trait of the nineteenth-century repertoire, Tilly also creates a tension. For Tarrow, their modular nature is what accounts for the success of established patterns of protest. Actors revive known forms because the latter make it possible to mobilize without the burden of learning or inventing wholly new techniques of contention. To the extent that modularity facilitates mobilization by reducing start-up costs, however, it should be a characteristic of repertoires *in general*. The conditions of late-modern social life may accelerate the rate of propagation, but the modular advantage might be expected to apply to *all* forms of repertorial action.

In Tilly's own judgment, the repertoire concept has been something less than a "roaring success." He acknowledges that, in its original formulation, the notion of the repertoire is more a suggestive metaphor than a precise analytical tool. As he also notes, instances of parallel invention abound. A recently translated work by the historians Farge and Revel (1991) provides a further example. The authors examine a flurry of rumors concerning the abduction of children in mid-eighteenth-century Paris which sparked attacks against police and suspected police informers. The spread of these rumors and the outbreak of mob actions are observed to follow a "scenario of conflict" that exhibited considerable stability over time. In a chapter entitled "The Rules of Rebellion," Farge and Revel describe how participants' actions appear to be at once constrained by accepted patterns of collective action and open to reinterpretation and innovation: "The events unrolled like a play that takes its framework from tradition but is improvised and scripted by the actors. The development was not a random affair however; the rioters themselves chose their locations and forms of expression and in exercising this choice they were constantly in the process of creating the significance of their own protest" (ibid.: 57). Like Tilly, Farge and Revel see the origins of such patterns in the rhythms of daily life and their significance in what they tell us of the interaction between contenders and authorities. They conclude that in the Parisian case they examined, mob action was aimed at establishing a "common, unwritten code of conduct between Parisians and the police" (66, 72).

My own attempt to apply the repertoire perspective to the use of barricades in France, beginning in 1588, arrives at similar conclusions. Just as Tilly leads one to expect, barricades originated as a by-product of everyday practices. And just as he suggests, the detailed examination of the evolution of their form and function over the course of the nineteenth century reveals, through the mutual adaptations of insurgents and social control forces, the interactive nature of what at first glance appears to be an almost ritualized behavior.

The study of barricades is also used to shed light on Sewell's and Tilly's alternative periodizations of the great sea change in forms of European contention. But neither of their models nor the repertoire concept itself is very effective in accounting for the remarkable persistence of the barricade across a span of time that encompasses what are supposed to be two distinct styles of collective action. To some extent, the notion of two separate repertoires is rescued by the observation that the use of barricades undergoes a fundamental transformation in the course of the nineteenth century, so that earlier, utilitarian barricades and later, symbolic barricades become distinctive elements in different styles of contention.

engendered directly by the crown's efforts to mobilize for war. The newspaper also reported multiple prosecutions of women and men who, the previous year, had joined in public resistance to the militia draft or in the "pillaging" of food supplies. Local conflicts occurred more frequently than events concerning nationally articulated issues. The rarer war-connected struggles, however, made more highly visible connections between contention and the structure of power. Those connections, although less obvious at a local scale, actually informed local events as well. Battles between smugglers and troops, vengeance against pub owners and child molesters, destruction of enclosures, and pulling down of dangerous houses did the work of everyday popular politics.

Through these vignettes of popular contention—of occasions on which people gathered and made claims on other people, including holders of power—we glimpse the issues that brought eighteenth-century Britons into open confrontation with each other, as well as the kinds of actors who joined the fray. Clearly, military men often participated in conflicts with the state, on both sides of the line. Patently, vengeance against moral and political offenders occupied a prominent place in the contention of ordinary people. Evidently, local people and local issues, rather than nationally organized programs and parties, entered repeatedly into the day's collective confrontations. As compared with today, these British conflicts of 1758 breathe the musty air of antiquity. In popular contention a great deal has changed since then.

CONTENTION IN 1833

Instead of being spread out evenly over the succeeding two centuries, however, many of the critical changes in popular contention from 1758 to the present crowded into a few decades around the end of the eighteenth century. More like a volcano than a glacier, the forms of conflict changed in bursts. By the 1820s and 1830s, as a result, many features of today's contention were already visible. A comparison of 1833's conflicts with those of 1758 will help us see them.

Three-quarters of a century after 1758, Great Britain had been at peace in Europe and America for 18 years. The vast effort of the Napoleonic Wars had outstripped any previous mobilization and had propelled Britain into becoming the world's most powerful

state. In the midst of war (1801) Great Britain had become part
of the (forcibly and uneasily) United Kingdom of Great Britain
and Ireland. The wars with Napoleon ended, Britain had shifted
its warmaking power to Asian conquests and—with the critical
exception of Ireland—deployed its troops less and less at home.

Not that domestic conflict had ended or contentious claims
ceased. Consider a series of events that occurred in Great Britain during the first few days of January 1833. Factory weavers of
Paisley, near Glasgow, capped a long struggle by holding a public
meeting with the town's cloth manufacturers and by bargaining to
gain a minimum wage. In Nairn (Inverness) a "rabble" attacked
the coach of newly elected MP Colonel Baillie as he changed
horses on his way south. ("The better classes," tut-tutted a report
the *Morning Chronicle* of 10 January reprinted from the *Inverness Journal*, "were scandalised by so lawless an outrage.") In
Edinburgh another MP, George Sinclair, chaired a meeting of the
Society for the Abolition of Church Patronage; unsurprisingly, the
participants sent a petition to Parliament urging the abolition of
church patronage in Scotland. A wardmote (that is, a general assembly of the ward) in Cripplegate Without, London, resolved to
petition the Court of Common Council for the regular election of
aldermen and for open meetings of the court. In Chelsea a group
of men who were playing dominoes in a pub left their game and
beat a man they accused of being a common informer.

Nor was that all. A dinner of 150 to 200 Midlothian Whig
electors cheered their MP, Sir John Dalrymple, in Dalkeith as
he proclaimed the need for further reforms in government. In
Withyam (Sussex) a group of unauthorized hunters—poachers in
authorities' eyes—fought a "desperate affray" with Lord De La
Warr's gamekeepers, breaking a warden's arm in two places. At a
meeting in Liverpool reelected MP Lord Sandon described himself as satisfied with the recent Reform Bill, prepared to press for
church reforms, but was hostile to such innovations as the vote by
ballot.

Amid all the news from England, Scotland, and Wales filtered
reports of a Tithe War in Ireland: resistance by Catholic cottagers
to Anglican divines' collections of the obligatory ecclesiastical
tithe. These abundant reports only take us through the first four
days of January 1833 (LT [*Times* of London] 3, 7, 9, 11, 19 Jan.,
2 Feb. 1833; MC [*Morning Chronicle*] 3, 7, 10, 11, 18 Jan. 1833;
MOP [*Mirror of Parliament*] 11 Feb. 1834); the remainder of the

year saw more than 600 similar events—events in which people gathered publicly and made visible claims on others, including powerholders—occur somewhere in Great Britain.

Claim-making events of 1833 shared some features with those of 1758. In 1833, poachers continued to ply their trade and to battle gamekeepers. Unmasked informers were no more likely to escape a beating in 1833 than 75 years earlier. Disgruntled citizens still stoned the coaches of unpopular public figures, although that particular form of direct action was fading from prominence.

Other forms of contention had altered greatly. Pubs and coffee-houses figured much more often as the sites or starting points of contention in 1833 than they had in 1758. By 1833 the proportion of claim-making events that included physical violence had greatly declined. Attacks on prisoners pilloried for sexual offenses, common in the 1750s, had virtually disappeared, as had the public tribute to a popular figure who was placed in the stocks or otherwise subjected to judicial humiliation; indeed, public whipping and the pillory were on their way out, in favor of various forms of transportation and incarceration (Beattie 1986: 450–618).

Still more had changed between 1758 and 1833. Turnouts were occasions on which workers in a trade of a given town gathered, deliberated, decided to quit work, went from shop to shop inducing those who were still working to join them, deliberated again, then presented common demands to all the local masters; such turnouts had become more frequent by 1833. Public assemblies such as wardmotes and vestry meetings had gained importance. Named associations—the Society for the Abolition of Church Patronage, the National Political Union, the Society for Improving the Condition of Factory Children, and so on—had taken on new prominence. Above all, in 1833 the apparatus of public meetings recurred constantly: advertised assemblies open to all who shared an interest, elections of chairmen, presentations of speakers, resolutions, votes, acclamations, petitions.

Some meetings featured open debates, and a few of them conducted organizational business, but many of them consisted essentially of public displays of united will. At the meeting on abolition of church patronage in Edinburgh, for example, MP Sinclair opened the session by declaring:

> we come before you a society already established and some years in operation, and none can be expected to take a part

in our proceedings who is not himself a member of the institution, and consequently an approver of its objects. I know there are many men of great piety, intelligence, and respectability, who consider that to be the bulwark of our church which we consider to be its bane. If those individuals choose to hold any meeting for the purpose of expressing their opinions, they shall not experience from any member of this association the least interruption, and, on the other hand, I may venture to hope we shall experience no interruption to our proceedings. The object this society has in view is the entire and unqualified abolition of patronage. (LT 19 Jan. 1833, from the *Edinburgh Observer*)

Not all meetings proceeded so decorously. In the spring of 1833 radical and reformist organizers in the National Union of the Working Classes began planning a national convention bringing together delegates from different towns throughout Britain. Since the French Revolution, the idea of a grass-roots convention had stated an essentially Jacobin claim to popular sovereignty (Belchem 1978, 1981, 1985; Epstein 1990; Parssinen 1973). "The plan," noted Francis Place, "was such that they might evade the law at their first set out, for they could call it an universal suffrage association; even honest Lord Althorpe could not find fault with it, since he had his own Agricultural Association, which was similar as a body, to the proposed delegates" (BL Add [British Library, Additional Manuscripts] 27797). On 4 May the *Poor Mans Guardian* announced a general meeting in Cold Bath Fields for 13 May. The meeting's organizers, speaking for the National Political Union and the National Union of the Working Classes, issued a manifesto entitled "A National Convention, the Only Proper Remedy." It began:

FELLOW CITIZENS, The majority of the hereditary legislators obstinately and impudently oppose our just claims to representation. Treat their opposition with contempt; set the privileged villains and usurpers at defiance. This political club of hereditary self-elected law-makers has no proper authority either to concede or to withhold our just and irrefragable right to representation. Their privilege of nullifying the expressed will of the majority of the national is an unjustifiable usurpation, repugnant to reason and justice, which ought not to be tolerated for an instant longer. (Black 1969: 85)

It went on to propose a duly elected national convention. The petition that organizers had prepared for the meeting protested against individual land ownership, primogeniture, the funding system, and legislation protecting large landowners (Chase 1988: 161).

Despite the government's prohibition of the meeting in a proclamation of 11 May, 300 people assembled; after the Metropolitan Police arrived, the crowd swelled to 3,000 or 4,000. Altogether, about 1,800 policemen gathered to contain them. As the meeting's elected chairman (James Mee, who described himself as a "poor, industrious mechanic") spoke, 400 policemen marched into the crowd swinging truncheons; one policeman was killed and many civilians were wounded. (A jury ruled the policeman's death justifiable homicide, and Richard Carlile's radical *Gauntlet* published the jurymen's names in gold letters [Wiener 1983: 193].) Police captured four flags: an American flag; a tricolor with a beehive and the inscription "Equal rights and equal laws"; a small flag with a beehive, a bundle of sticks, and united hands; and a black flag featuring a death's head, crossbones, and the motto Liberty or Death (BL Add 27797, as well as multiple mentions in MC, LT, AR, HPD, and MOP). The Cold Bath Fields meeting turned into something very like a violent demonstration. Generally, the open meeting had become a kind of demonstration—indoor or outdoor—a coordinated way of publicizing support for a particular claim on holders of power. Frequently, a special-purpose association, society, or club called the meeting, and many meetings concerned national issues, emphatically including issues that the government and Parliament were on their way to deciding.

Although British people had assembled and made demands in other ways for many centuries, as of 1833 they had not long used the special-purpose association and its meetings for that purpose. Members of the eighteenth-century ruling classes, it is true, frequently formed associations for discussion, celebration, commemoration, or diversion, and sometimes they turned their associations to the ends of national politics. The early years of the French Revolution, furthermore, saw a proliferation of politically oriented associations before the government, at war with France, closed them down in 1794 and after. Except for the more conventional religious congregations, however, any sort of mass-membership organization remained suspect, and subject to tight control by public authorities, into the 1820s. The lobby—which was, literally, an organized effort to buttonhole MPs in the Parliament building's lobby—on behalf of recognized interests came into its own only during the eighteenth century. Whether local interests and ordinary people had a right to exert the same sort of pressure kept controversy going into the nineteenth century. A fortiori, general public meetings and street demonstrations on behalf of a self-defined interest took a long time to gain acceptance.

At the start of 1780, for example, the sheriff of Surrey had called a meeting of "noblemen, gentlemen, clergy, and freeholders" to discuss ways of trimming war-swollen governmental expenditures and to form, on the American model, Committees of Correspondence to coordinate discussion with like-minded people in other parts of Great Britain (LC 7 Jan. 1780: 26). Promoted by the Reverend Christopher Wyvill and members of the parliamentary opposition, similar meetings were taking place in much of Britain. But on 7 February another meeting of Surrey freeholders, convened by Lord Onslow, adopted a resolution declaring:

> Lest the proceedings of the Meeting called by the late High Sheriff of the County, on the 21st day of January last, should be considered the general sense of the County, we whose names are hereunto subscribed, the Sheriff, Lieutenant, Noblemen, Gentlemen, Clergy, and Freeholders of the County of Surrey, having taken into our serious consideration the said proceedings, do not object to the general prayer of the petition then agreed to, but we do, as good and loyal subjects, strongly protest against the Resolution for an Association and Committee of Correspondence, for the purposes therein mentioned, because we think such Associations and Committees of the most dangerous tendency, and coupled with Petitions, can, as we conceive, have no other meaning, than to overawe and control the free discussion and determination of the several matters contained therein by parliament, the only power intrusted by the constitution to judge and decide upon the same, thereby assuming a self-constituted power to overturn the legislature, the establishment of which was the great object of the glorious Revolution. (LC 8 Feb. 1780: 135)

Responding exactly one month later to a series of petitions against wastefulness in public expenditure from the newly formed Yorkshire Association, William Burrell said in Parliament:

He for one approved of petitions; he was himself a peti-
tioner, but he totally disapproved of committees and associations. . . . He knew of no way to collect the voice of the
majority of the people, but by the majority of the freeholders;
and . . . not above an eighth of that description had signed
the petitions. . . . They plainly aimed at the destruction of
the independency of parliament, by tying down the members
to certain measures. (Butterfield 1968: 253)

Formidable coalitions, organized at a national scale, crystallized
on both sides of the issue. The right to form associations and make
demands in their names—which indirectly asserted popular sovereignty—remained essentially contested in 1780. So did any other
public and collective effort to influence Parliament's decisions. By
1833 these practices were routine and uncontested.

REPERTOIRES THROUGH ALIEN EYES

Nevertheless, foreign visitors to Great Britain found British popular politics perplexing. Alexis de Tocqueville, who in August 1833
attended a London gathering on behalf of aid to exiled Poles,
considered British public meetings an impressive instrument of
democracy, where ordinary workers had the chance to speak up
and be heard (Spring 1980). "An extraordinary feature of the meeting," he mused, "was the way the aristocrats who were present had
to give way without saying a word; indeed, they were obliged to
flatter popular passions and prejudices in order to get indulgence
and applause" (Tocqueville 1958: 17).

Tocqueville's countryman baron d'Haussez, who visited England the same year, found the public *méting* (as he called it)
ridiculous and offensive, for essentially the same reasons that
made Tocqueville admire it. It was in the public meeting, thought
d'Haussez, that one saw the English people "deliberate on the
law, criticizing the behavior of the Cabinet, deciding everything,
and returning home sure that it has done great things, that it has
a will, that it thought everything the speakers said, in fact that
the speakers said nothing the people had not inspired" (d'Haussez
1833: 189–90). D'Haussez complained of strident, promise-filled
oratory, of petitions prepared in advance, of the presence of shopkeepers and badly dressed workers. "A meeting," he continued,

only brings together the lowest social classes, the most inflammable, the least likely to be guided by reason, and to balance the good and bad in a particular program. It will follow the plans of the turbulent, anxious, and dangerous party, and will lend popular support to its leaders" (d'Haussez 1833: 193). In short, public meetings smacked of direct democracy and popular sovereignty.

Tocqueville and his countrymen saw that the British had fashioned a new political instrument, and were using it enthusiastically. In 1833 the great themes of public meetings were elections, the behavior of the national government, treatment of the Irish, administration of local affairs, maintenance of trade, the abolition of slavery, and taxes—essentially the same issues as Parliament was debating that very year. Although meetings also tended local affairs and private interests, they had become a major device for exerting pressure in national politics. Over the previous few decades a new variety of claim-making had taken shape in Britain. Today, to a large degree, citizens of Britain and other Western countries still make their claims by means of the same routines. British contention had moved from the alien world of the eighteenth century into our own era. Mass popular politics had taken hold at a national scale in Great Britain.

It is useful, I think, to organize an analysis of that great transformation around an unfamiliar concept: repertoires of contention. The word *repertoire* identifies a limited set of routines that are learned, shared, and acted out through a relatively deliberate process of choice. Repertoires are learned cultural creations, but they do not descend from abstract philosophy or take shape as a result of political propaganda; they emerge from struggle. People learn to break windows in protest, attack pilloried prisoners, tear down dishonored houses, stage public marches, petition, hold formal meetings, organize special-interest associations. At any particular point in history, however, they learn only a rather small number of alternative ways to act collectively.

The limits of that learning, plus the fact that potential collaborators and antagonists likewise have learned a relatively limited set of means, constrain the choices available for collective action. The means, furthermore, articulate with and help shape a number of social arrangements that are not part of the collective action itself, but channel it to some degree: police practices, laws of assembly, rules of association, routines for informal gatherings, ways of displaying symbols of affiliation, opposition, or protest, means of reporting news, and so on. By analogy with a jazz musician's improvisations or the impromptu skits of a troupe of strolling players (rather than, say, the more confining written music interpreted by a string quartet), people in a given place and time learn to carry out a limited number of alternative collective-action routines, adapting each one to the immediate circumstances and to the reactions of antagonists, authorities, allies, observers, objects of their action, and other people somehow involved in the struggle.

Like their theatrical counterparts, repertoires of collective action designate not individual performances, but means of *inter*action among pairs or larger sets of actors. A company, not an individual, maintains a repertoire. The simplest set consists of one actor (say a group of workers) making collective claims, and another actor (say the workers' boss) becoming the object of those claims. That simple set compounds into pairs making claims on each other, into trios of claimants, up to the complex arrays of national politics. Not all collective claims involve overt conflict. Participants in collective celebrations often make claims only on each other, demanding little more than shared affirmation of identity; leaders call on followers for support, and followers declare their solidarity, without necessarily arousing conflicts of interest. When the claims in question would, if realized, affect the interests of other actors, we may speak of *contention*. Thus, repertoires of contention are the established ways in which pairs of actors make and receive claims bearing on each other's interests.

We confront a metaphor. A weak version of the metaphor asserts simply that participants in action attend to each other's assigned parts in the drama and to shared memories of similar events. As a guide to interpretation, even a weak version helps. But I mean a strong version, which implies: (a) social relations, meanings, and actions cluster together in known, recurrent patterns and (b) many possible contentious actions never occur because the potential participants lack the requisite knowledge, memory, and social connections. In a strong version the appearance of new forms results from deliberate innovation and strenuous bargaining, as in the process by which employers, workers, and agents of the British state struggled over the boundary between acceptable and unacceptable forms of strike activity. While contenders are constantly innovating, furthermore, they generally innovate at the perimeter of the existing repertoire rather than by breaking entirely with old ways.

Most innovations fail and disappear; only a rare few fashion long-term changes in a form of contention. Durable innovations generally grow out of success, as other actors rapidly borrow, then institutionalize, a new form of action that visibly advances its users' claims. When that happens, all parties to the action, including authorities and objects of claims, adapt to the new presence. Thus, in France of the 1830s the venerable charivari politicized, moving from its sphere of commentary on marital and sexual delinquency to the expression of opposition to corrupt officials or other candidates for office. Only rarely does one whole repertoire give way to another; for example, British experience from the 1750s to the 1830s features just one such massive change in repertoire. For these reasons, repertoires of contention have their own distinct histories.

THINKING ABOUT REPERTOIRES

The concept of repertoires of contention itself has a distinct history. So far as I know, I introduced the notion of repertoire into the study of collective action in 1977. For several years I had been using crude taxonomies of forms I had devised to improve on the prepolitical/political dichotomy employed by E. J. Hobsbawm and George Rudé. By 1977 I was proposing this trio: *competitive* (playing out rivalries within a constituted system), *reactive* (defending threatened rights), and *proactive* (claiming rights not yet enjoyed). But I also was beginning to recognize that a form such as the strike sometimes appeared in all three contexts; the categories actually described claims, not forms, of action. What is more, the trio's teleological tone bothered me, especially when other authors adopted it as an evolutionary scheme. It sounded suspiciously like modernization theory.

The comparisons that my collaborators and I had undertaken in *The Rebellious Century* (1975), in the work on Great Britain I had then recently begun, and in the research on France I was starting to synthesize made the weaknesses of the tripartite scheme apparent. Dissatisfaction with the taxonomy led me to introduce the concept of repertoire, which first reached print in my "Getting It Together in Burgundy" (1977). For two or three years (notably in

From Mobilization to Revolution, 1978) I held to the competitive, reactive, and proactive categories while writing increasingly of repertoires. Eventually I realized that the two were incompatible; at that point I finally expunged the residues of modernization theory from my concepts, if not necessarily from every aspect of my analysis.

Let me not exaggerate the idea's originality. Every historian of popular collective action realizes that the predominant forms of contention vary decisively by time and place. Ian Gilmour's recent overview, for example, includes separate chapters on the press gang, poaching, election conflicts, food riots, industrial disputes, and dueling, each treated as distinct from the others (Gilmour 1992). When Andrew Charlesworth and his collaborators mapped "rural protest" in Great Britain, they distinguished among land protests, food riots, turnpike disturbances, agricultural laborers' protests, and a variety of other conflicts (Charlesworth 1983). A distinguished string of publications singles out Rough Music (charivari in France, Katzenmusik in Switzerland, and so on) for separate historical treatment (see, e.g., Le Goff and Schmitt 1981).

The historical literature, in short, does not lack documentation or analysis of particular contentious forms. What it does lack is systematic discussion of their covariation and change. On the whole, analysts of particular action forms have taken one of these historical tacks: absorbing them into general narratives of political struggle and/or changing class consciousness; adopting gross categories and periodizations on the order of prepolitical vs. political; treating them hermeneutically in context. With the introduction of a new term, I hoped to accomplish three things: (1) to help codify the existing knowledge of social and political historians with respect to the forms of popular collective action, (2) to generalize the question of why such forms change and vary, (3) to forward the hypothesis that the prior history of contention strongly constrains the choices of action currently available, in partial independence of the identities and interests that participants bring to the action.

I soon recognized a significant weakness in my initial formulations concerning repertoires. Since authorities such as police, justices of the peace, and home secretaries created and kept many of the records describing popular collective action, archival research immediately brings out the significant involvement of governmental agents as interlocuters, regulators, and even agents provocateurs. Judicial proceedings, it is true, tilt their mirror away from officials and toward the defendants, while newspapers typically adopt conventions that make popular collective action seem relatively self-contained: "Another food riot occurred near Maidstone," and so on. But police dossiers reveal a continual play of strategic interaction—appeals to authorities, forbidden meetings, threatening letters, arrested leaders, secret consultations, instructions to participants, testing of limits, show trials, negotiated sentences—that amount to bargaining out ground rules for different forms of action.

Somehow my first theorizing about repertoires neglected this obvious archival lore. Contrary to the interactive process I was observing in my comparative studies of collective action, my first statements assumed that a single actor (individual or collective) owned a repertoire of means and deployed it strategically. That was a mistake. Each routine within an established repertoire actually consists of an *interaction* among two or more parties. Repertoires belong to sets of contending actors, not to single actors.

The elementary case—for example, a group of weavers who break the loom of a fellow worker who produces for less pay than the going rate—involves a claimant and an object of claims. Even that simple case typically entails interaction with other parties, such as the merchants or employers who are paying substandard rates, local authorities and police who intervene, and other workers who are violating (or are tempted to violate) local standards. The action takes its meaning and effectiveness from shared understandings, memories, and agreements, however grudging, among the parties. In that sense, then, a repertoire of actions resembles not individual consciousness but a language; although individuals and groups know and deploy the actions in a repertoire, the actions connect *sets* of individuals and groups.

Q.E.D.

Consider the street demonstration, a form of action that crystallized in Western Europe and North America between 1780 and 1850, in tandem with the expansion of electoral politics. It consists of gathering deliberately in a visible, symbolically important place, displaying signs of shared commitment to some claim on authorities, then dispersing. Demonstrations have many variants: with or without marches through the streets, with or without speeches, with or without the trappings of parades such as uniforms, costumes, banners, signs, musicians, songs, and chanted slogans. Demonstrations broadcast a multiple of numbers and commitment to a cause, with signs of intense commitment compensating to some degree for small crowds.

In all their variants, demonstrations involve at least four actors: demonstrators, objects of their claims, specialists in official control of public space (usually police), and spectators. They often involve others: reporters for mass media; counterdemonstrators; allies such as dissident members of the ruling class; spies; operators of nearby establishments that crowd action might engage or endanger; pickpockets; gangs itching for a fight; political scientists eager to observe street politics, and so on.

In France the demonstration emerged as a way of doing political business during the July Monarchy (1830–48), became a major form of action during the Second Republic (1848–51), and remained a standard element of collective-action repertoires thereafter despite becoming less used during moments of severe repression such as the early 1850s and the German occupations of 1870–71 and 1940–44. The French forms of the demonstration emerged from intense, continuous bargaining between various political claimants and public authorities, especially police officials, from the 1830s through the early twentieth century. The result was a dramatic narrowing and standardization of the actions that made up a demonstration, an increasing differentiation of demonstrations from public meetings, processions, parades, funerals, festivals, strikes, and insurrections (Favre 1990).

In Great Britain the demonstration took shape earlier than in France but through a similar process of experimentation, bargaining, and standardization shaped by intense interaction between demonstrators and authorities. During the later eighteenth century, British people commonly displayed their electoral preferences vociferously at the hustings, participated in marches to present petitions, gathered to demand that householders illuminate their windows in honor of popular heroes or victories, took advantage of authorized public celebrations to voice their own complaints, and attended public meetings at which all comers voted petitions or resolutions concerning current issues. They did not, however, engage in demonstrations as distinct displays of massed will. By

the 1820s political organizers and public authorities were clearly
negotiating agreements about street demonstrations, although the
word itself gained currency only in the 1830s. (The term apparently
leaped almost immediately from its military version, a deliberate
show of force for intimidation of potential opponents, to a civilian
analog.)

TO STUDY BRITISH REPERTOIRES

The analyses I have undertaken of Britain's changing repertoires
concentrate on moments in which people gathered to make vigorous, visible, public claims, acted on those claims in one way
or another, then turned to other business. In stressing open, collective, discontinuous contention, the analyses neglect individual
forms of struggle and resistance as well as the routine operation of
political parties, labor unions, patron-client networks, and other
powerful means of collective action, except when they produce
visible contention in the public arena. They do so in an effort to
make the analysis of collective action manageable, in the convic-
tion that contention is an important subject for its own sake, and
in the hope that the careful analysis of collective contention will
also lend insight into individual action, continuous contention, and
noncontentious collective action.

My central body of evidence comes from a machine-readable
catalog of slightly more than 8,000 contentious gatherings (CGs)
that occurred in southeastern England (Kent, Middlesex, Surrey,
or Sussex) during 13 years scattered from 1758 through 1820 and in
Great Britain as a whole during the seven years from 1828 through
1834. Although I have compared the inventory of CGs extensively
with official correspondence (notably of the Home Office) and
with the compilations of other historians, the basic catalog comes
from the full reading of periodicals: the *Times*, *London Chronicle*,
Morning Chronicle, *Hansard's Parliamentary Debates*, *Mirror of
Parliament*, *Annual Register*, *Gentleman's Magazine*, and *Acts and
Proceedings of Parliament*.

A *contentious gathering* is an occasion on which a number
of people (here, a minimum of 10) outside of the government
gathered in a publicly accessible place and made claims on at least
one person outside their own number, claims which if realized
would affect the interests of their object. The definition takes in

just about every event for which authorities and observers used such terms as riot, disorder, disturbance, or affray, but it also includes a great many peaceful meetings, processions, and other assemblies that escaped the wrath of authorities. Since salutes, cheers, and professions of support count as claims, the word contentious slightly misstates the character of events in the catalog. Even professions of support for one party, however, typically involved opposition to another party. Almost all of the gatherings identified by the definition entailed genuine conflicts of interest; they involved the public taking of stands that could—and often did—cost the actors and the objects of their action something.

In Great Britain contentious repertoires changed fundamentally between the 1750s and the 1830s. During the eighteenth century, Britain's prevailing forms of open conflict above a very small scale included seizures of grain, tollgate attacks, disruptions of ceremonies or festivals, group hunting on forbidden territory, invasions of land, orderly destruction of property, shaming routines such as Rough Music, and similar events. Most of these contentious forms had existed for several centuries with relatively little change; the largest alterations in Britain's contentious repertoires from the sixteenth to eighteenth centuries seem to have been the decline of depredations by private armies and gangs of retainers rather than the introduction of distinctively new forms of action (Charlesworth 1983; Cockburn 1991; Colley 1980; Fletcher 1968; Fletcher and Stevenson 1985; Gilmour 1992; Harris 1987; Mac-Culloch 1979; Manning 1988; Outhwaite 1991; Reed and Wells 1990; Rogers 1989; Sharp 1980; Stone 1947; Stone 1983; E. P. Thompson 1991; Walter and Wrightson 1976; Zagorin 1982).

Like political life as a whole, we might characterize the eighteenth century repertoire as parochial, particular, and bifurcated. It was *parochial* because most often the interests and action involved were confined to a single community. It was *particular* because forms of contention varied significantly from one place, actor, or situation to another. It was *bifurcated* because when ordinary people addressed local issues and nearby objects they took impressively direct action to achieve their ends, but when it came to national issues and objects they recurrently addressed their demands to a local patron or authority who might represent their interest, redress their grievance, fulfill his own obligation, or at least authorize them to act.

Thus, the collective seizure of grain, which authorities called a "food riot," stated both a grievance against local merchants and the claim that local authorities should act to keep food in the community at a price that poor people could afford, while the breaking down of enclosures stated the claim that landlords and authorities should maintain the rights of community members to glean, pasture, gather, or otherwise use unplanted lands to their advantage. The parochial, particular, and bifurcated eighteenth-century repertoire likewise included a good deal of ceremonial, street-theater deployment of strong visual symbols and destruction of symbolically charged objects (Bohstedt 1983; Brewer 1976, 1979–80, 1980; Dobson 1980; Fletcher and Stevenson 1985; Gilmour 1992; Laqueur 1989; Manning 1989; Muskett 1980; Rule 1981, 1986; E. P. Thompson 1991).

Although some of these eighteenth-century routines survived well into the nineteenth century, they rapidly lost their relative prominence among the means of righting wrongs. Instead, demonstrations, strikes, rallies, public meetings, and similar forms of action came to prevail during the nineteenth century. As compared with their predecessors, the nineteenth-century forms had a national, modular, and autonomous character. They were *national* in often referring to interests and issues that spanned many localities or affected centers of power whose actions touched many localities. They were *modular* in that the same forms served many different localities, actors, and issues. They were *autonomous* in beginning on the claimants' own initiative and establishing direct communication between the claimants and those nationally significant centers of power. Yet they involved less direct action and immediate redress of grievances than their eighteenth-century predecessors. Figure 1 shows one of the by-products of these changes: a dramatic decline in the physical violence of contention, as illustrated by the near-disappearance of deaths in the course of the interaction; the trends are similar for number wounded and arrested, except that the rate of arrests again rose slightly after 1828, probably as a result of expanded policing.

The change from repertoire to repertoire occurred in irregular surges: critics of government policy during the American troubles, including John Wilkes, adopted the popular association, but used it only intermittently; Lord George Gordon molded his anti-Catholic followers into a temporarily effective Protestant Association in

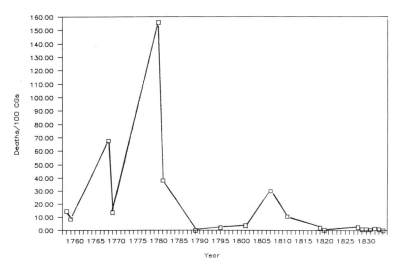

Figure 1: Deaths per 100 CGs, Southeast England, 1758–1834

1780; London's radicals built extensive associations with relatively small followings during the French wars; in 1816 and 1817 Henry Hunt launched a campaign of "cumulative, constitutionally sanctioned protest, open to all, for a programme demanding the constitutionally decreed rights of all" (Belchem 1985: 22); during the following decade, Daniel O'Connell's Catholic Association provided the base for a national—indeed, international—set of demands; by the time political unions and similar organizations waged the fight for Reform between 1830 and 1832, national and autonomous popular politics had become Britain's regular style.

   In this regard, as in so many others, the period of the French Revolution and Empire was pivotal; an increasingly powerful and demanding state called forth a new form of politics. The repertoire changed accordingly. Figure 2 shows the joint trend in two important variables: the proportion of all CGs that took the form of public meetings, and the proportion of all claims for which Parliament was the object. The graph shows both a decisive movement toward public meetings plus claims on Parliament and a point of inflection between 1789 and 1807.

   In the same process, contested elections became more common (Phillips 1982). Citizens who lacked the right to vote followed elec-

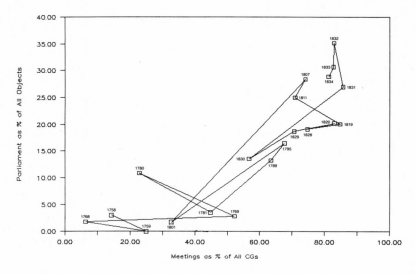

Figure 2:   Meetings and Parliament, Southeast England, 1758–1834

tions and participated in the campaigning more and more actively. The rudiments of a two-party system came into being (O'Gorman 1982, 1989). Merchants, entrepreneurs, financiers, and members of established trades pressed their claims on the state ever more openly and directly. Voluntary associations formed, especially among the middle classes, to promote self-help, recreation, education, moral reform, and political action (Morris 1983, 1990). Pubs and coffeehouses became increasingly important gathering places and bases for special-interest associations; for example, "box clubs" bringing together members of a particular trade met regularly in pubs, with the innkeepers holding the groups' funds and papers in locked boxes. Thus was seen the dramatic rise in the proportion of all CGs that were meetings from a typical one-fifth of all CGs in the 1750s and 1760s to a typical four-fifths in the 1820s and 1830s.

Labor unions emerged from the informal trade networks that already prevailed during the eighteenth century. Newspapers carried more and more information about the doings of government, Parliament, and powerholders. Within Parliament, private bills on behalf of local constituents first multiplied, then gave way to a proliferation of public bills. Issues of national action—rights of religious minorities, parliamentary reform, slavery, taxes, and so on—came to preoccupy public discussion. In short, associationally based popular politics took shape on a national scale. As all this happened, ordinary Britons came to identify with the national state as never before (Colley 1986, 1992). Bourgeois and skilled workers led the way, but other workers—even agricultural workers, in the long run—followed the same path.

Britain's surges of collective activity represented the birth of what we now call the social movement—the sustained, organized challenge to existing authorities in the name of a deprived, excluded, or wronged population. In most cases the appearance of a social movement incited the formation of countermovements by those whose interests the movement threatened; thus, supporters of the Church of England rallied against Catholic Emancipation, using many of the emancipators' tactics. In the 1820s and 1830s the struggles around Catholic Emancipation, Test and Corporation Acts, the abolition of slavery, the New Poor Law, and, preeminently, parliamentary Reform, all took shape as social movements and countermovements.

Social movements parallel and feed on electoral politics, precisely because they signal the presence of mass support—and even of potential votes—for programs that lack strong voices in existing legislatures. In the West as a whole the national social movement became a significant element of popular politics as participation widened, whether through expansion of the suffrage or through popular pressure on those who had the vote. In Great Britain the flourishing of extraparliamentary (or, better, paraparliamentary) politics followed just such a course; calls for a mass platform, a national convention, or even a people's charter conveyed the idea that the existing representative process excluded people who had a right to be heard (Beer 1957; Belchem 1978, 1981, 1985; Bradley 1986; Brewer 1976, 1979–80, 1980; Dinwiddy 1990; Epstein 1990; Kramnick 1990; Lottes 1979; Morgan 1988; Parssinen 1973). Indeed, one can make a reasonable case that British political entrepreneurs from John Wilkes to Francis Place invented the national social movement as a standard way of making claims; they coordinated marches, meetings, petitions, slogans, publications, and special-purpose associations into nationwide challenges to the existing distribution or use of state power (Tilly 1982a).

British popular politics thus provided a new model for the citizens of other Western states.

CONCLUSION

Judged by the response of other scholars, I cannot say that the notion of contentious repertoires has been a roaring success. Although a weak version of the metaphor has seeped into a number of academic discussions (e.g., Ennis 1987; McPhail 1991), only a small number of researchers have adopted a strong version, actually attempting to integrate the concept into their theories and analyses of evidence: Sidney Tarrow in his analysis of the protest cycle in postwar Italy, Mark Beissinger in his study of Soviet and post-Soviet ethnic conflicts, Marco Giugni and collaborators in their work on new social movements in Europe, but not many more (Beissinger 1991; Giugni 1991; Tarrow 1989a; Tarrow and Soule 1991). If Tarrow had not spread the word, indeed, he and I might be the only researchers trying to implement the study of repertoires.

Why is that? There are several possibilities: (1) the idea is wrong; (2) it is redundant; (3) it is obscure; (4) no one has demonstrated its utility with sufficient clarity and concreteness. In this interim report I have tried to counter the first three objections, but I have not really addressed the fourth.

What will it take? Most of all, a series of empirical applications that go beyond the post factum labeling of contention's varieties. First, someone will have to devise reasonable a priori tests of a repertoire's actual existence: evidence that claim-making clusters in a limited number of forms that recur with only minor variations and form the array among which potential actors select in a more or less deliberate way. I am trying to assemble that evidence by close examination of the sequences of actions within CGs in different eras and settings, but the effort will eventually require studies of action and deliberation before CGs begin.

Second, someone will have to determine whether innovations actually alternate (as Tarrow has hypothesized) between incremental experimentation at the edges of existing forms during routine periods of contention and brash invention in the course of protest cycles and revolutionary situations. This demonstration will require not only descriptions of a precision few researchers have ever assembled on a large scale, but also aggregation of events to distinguish reliably between routine and exceptional circumstances. Finally—and most ambitious of all—someone will have to show that the prior history of particular forms of contention in a locale constrains their subsequent use. That will require close comparisons of different times and places in which similar forms of claim-making could, in principle, have appeared. To say the least, none of these is easy. It will take a good deal of collaboration, and more than one careful investigation, to advance our understanding of contentious repertoires.

NOTE

1 The National Science Foundation has long supported the research reported in this study. I have adapted the introduction, "From Mutiny to Mass Mobilization in Great Britain, 1758–1834," Working Paper 109, Center for Studies of Social Change, New School for Social Research, March 1991, which contains a more general introduction to the study. "How to Detect, Describe, and Explain Repertoires of Contention," CSSC Working Paper 150, October 1992, says much more about problems of explanation. Let me blame Mark Traugott, who asked me to reflect out loud, for the essay's excessively personal tone.

REFERENCES

Beattie, John (1986) Crime and the Courts in England, 1660–1800. Princeton, NJ: Princeton University Press.
Beer, S. (1957) "The representation of interests in British government: Historical background." American Political Science Review 51: 613–50.
Beissinger, M. (1991) "Protest mobilization among Soviet nationalities." Unpublished paper, Department of Political Science, University of Wisconsin, Madison.
Belchem, J. (1978) "Henry Hunt and the evolution of the mass platform." English Historical Review 93: 739–78.
———(1981) "Republicanism, popular constitutionalism and the Radical platform in early nineteenth-century England." Social History 6: 1–32.
———(1985a) " 'Orator' Hunt, 1773–1835." History Today 35: 21–27.
———(1985b) "Orator Hunt: Henry Hunt and Working-Class Radicalism. Oxford: Clarendon Press.
Black, E. (1963) The Association: British Extraparliamentary Political Organization, 1769–1793. Cambridge, MA: Harvard University Press.
Bohstedt, J. (1983) Riots and Community Politics in England and Wales, 1790–1810. Cambridge: Harvard University Press.
Bradley, J. (1986) Popular Politics and the American Revolution in England: Petitions, the Crown, and Public Opinion. Macon, GA: Mercer University Press.

Brewer, J. (1976) Party Ideology and Popular Politics at the Accession of George III. Cambridge: Cambridge University Press.

———(1979–80) "Theater and counter-theater in Georgian politics: The mock elections at Garrat." Radical History Review 22: 7–40.

———(1980) "The Wilkites and the law, 1763–74: A study of radical notions of governance," in John Brewer, and John Styles (eds.) An Ungovernable People: The English and Their Law in the Seventeenth and Eighteenth Centuries. New Brunswick, NJ: Rutgers University Press.

Butterfield, H. (1968 [1949]) George III, Lord North, and the People, 1779–80. New York: Russell and Russell.

Charlesworth, A. (ed.) (1983) An Atlas of Rural Protest in Britain, 1548–1900. London: Croom Helm.

Chase, M. (1988) "The People's Farm": English Radical Agrarianism, 1775–1840. Oxford: Clarendon Press.

Cockburn, J. S. (1991) "Patterns of violence in English Society: Homicide in Kent, 1560–1985." Past and Present 130: 70–106.

Colley, L. (1980) "Eighteenth-century English radicalism before Wilkes." Transactions of the Royal Historical Society 31: 1–19.

———(1986) "Whose nation? Class and national consciousness in Britain, 1750–1830." Past and Present 113: 97–117.

———(1992) Britons: Forging the Nation, 1707–1837. New Haven, CT: Yale University Press.

Dinwiddy, J. R. (1990) "Conceptions of revolution in the English radicalism of the 1790s," in Eckhart Hellmuth (ed.) The Transformation of Political Culture: England and Germany in the Late Eighteenth Century. London: German Historical Institute and Oxford University Press.

Dobson, C. R. (1980) Masters and Journeymen: A Prehistory of Industrial Relations, 1717–1800. London: Croom Helm.

Ennis, J. (1987) "Fields of action: Structure in movements' tactical repertoires." Sociological Forum 2: 520–33.

Epstein, J. (1990) "The constitutional idiom: Radical reasoning, rhetoric and action in early nineteenth century England." Journal of Social History 23: 553–74.

Favre, P. (1990) ed., La manifestation. Paris: Presses de la Fondation Nationale des Sciences Politiques.

Fletcher, A. (1968) Tudor Rebellions. London: Longmans.

Fletcher, A., and J. Stevenson (eds.) (1985) Order and Disorder in Early Modern England. Cambridge: Cambridge University Press.

Gilmour, I. (1992) Riot, Risings and Revolution: Governance and Violence in Eighteenth-Century England. London: Hutchinson.

Giugni, M. (1991) "La mobilisation des nouveaux mouvements sociaux en Suisse," Département de Science Politique, Université de Genève, Travaux et communications, no. 2.

Harris, T. (1987) London Crowds in the Reign of Charles II. Cambridge: Cambridge University Press.

d'Haussez, Baron (1833) La Grande Bretagne en mil huit cent trente trois. Paris: Urbain Canel. 2 vols.

Kramnick, I. (1990) Republicanism and Bourgeois Radicalism: Political Ideology in Late Eighteenth-Century England and America. Ithaca, NY: Cornell University Press.

Laqueur, T. (1989) "Crowds, carnival and the state in English executions, 1604–1868," in A. L. Beier, David Cannadine, and James M. Rosenheim (eds.) The First Modern Society: Essays in English History in Honour of Lawrence Stone. Cambridge: Cambridge University Press.

Le Goff, J., and J.-C. Schmitt, eds. (1981) Le Charivari. Paris: Mouton.

Lottes, G. (1979) Politische Aufklärung und plebejisches Publikum. Zur Theorie und Praxis des englischen Radikalismus im späten 18. Jahrhundert. Munich: Oldenbourg.

MacCulloch, D. (1979) "Kett's Rebellion in Context." Past and Present 84: 36–59.

McPhail, C. (1991) The Myth of the Madding Crowd. New York: Aldine De Gruyter.

Manning, R. (1988) Village Revolts: Social Protest and Popular Disturbances in England, 1509–1640. Oxford: Clarendon Press.

Morgan, E. (1988) Inventing the People: The Rise of Popular Sovereignty in England and America. New York: Norton.

Morris, R. J. (1983) "Voluntary societies and British urban elites, 1780–1850: An analysis." Historical Journal 26: 95–118.

———(1990) "Clubs, societies, and associations," in F. M. L. Thompson (ed.), The Cambridge Social History of Britain, 1750–1950. Volume 3. Social Agencies and Institutions. Cambridge: Cambridge University Press.

Muskett, P. (1980) "A picturesque little rebellion? The Suffolk workhouses of 1765." Bulletin of the Society for the Study of Labour History 41: 28–31.

O'Gorman, F. (1982) The Emergence of the British Two-Party System 1760–1832. London: Arnold.

———(1989) Voters, Patrons, and Parties: The Unreformed Electoral System of Hanoverian England 1734–1832. Oxford: Clarendon Press.

Outhwaite, R. B. (1991) Dearth, Public Policy and Social Disturbance in England, 1550–1800. London: Macmillan.

Parssinen, T. M. (1973) "Association, convention and anti-Parliament in British radical politics, 1771–1848," English Historical Review 88: 504–33.

Reed, M., and R. Wells (eds.) (1990) Class, Conflict and Protest in the English Countryside, 1700–1880. London: Frank Cass.

Rogers, N. (1989) Whigs and Cities: Popular Politics in the Age of Walpole and Pitt. Oxford: Clarendon Press.

Rule, J. (1981) The Experience of Labour in Eighteenth-Century Industry. London: Croom Helm.

———(1986) The Labouring Classes in Early Industrial England, 1750–1850. London: Longman.

Sharp, B. (1980) In Contempt of All Authority: Rural Artisans and Riot in the West of England, 1586–1660. Berkeley: University of California Press.

Spring, D. (1980) "An outsider's view: Alexis de Tocqueville on aristocratic society and politics in 19th century England." Albion 12: 122–31.

Stone, L. (1947) "State control in sixteenth-century England." Economic History Review 17: 103–20.

——— (1983) "Interpersonal violence in English society, 1300–1980." Past and Present 101: 22–33.

Tarrow, S. (1989) Democracy and Disorder: Social Conflict, Political Protest and Democracy in Italy, 1965–1975. New York: Oxford University Press.

Tarrow, S., and S. Soule (1991) "Acting collectively, 1847–49: How the repertoire of collective action changed and where it happened." Paper presented to Social Science History Association, New Orleans.

Thompson, E. P. (1991) Customs in Common. London: Merlin Press.

Tilly, C. (1977) "Getting it together in Burgundy." Theory and Society 4: 479–504.

——— (1978) From Mobilization to Revolution. Reading, MA: Addison-Wesley.

——— (1982) "Britain creates the social movement," in James Cronin and Jonathan Schneer (eds.), Social Conflict and the Political Order in Modern Britain. London: Croom Helm.

Tocqueville, A. de (1958) Voyages en Angleterre, Irlande, Suisse et Algérie, ed. J. P. Mayer. Paris: Gallimard. Oeuvres, papiers et correspondances d'Alexis de Tocqueville, V.

Walter, J., and K. Wrightson (1976) "Dearth and the social order in early modern England." Past and Present 71: 22–42.

Weiner, J. (1983) Radicalism and Freethought in Nineteenth-Century Britain. The Life of Richard Carlile. Westport, CT: Greenwood.

Zagorin, P. (1982) Rebels and Rulers, 1500–1660. Cambridge: Cambridge University Press. 2 vols.

Barricades as Repertoire: Continuities and Discontinuities in the History of French Contention

MARK TRAUGOTT

CHARLES TILLY HAS INTRODUCED to historical and sociological discourse the concept of the repertoire of collective action.[1] The concept is rooted in the observation that "any given population tends to have a fairly limited and well-established set of means for action on shared interests. . . ." (Tilly 1977: 39) The repertoire of collective action, like its theatrical counterpart, implies a group of actors who choose among a restricted number of performances with which they are familiar. Their options are circumscribed both by prior experience and by the material, organizational, and conceptual resources they find readily at hand (Tilly and Tilly 1981: 19). Tilly also likens the repertoire of collective action to a

Mark Traugott is professor of history and sociology at the University of California at Santa Cruz. His research interests include the social history of nineteenth-century France (*The French Worker*), the sociology of social movements (*Armies of the Poor*), and the history of sociological thought (*Emile Durkheim on Institutional Analysis*). The research on which this essay is based forms part of a larger study on the use of barricades throughout the nineteenth century in France. An earlier version of this essay was presented at the 1991 annual meeting of the Social Science History Association in New Orleans. The author would like to acknowledge the helpful comments received from Michael Hanagan, the other members of the SSHA panels, and *Social Science History*'s anonymous reviewers. This research has been supported in part by grants from the John Simon Guggenheim Foundation and the University of California, Santa Cruz, Faculty Research Committee.

game that involves a set of basic rules around which a considerable degree of extemporization is not only permitted but required. The result is a "paradoxical combination of ritual and flexibility" (Tilly 1977: 22; Tilly 1986b: 33, 37) in which neither element must be allowed to displace the other, lest the performance lose either its creative edge or its ready communicability.

In more formal terms a repertoire of collective action consists of the "whole set of means" that a group has available for use in making claims and to which its members turn consistently, "even when in principle some unfamiliar form of action would serve their interests much better." (Tilly, 1986b: 4)[2] Although Tilly emphasizes that such behaviors are learned, the mechanisms by which such knowledge is transmitted to new initiates, other than by direct experience, are not specified. He downplays the strong version of the concept that would see the repertoire as the result of deliberate choices on the part of collective actors, appearing to favor a weaker version in which the loosely structured interaction between contenders and authorities makes certain forms of protest "more feasible, attractive, and frequent" than the alternatives.[3]

The distinctive features that set the repertoire apart are the considerable stability it exhibits over long swaths of time and the constraining influence it exercises over participants in collective action, as it shapes their activities in patterns that are sometimes wondrously, sometimes infuriatingly, self-consistent. Tilly's original model attributes this patterning to the rootedness of all collective action in the organization of everyday life and to the usefulness of repertoires for the purposes of "signaling, negotiation, and struggle" with other parties (Tilly 1986b: 4).

But the continuity exhibited by repertoires over time is just one aspect of their nature. Tilly also is concerned with the changes they undergo. These include the small, incremental modifications that occur continuously across generations of use as actors adapt to the changing political, economic, and social context in which they operate, and as new interests and opportunities emerge (Tilly 1977: 22). They also embrace the even more fascinating, epochal transformations in an entire people's repertoire of contention that occur at long intervals.

In the French context, Tilly identifies one eighteenth-century repertoire, which actually survives well into the 1800s, and another nineteenth-century repertoire, which sets the stage for and persists into the twentieth. The former includes food riots and grain seizures but also embraces the charivari, the draft riot, the intervillage brawl, invasions of fields and forests, armed rebellions against tax collectors, and a wide variety of public rituals, often involving the use of costumes, disguises, and effigies, including mock trials and executions. Among the distinctive features of this earlier style of protest are the reliance on tactics normally reserved for use by the authorities, often subjected to some symbolic or parodic reversal, and the tendency to direct such actions to third parties who are invited to intervene on behalf of participants.[4]

More typical of the nineteenth-century pattern are strikes, demonstrations, electoral rallies, petition marches, public assemblies of all kinds, especially those organized around programmatic objectives and involving visible public actions, including the use of signs, banners, and pamphlets. Tilly explicitly states that the "planned insurrection" is specific to this repertoire, a point to which we shall return. The thread which binds these disparate activities together is that, in relation to the forms of protest that preceded them, they are less likely to be communal and more likely to be national in scope; they rely more heavily on formal organization (in the sense of associations, clubs, societies, etc.); and they are more autonomous (in the sense of using tactics that are distinct from those employed by the constituted authorities).[5] Such activities, which carry over into the twentieth century, are more likely to present direct challenges to their targets (especially those who hold power), to operate on a larger scale, and to make more effective use of explicit and well-elaborated programs of action.[6]

Although the transition from an old to a new repertoire usually takes place over a span measured in decades or generations, Tilly believes it possible to isolate what he terms the "hinge": the moment, typically associated with a landmark set of events, when the predominance of an earlier style of protest is irreversibly supplanted by that of its successor. At such pivotal junctures in history those sociological forces that normally channel collective action into previously established patterns are temporarily suspended. In the heat of some great cataclysmic confrontation the attention of contending parties becomes fixated on new alternatives that hold promise for change. Suddenly, forces are realigned in support of the emergent repertoire, which now rapidly displaces the older style of protest with which it had coexisted for some time. Tilly suggests that one such moment of transformation occurred at the time of the Fronde (i.e., the mid-seventeenth century), and he specifically places the crucial watershed between the eighteenth- and nineteenth-century repertoires in 1848.

WHEN DID STYLES OF COLLECTIVE ACTION CHANGE IN FRANCE?

In a 1990 article William Sewell, Jr., both praises Tilly's contributions, empirical and theoretical, to our understanding of the history of contention in France. He also raises questions about Tilly's "novel periodization." Sewell's exposition of Tilly's framework avoids explicit reference to the concept of repertoire but does rely on the contrast between communal and associative styles of protest, thus echoing Tilly's distinction between eighteenth- and nineteenth-century repertoires and usefully tying the shift to changing forms of social organization. However, in contrast to Tilly's "hinge" of 1848, Sewell locates what might be termed a "wedge," driven between the two divergent styles of collective action, in the radical phase of the great French Revolution, 1789–95. In his view, it was the attempt to destroy the corporation—the institutional form around which Old Regime society had been structured—that defined the revolutionary period and launched the century-long struggle by French citizens to regain the right of association that the attack on privilege had severely restricted. Thus, for Sewell, the French Revolution mattered more than 1848.

In part, we see revealed in this debate the difference between those (like Sewell) for whom the moment of origin carries within it the as-yet-unrealized germ of later transformations, and those (like Tilly) for whom the shift in the preponderant style of collective action is what is significant because it encapsulates the trend of larger historical forces. Tilly's interpretive style emphasizes more structural and encompassing (but also more diffuse) factors like the growth of state power and the degree of urbanization, whose impact on events becomes apparent only across long stretches of time. Sewell's style, in contrast, stresses the cultural and linguistic dimensions of collective violence and the way in which short-term and situationally specific factors account for the form in which change becomes manifest. Sweeping historical consequences are seen as unfolding in a gradual and contingent manner from ostensibly modest beginnings.

There is one point on which Sewell (1990: 540) agrees with Tilly and that I mention because I wish to take issue with them both: that the insurrection represents a new category of collective violence specific to the late-modern period. It is true that each qualifies his assertion in such a way as to allow for the occurrence of at least superficially similar events before the end of the eighteenth century. Tilly specifies that it is their planned character that sets the insurrections of the second half of the nineteenth century apart. Sewell situates the novelty chiefly in the newly positive connotations associated with the term insurrection (as opposed to revolt, mutiny, rebellion, sedition, etc.), the increased frequency of such events, and their enlarged role in legitimating new forms of the state. Despite these stipulations, I have found it impossible to distinguish in unambiguous terms the insurrections of the nineteenth century from others that long predated them. A review of the history of barricade use in France will make the nature of the problem clearer.

A VIEW FROM THE BARRICADES

From their beginnings, barricades have been associated with urban insurrection. Yet until the mid-nineteenth century, urban insurrection was associated with barricades only in France. The origin of the modern tradition of barricade construction can, in fact, be retraced to Paris in 1588. It is even possible to specify the individual—a count of Cossé de Brissac—who is said to have invented the tactic. Yet the building of barricades, like most elements of popular repertoires irrespective of period or setting, originated as a by-product of everyday experiences, just as Tilly has suggested. Sixteenth-century Parisians had long since devised a means of protecting their neighborhoods by embedding one end of a heavy iron chain in the foundation of a corner building. It was the custom each evening to stretch such chains across the mouths of adjoining streets as a way of blocking access and preventing outsiders from disturbing the sleep of residents. However, chains also were used in daylight hours to secure the Parisian *quartier* whenever unrest in the city threatened disruption. The great innovation of 12 May 1588 was to fortify the line of demarcation represented by the chains and to use the barriers thus created to impede the movements of King Henri III's Royal Guards.

Henri had ordered his troops to enter Paris against the chance that the arrival of the enormously popular and ultra-Catholic Duke of Guise would incite unrest. Their deployment prompted precisely the result it was intended to forestall. Parisians, enraged at this armed intrusion, followed the instructions of Cossé de Brissac and reinforced the chain barriers by heaping earth and paving stones into wooden barrels (or *barriques*, in the French of that day, whence the term barricades). The Royal Guards suddenly found themselves isolated in small units. With their lines of communication broken, they became highly vulnerable to the barricade-builders who had so quickly asserted control over the capital. After initial collisions in which a few guardsmen were killed and many others disarmed, the troops—and eventually the king himself—were forced to withdraw from the city.

The important role played by the *Seize* (delegates of the 16 quarters of Paris) and by the Duke of Guise's aristocratic lieutenants, who coordinated popular resistance, gave to this Day of the Barricades a planned character that is difficult to differentiate sharply from such events as the February and June Days of 1848. As with virtually all events of this type, the 1588 rising of the Parisian population combined elements of organization and spontaneity.

The lessons of that victory were not lost on subsequent generations of Parisians. In 1648 a second major event took place (also referred to, somewhat confusingly, as the Day of the Barricades). During Louis XIV's minority, France was effectively ruled by Anne of Austria, acting as regent, and Cardinal Mazarin, as head of the king's council. By the late 1640s, the cardinal's foreign adventures had seriously depleted the royal treasury. Mazarin's plans to levy new taxes met resistance in the capital. A crisis ensued in August 1648, culminating in an order for the arrest of the widely respected and beloved councilor of the Paris parliament, Pierre Broussel, among others. All Paris rose to his defense. The idea of erecting barricades is said to have been planted by agents of Cardinal de Retz, ringleader of the opposition forces, although the concept appears to have been generally familiar to the residents of Paris, even if few veterans of the 1588 rebellion could still have been alive (Anquetil 1851: 517; DeRetz 1872). Contemporary sources claimed that no fewer than 1,260 barricades were erected.

Only after the queen grudgingly granted concessions, including the release of Broussel, was calm restored to the city. The truce was only temporary, however, for these events marked the onset of the period of civil war known as the Fronde, which lasted through 1653.

With the death of Mazarin in 1661, Louis XIV began the 54-year personal rule that succeeded in consolidating the authority of the Bourbon monarchy over France. With this strengthening of the state, the phenomenon of barricade construction went into eclipse. I have been unable to identify a single, further instance of their use until the period of the French Revolution.[7] Thus, barricades, and the urban insurrections from which they were inseparable, flourished for a time in the late 1500s and mid-1600s, before disappearing for nearly 150 years. Their earlier occurrence needs to be reconciled with the notion of a distinctive and period-specific nineteenth-century repertoire of urban insurrection.

BARRICADES IN THE AGE OF REVOLUTION

Between the end of the Old Regime and the fall of the Paris Commune, at least 21 independent occurrences of barricade construction took place in France.[8] These events can be roughly grouped into three subperiods corresponding to stages in the further elaboration of a repertoire of barricade construction.

The initial stage extended from 1795 to 1827. In the first of those years the French capital witnessed the only instance of barricade construction to occur during the great Revolution. A generation later, the period closed with the abortive coup attempt in which Auguste Blanqui and a cohort of young radicals served their apprenticeship in insurrection.[9] But this resurgence of the use of barricades occurred within a changed context. Whereas insurrections in the sixteenth and seventeenth centuries might paralyze the monarchy, by the nineteenth century they at times achieved the outright overthrow and reconstitution of the state. In the earlier period, because the nation was less well-integrated and administrative control less complete, it was harder for a popular rebellion to conceive, much less carry out, an actual takeover of the governmental apparatus and the conscious redirection of social policy. By the nineteenth century a shift in the calculus of power had taken place, and capital cities, where the intellectual and political as well as material resources of the nation were concentrated, could impose their will over the more numerous but more dispersed population of the provinces.

A second phase, which ran roughly from 1830 to 1848, witnessed the diffusion of the barricade as a technique of insurrection. It began with the July Days that toppled the last of the Bourbon kings and within a month had spawned barricades in Belgium, the first such use I have been able to document outside their country of origin. It concluded with the great conflagration of 1848, when barricades spread across the Continent and achieved a genuinely international status as a tactic of revolt. They appeared for the first time in Vienna, Berlin, Munich, Milan, Naples, Budapest, Frankfurt, Prague, and Dresden. In barely more than six months, these and other cities were rocked by rebellion, arguably the most temporally concentrated and spatially diffused outburst of insurrectionary activity that had ever been observed. It is reasonable to conjecture (although I have found it impossible to establish systematically) that the carriers of this epidemic of barricade construction included emigrant workers and intellectuals, whether because they were forced to leave France behind by the economic crisis of 1846–47 or were simply inspired by the February Revolution to bear the torch of democratic reform back to their homelands. But it also is clear that the outbreak of insurrection might be prompted by nothing more than the arrival of scattered news dispatches concerning events that had taken place in Paris or elsewhere. Barricades, which became a widespread and increasingly ritualized element in this wave of unrest, served as both an instrument and an index of the pan-European sense of solidarity that developed among proponents of democratic change.

By the start of the third stage, barricades were rapidly losing much of their purely military efficacy. Despite the victories of popular forces in the July Days and February Days, the 1830 introduction of cannons, and especially their unrestricted use against the domestic population during the June Days, marked the beginning of the end for the barricade as a strictly pragmatic tactic of insurrection. Where the government and its forces of social control were determined to resist insurrectionary challenges by such means, the result was inevitably the defeat of the insurgents. Moreover, army and militia commanders had learned the lessons of previous revolutions in which troops had immediately been dispersed to prevent the construction of barricades spread across the capital. This approach exposed the rank and file to appeals by insurgents and to the risk of being disarmed. Based on this experience, the June insurrection was allowed to develop more completely before troops were dispatched in massed units with orders to attack.

Yet the barricade did not disappear. Instead, its symbolic and sociological functions, which had always played a real if less visible role, came increasingly to the fore. The great barricades of the Commune were for the most part elaborate showpieces that did little to inhibit the invasion of the capital. Their primary contribution was to mobilize prospective combatants and reinforce the bonds of solidarity among them by expressing the participants' sense of identification with the actions and values of generations of insurgents who had come before. In this way the barricade became as much a representation of the revolutionary tradition as an instrument of combat pure and simple.

CONCLUSION

While the construction and defense of barricades may lack the comprehensive character that would qualify it as a repertoire unto itself, it exhibits many of the attributes described by Tilly. Originating in France as an outgrowth of customary practices, barricades became a standard tactic to which participants in collective action had consistent recourse. From 1588 to 1968 the French have built barricades in each of the last five centuries. Yet during that time the technique of barricade construction not only has crossed national borders, but has violated the chronological boundaries that are supposed to separate the discrete repertoires that Tilly assigns to the period. Indeed, barricades are so broadly distributed that one is forced to conclude that they (like the insurrections with which they are so closely associated and unlike other forms of repertorial action) are non-period-specific.

On closer examination, the remarkable longevity of the barricade seems due in part to its ability to adapt in form and function as a response to a changing social context. The barricades of the sixteenth and seventeenth centuries were relatively modest, essentially defensive structures thrown up by small groups of neighbors drawn from a highly restricted local area. During the long nine-state in France. When barricades returned in 1795, it was again at a moment when fiscal crisis and administrative disarray had opened the legitimacy and efficacy of the state to renewed question. The French Revolution ushered in a century so rich in political contention and attempted insurrections that the practice of barricade construction was nearly continuous in the experience of four successive generations. No fewer than eight different forms of government ruled France during this period.[12] These changes produced an unprecedented level of violent social conflict right up until the 1870s, when the founding of the Third Republic brought a measure of political calm.[13]

If one considers the history of collective action in France solely from the perspective of when barricades have been erected, then the periodizations of both Sewell and Tilly are wrong. Neither 1789 nor 1848 seems to mark a radical break in a pattern of barricade construction that stretches from 1588 to 1968. This apparent continuity makes it difficult to distinguish a clear watershed between sharply divergent styles of protest on the grounds of barricade use alone. Furthermore, the contention, advanced by Sewell and Tilly alike, that the insurrection is a strictly modern occurrence is even more difficult to sustain. In its nineteenth-century manifestation, it may well have possessed a distinctive potential for effecting social and political change, but this was mainly because such events were by then embedded within revolutionary movements (or benefited from structural conditions that *were* specific, in the European context, to the nineteenth century) rather than because of characteristics inherent to the urban insurrection.[14]

But if we also consider qualitative changes in barricade use, then both Sewell and Tilly may claim some vindication. Consistent with Sewell's dating, the revival of barricades during the French Revolution, after a 150-year absence, coincided with the new and enlarged role of the common people in the political and social affairs of the nation. This was indeed the moment when the attack on the corporate basis of Old Regime society, the rise of novel forms of organization, and the shift to a larger scale of collective action all began.

It also is true that 1848 was the year that most clearly confirmed the trends to which the French Revolution had pointed. In 1789 old and new styles were juxtaposed—the food riot alongside the public rally, attacks on the homes of factory owners alongside the birth of the modern political movement. By mid-century the newly dominant forms of collective action had largely displaced the old. Both the program and the activities of the republican and democratic-socialist movements of 1848 aimed at being, in Tilly's terms, national and autonomous. From this point of view there is no necessary contradiction in Sewell seeing the French Revolution as the modern repertoire's moment of origination and Tilly specifying 1848 as the point at which the transformation irreversibly took hold.

Perhaps more satisfying, however, is the alternative conceptualization offered in Goldstone's examination of *Revolution and Rebellion in the Early Modern World*. For him, the linearity of the dominant models of social change—from the classic formulations of Marx, Durkheim, and Weber to the more focused efforts of contemporary theorists such as Tilly and Sewell—is at odds with the empirical record. Goldstone (1991: 38–44) is struck by a remarkable global synchronicity in the great waves of social change that occurred during the seventeenth century and during the late eighteenth to early nineteenth centuries. The first included not just the English Revolution but crises in Ottoman Turkey and Ming China. The second encompassed not just the French Revolution but further paroxysms in China, the Ottoman Empire, and Tokugawa Japan. From this perspective, patterns of large-scale social upheaval must be seen as worldwide in scope and cyclical in character. Their rhythms are tied to secular processes such as state-making, the expansion of the market economy, and demographic fluctuation. Only when a conjuncture among such forces takes place are its consequences felt on a global scale, but when such rare events occur, they need to be recognized and explained in their own terms rather than as part of a preordained, linear progression.

A thorough assessment of so ambitious and broad-ranging a thesis lies beyond the scope of this essay. Still, a remarkable convergence exists between the observed peaks of barricade use in France and the great waves of revolution and rebellion, in France and elsewhere, between 1500 and 1900. Moreover, the incidence of barricade construction suggests that rather than fitting a pattern of successive, discrete repertoires, barricades respond to long cycles of conjunctural social change.

The cycles in question do not, of course, produce simple repetitions of what has gone before. The form and function of barricades are powerfully inflected by the social and historical context in which they arise. We have seen how their initially tactical, military utility receded in importance, and how an alternative set of organizational and mobilizational advantages increased in importance until, by the second half of the nineteenth century, the symbolic significance of barricades became the predominant reason for their continued use.

This dynamism explains why the barricade, which originated as a weapon in early-modern struggles against the centralizing state, could prove just as useful in waves of revolutionism two centuries later, and even in countercultural social movements like that of May 1968. In the process, what began as a uniquely Parisian tactic of resistance became first a French, then a European, and ultimately a global symbol of revolt. It is this facility for adaptation and assimilation across both temporal and cultural boundaries that explains how the barricade has succeeded in overcoming the period-specificity exhibited by many other forms of collective action and acquired its central place in a popular culture of insurrection that now spans the contemporary world.

NOTES

1 References to repertoires of collective action, explicit or otherwise, are scattered throughout Tilly's writings. In assembling this overview, I have relied primarily on the following four sources, where the concept is discussed at length: Tilly (1977); Tilly and Tilly (1981: 13–25); Tilly (1986a); Tilly (1986b).

2 Under this definition, it is not clear that barricade-building properly qualifies as a repertoire unto itself. It would be logical to apply the term only to the complete array of alternative courses of action among which participants in collective action make knowing choices. In its practical application the concept has been used to designate activities, like the construction of barricades, to which rebels predictably resort, even when the behavior is actually part of a larger pattern like the urban insurrection.

3 See Tilly (1986a: 17).

4 On the eighteenth-century repertoire in France, see Tilly (1977: 22, 24–25); Tilly and Tilly (1981: 20); and Tilly (1986a: 14).

5 In the earliest formulations, participants in the kinds of events that constitute the nineteenth-century repertoire were seen as adopting a more "pro-active" orientation, versus the essentially reactive stance that typified collective action in the eighteenth-century repertoire. Note, however, that the pro-active/reactive distinction used in Tilly's original conceptualization of the

repertoire disappeared by the late 1970s, although it persists in others' appropriations of Tilly's ideas.

6 On the nineteenth-century repertoire in France, see Tilly (1977: 25, 29); Tilly and Tilly (1981: 19); Tilly (1986a: 14, 36); and Tilly (1986b: 391).

7 To be more precise, barricades are said to have been used in Paris during the skirmishes that followed the pitched battle between the opposing armies of Condé and Turenne in July 1652, and again in 1657. For a variety of reasons—principally because they were used in conflicts between opposing armies rather than by irregular formations of civilian insurgents— these structures would not properly qualify as barricades in the sense employed here.

8 Independence is difficult to establish, and such independence would be relative at best, as the concept of repertoire implies. In the present context I have counted as a single occurrence all those incidents of barricade-building that may have taken place in scattered locales within a few days or weeks. Thus, the barricades of the July Days of 1830 or those erected under the Paris Commune have been treated as discrete and unitary events. It is, however, often impossible to demonstrate that such incidents were interconnected by mechanisms more concrete than imitation or the inspiration of example.

9 The 1827 rising is incorrectly treated as the first modern use of barricades by Duveau (1967), who also states categorically and erroneously that barricades were not used during the French Revolution. I sympathize wholeheartedly with Duveau for these lapses, since anyone reporting on what are intrinsically rare events taking place over long blocks of time in far-flung locations is unlikely to unearth them all. Invariably, it seems, when missing cases are finally uncovered, they contradict conclusions based on an incomplete subsample. In my attempts to make sense of patterns of barricade use, I have been forced to proceed as if I possessed complete information, relying on others to fill in the gaps in my knowledge. For the record, I am reasonably confident that my enumeration of events in Paris is comprehensive for the modern period, whereas my coverage of events in the rest of France remains spotty and my knowledge of events in other European countries is rudimentary.

10 Although there is little evidence that they actually exerted the intended influence, Blanqui's treatises on the art of insurrection and explicit instructions on how to construct a barricade give evidence of this change in orientation.

11 While I have not made the barricades of twentieth-century France a focus of my research, the details of May 1968 (another peak of collective action, and on a global scale) illustrate the extent to which the symbolic or representational aspects of barricade use had come to predominate by that time.

12 These governments were the Old Regime, the First Republic, the First Empire, the Restoration, the July Monarchy, the Second Republic, the Second Empire, and the Third Republic.

13 Although the Third Republic was relatively long-lived, the disappearance of barricades for the remainder of the century was likely due less to the new government's inherent strength than to the opportunities that this more liberal regime created for pursuing alternative paths to political and social change.

14   I attempt to discuss some of the factors that created a period-specific potential for urban insurrections to capture national states in a forthcoming manuscript, "Capital Cities and Revolution."

REFERENCES

Anquetil, Louis-Philippe (1851) Histoire de France. Paris: Gabriel Roux.
De Retz, Cardinal (1872) Oeuvres du Cardinal de Retz. Vol. 2, Mémoires du Cardinal de Retz. Paris: Hachette.
Duveau, Georges (1967) 1848: The Making of a Revolution. New York: Vintage.
Goldstone, Jack A. (1991) Revolution and Rebellion in the Early Modern World. Berkeley: University of California Press.
Sewell, William H., Jr. (1990) "Collective violence and collective loyalties in France: Why the French Revolution made a difference." Politics and Society 18: 527–52.
Tarrow, Sidney G. (1983) Struggling to Reform: Social Movements and Policy Change during Cycles of Protest. Ithaca, NY: Cornell University Press.
Tilly, Charles (1977) "Getting it together in Burgundy, 1675–1975." Theory and Society 4 (Winter): 479–504.
———— (1986a) "European violence and collective action since 1700." Social Research 53: 159–84.
———— (1986b) The Contentious French. Cambridge, MA: Harvard University Press.
Tilly, Louise, and Charles Tilly (eds.) (1981) Class Conflict and Collective Action. Beverly Hills, CA: Sage.

The Roar of the Crowd: Repertoires of Discourse and Collective Action among the Spitalfields Silk Weavers in Nineteenth-Century London

MARC W. STEINBERG

ON FRIDAY, 9 MAY 1823, Thomas Wilson, M.P. for London, rose from the bench to present a petition to the Commons from the silk manufacturers of London and Westminster. The petitioners, among them the largest and most prosperous in the trade, requested the repeal of the Spitalfields Acts, laws passed in the late eighteenth century to placate rioting weavers. Among their clauses, the Acts prohibited the importation of foreign wrought silks, provided for minimum piece rates among the silk weavers in the London area, and authorized magisterial intervention in determining these rates (Bland et al. 1919: 547–51; Clapham 1916; Plummer 1972). To free traders these protective laws were the sorry relics of a previous era; to the manufacturers they were vexatious regulations that fettered their business. They objected to the Acts not only on economic grounds, but on political principles as well. The law, they argued, should not infringe on but protect their rights as English citizens to freely use their property, capital. As they stated, they wished

> to be exempted from the arbitrary, injurious, and impolitic
> enactment which prevents them, while they continue to re-
> side in certain districts, from employing any portion of their

Marc W. Steinberg teaches sociology at Smith College. He is currently completing a book, *Fighting Words*, on patterns of discourse, ideology, and collective action among working-class trade groups in early nineteenth-century England. He wishes to thank Sidney Tarrow, Charles Tilly, Mark Traugott, and the anonymous reviewers of *Social Science History* for their comments on previous drafts.

capital in such other parts of the kingdom as deemed most
beneficial; thereby depriving them not only of their fair exercise of their privileges as free subjects, and totally preventing
all the public benefit which would arise from a competition
between London and the country manufacturers, but depriving them also of all hope of ever participating in the foreign
trade of the Empire. (*Hansard's*, n.s., v. 9, 1823, c. 148–49)

David Ricardo, at the height of his power in Parliament, readily
supported the petition. He broadened the argument on the limitations of civic liberty and the public good by arguing that the Acts
"were not merely an interference with the freedom of trade, but
they cramped the freedom of labor itself" (*Hansard's*, n.s., v. 9,
1823, c. 149).

The Spitalfields silk weavers, who saw the Acts as a great shield
of security, mobilized rapidly to defend them and counter the petition. They responded with a sweeping lobbying effort of both the
Commons and Lords, producing several widely circulated petitions, including one containing 21,000 signatures addressed to the
Lords in June 1823, and lobbied members as they entered Westminster before crucial votes (*An Account* 1823: 29). Additionally,
a member of the journeymen's committee personally addressed
a response to one of the manufacturers petitioning for repeal.
Replying to the manufacturers' depiction of just laws and the public good, this representative maintained that the extant regulation
of labor was indeed just and provided freedom for artisans and
benefits to the larger community through its protection.

Not just, Sir, why not? is not all acquired property protected
by the law, and is not that just? Why then should it not be
just to protect natural property which is labour. Labour is the
only property a poor man has, which is the root and origin of
all the riches of the great and mighty, who are able to protect
themselves, while the poor have neither the means nor the
power of self-defence without the assistance of the law. The
law was designed at the first formation of civil society, for
the mutual protection of the community at large. (*An Account*
1823: 60–61)

This rhetorical sparring was to continue through the repeal of
the Acts the following year and through the end of the decade.

In form and content it was not a free-for-all; rather, it assumed a distinctive patterning in the form of a discursive repertoire of contention.

Charles Tilly defines repertoires of contention as "the established ways in which pairs of actors make and receive claims bearing on each other's interests" (1992: 10; see also 1986). Those who have studied repertoires have concentrated on the socio-spatial forms of actions, targets of claims, and modes of expression, rather than on the making and receiving of the claims themselves. My argument below, to draw upon the metaphor, is that we must pay closer attention to the voices of the actors as well as their actions. To do so we must analyze the part of discourse in this process, the ways in which the collective articulation of claims operates as a piece of the collective knowledge of the repertoire.[1]

I pursue this analysis of discursive repertoires in four parts. First, I provide a theoretical account of how groups develop and use these repertoires and how discursive and largely instrumental repertoires interrelate. Second, I provide background for the case study of the silk weavers of London's Spitalfields district. In the third part I explicate how repertoires of discourse were developed by silk manufacturers and their allies and the weavers in the struggles of the 1820s. Finally, I explore why the weavers' instrumental repertoire remained stable in the face of persistent failure, focusing on how their instrumental and discursive repertoires mutually reinforced one another.

A THEORY OF DISCURSIVE REPERTOIRES

Recent trends in social movement theory have focused on the need to link processes of largely expressive and largely instrumental action.[2] In particular, social scientists have concentrated on the process of the framing of collective action. A collective action frame is defined as an "interpretive scheme that simplifies and condenses the 'world out there'" (Snow and Benford 1992: 137). Through frames, challenging groups construct the rationale for collective action and the political and moral bases for their claims (Snow and Benford 1986, 1992; Gamson 1992b; Tarrow 1992).

In this analysis I wish to extend this orientation to think of the frame itself as composed of a *repertoire of discourse* that is created and articulated through contention. We can use Tilly's notion of repertoires to investigate the ways in which contentious groups develop patterns of claims in struggle. Through these discursive repertoires contenders collectively articulate their morality of claims and remedies and their larger ideological vision of social equity and entitlement.

This struggle is best conceptualized as an ongoing *dialogue* between powerholders and challengers.[3] To a large extent this is accomplished through public and collective dialogues, in which moral boundaries for interaction are produced in the tug of ideological domination and resistance. Such dialogues are partly ongoing features of domination and resistance, but they become more focused and pronounced during contention when challengers must collectively articulate moral motives for stasis or change (Scott 1990).

When challengers develop a discursive repertoire they thus seek both to legitimize their claims within the existing ideology of domination and to subvert some of the powerholders' justifications. This is partly a process of what Alan Hunt has termed "counter-hegemony." As Hunt notes, "the most significant stage in the construction of counter-hegemony comes about with the putting into place of discourses, which whilst still building on the elements of the hegemonic discourses, introduce elements which transcend that discourse" (1990: 314).

Much as any challenging group has a limited action repertoire, so too does it have a limited discursive repertoire.[4] Constrained by the hegemonic talk of the powerholders, this counter-hegemony is generally piecemeal, with challengers often appropriating at the margins. They seize upon silences and contradictions in moral justifications of domination and negate or reverse those points in the dominant discourses (Hunt 1990: 314; see also Mouffe 1979).[5] Akin to instrumental repertoires, discursive repertoires are relatively stable and recurrent.

Discursive repertoires are not only limited but limiting. They bound the set of meanings through which challengers can articulate claims and ideologically mediate the decision to act instrumentally. By mediating between consciousness and action, discourse shapes conceptions of just claims and their legitimate pursuit and the targets for their redress. The knowledge of action repertoires provides collective wisdom on the whats, whens, whos, whys, and hows for the effective pursuit of claims. Discursive repertoires offer the collective morality for the whys and whens and the identification of the whos. They also provide ideological legitimation for the hows of collective action, justifications especially critical in the exercise of collective violence.

Discursive and instrumental repertoires clearly interact and can be mutually reinforcing and therefore stabilizing. This is particularly true when the process of acting affirms the moral rationale for action and vice versa. When powerholders recognize contenders as legitimate claimants, they can legitimate the possibility of contention. Conversely, to the extent that the two repertoires are not mutually reinforcing during contention, groups may be pressed to reexamine the cogency and validity of each. Stasis and change in both repertoires are functions of reciprocal affirmation. In the case of the silk weavers I document both the development of instrumental and discursive repertoires and the way in which this reciprocal affirmation reinforced the stability of each repertoire.

THE SILK WEAVERS AND SPITALFIELDS

By the 1820s the silk weavers were a distinctive trade community in the working-class East End (Warner 1921; Plummer 1972). Within the five parishes that composed the Spitalfields district lived some 13,000 to 14,000 weavers and their families, with many clustered in distinctive neighborhoods in the adjacent parishes of Christ Church Spitalfields and St. Matthew's Bethnal Green (Porter 1830: 80; P.P. 1834, XXXV, App. B. 2, Pt. IV, pp. 83i, 87i).

Silk-weaving was a trade anchored in the small domestic workshop, with weavers controlling, on average, three looms by the 1820s (P.P. 1835, VII, p. 10). In the idealized version of this enterprise the male weaver was the provider for the family and supervisor of wives and children assigned ancillary tasks (Jordan 1931: 12; P.P. 1818, IX, p. 148; P.P. 1835, VII, p. 11). However, economic realities necessitated that many wives wove alongside their husbands (Alexander 1976: 73, 95; Pinchbeck 1969: 160–61; L.S.P. 1823, CLVI, pp. 62, 102; P.P. 1818, IX, p. 44; P.P. 1835, VII, pp. 10–11). Weavers considered the apprenticeship of their offspring as an entailment of the trade, though by the period under review many readily accepted apprentices outside kin lines because of the extra income and labor they provided (Jordan 1931: 12, 156; P.P. 1818, IX, p. 44).

Wages in the trade were determined by an elaborate set of piece rates published sporadically in lengthy price books. Rates were highest in the fancy goods portion of the trade, which defined the luxury markets and legitimated silk weaving as a skilled trade. Up through the 1820s a third to a half of the trade was involved in such production (P.P. 1832, XIX, pp. 707, 716, 725; Rothstein 1977). Many small masters specialized in particular fabrics and designs, and they often sought to retain reliable weavers in their services (Jordan 1931: 3; P.P. 1832, XIX, p. 715; P.P. 1834, X, p. 590). The remainder of the trade was occupied in the production of various forms of broadloom cloth.

Throughout these decades weavers developed and maintained an ideology of trade and community respectability. They did so with their concepts of trade skill and independence, the elite nature of their product, and their status as productive artisans amidst the squalor of the plebeian East End. Their civility, independence, and patriotism were often noted during these years. As one master remarked in the Parliamentary hearings of 1832, "There does not exist in these realms, or in any part of the world, a class of people more industrious, more moral, and in every sense more deserving of the hand of government than the Spitalfields weavers" (P.P. 1832, XIX, p. 230).

Both the weavers' ability to maintain standardized piece rates and their status as honorable artisans rested firmly on the foundations of laws known as the Spitalfields Acts. The most significant of the Acts was passed in 1773 by an anxious Parliament, in response to several spates of large-scale collective violence conducted by the weavers protesting piece-rate cuts during the previous four years (Hammonds 1967; Rude 1962; Plummer 1972; Shelton 1972). The most significant provisions of the Acts mandated negotiation between masters and journeymen to establish piece rates, which were published in the abovementioned rate books. Binding arbitration was required if the parties could not agree, and once the prices were fixed they were considered inviolable. Piece rate disputes were to be adjudicated by local magistrates, which sometimes had the practical effect of discouraging masters from imposing fines as a means of lowering wages. Additionally, the Acts also prohibited masters who employed district weavers from contracting work outside of Spitalfields for below-book rates and fixed the maximum number of apprentices for each journeyman at two. Finally, the Acts prohibited the importation of foreign wrought silks, which severely limited competition from France and the East (Clapham 1916: 460–62; Plummer 1972: 328–29; P.P. 1818, IX, p. 190).[6] The Acts stood as a political sanctification of the weavers' claims of economic and social entitlement as productive and honorable artisans. As a weavers' committee later observed, the law could be used as a moral shield when workers were threatened with economic exploitation: "When men forget their moral obligations due between man and man, and as often as they can take poor men's labor without fair compensation, it is high time to call in the strong arm of the law, and convince them that they must not oppress with impunity" (*Letters* 1818, pp. 42–43). In so doing, the Acts gave de jure status to the weavers' moral economy of productive and community relations.[7] They legitimated both the communally derived standards of the value of labor and the workers' voice in trade relations.

For fifty years the Acts stood as ready legitimation of the weavers' standards of just remuneration and treatment, insuring an unbroken period of labor peace. The weavers were seen by magistrates and parish officers as responsible citizens among the plebeian rabble, trusted for their civil loyalty and deemed deserving of aid in hard times.

By the early 1820s the weavers found their world of trade and community respectability under imminent threat. The industry, which had traditionally been the realm of the resident small master, was being usurped by larger City wholesalers, leading one observer to warn that "the silk trade is very much under the influence of a few leading houses, who are extremely active, and distinguished for their zeal and perseverance" (British Library, Francis Place Newspaper Cuttings and Clippings Collection [hereafter Place Coll.], set 16, v. 2, fol. 32; Jordan 1931: 3; "Verax" 1822: 22–23). These "warehousers," as they were often termed, could control the output of several hundred looms and in so doing dominate the labor market. Unlike their diminutive counterparts, they had little if any experience in production, and virtually none lived in the East End (P.P. 1818, IX, pp. 143, 161, 168, 192; P.P. 1834, XXIX, pt. III, p. 112a). Economically, socially, culturally, and geographically, the weavers saw the gulf of class widen between them and their employers as the warehousers came to dominance.

By the 1820s these divisions found their most acute expression in dissension over the Spitalfields Acts, which became, in the words of one historian, "*the* test case for the further progress of the application of laissez faire" (Gordon 1979: 19; emphasis in original). On 9 May 1823, as I have noted, a group of manufacturers shot the opening salvo in what was to be their final campaign against the Acts. They depicted them as a yoke upon free trade, the employment of capital, the expansion of the industry, and as allowing the unwarranted influence of ignorant magistrates (*Hansards*, n.s., 1823, v. 9, c. 146–49). These City warehousers received substantial support from the large coterie of Tory and Whig free traders that had emerged in Parliament in the preceding decades.

For the next year the weavers sustained a well-coordinated campaign through their pub-based trade societies to stave off the onslaught of the warehousers and the champions of Political Economy. While the weavers won several of the initial skirmishes, the phalanx of warehousers and free traders was in the end their better. In June 1824 the repeal of the Acts was given royal consent. Through the campaign against repeal, however, the long-dormant weavers had laid the basis for a repertoire that would be the foundation for much contention in the succeeding years.

Contention between the weavers, manufacturers, and the state continued through the end of the decade. For the 1825–30 period the weavers mirrored England as a whole by making the public meeting and demonstration the dominant form of their repertoire (Tilly 1982, 1992; see also Belchem 1981; Parsinnen 1973). The weavers occupied most of their collective energies in public discussions on claims and in the petitioning of Parliament, ministries, and the royal family. Their action repertoire was quite standard. A committee called an assembly, the weavers met at a green or public house, discussed their grievances and the content of their petition, passed resolutions, and authorized the forwarding of the petition. Periodic meetings followed while waiting for a response and in the wake of a reply. Periods of petitioning were punctuated by strikes at two-year intervals starting in 1825, with the largest of these strikes being the May-June campaign of 1829.[8] Strike actions were more variable in their phases of action, though initially similar in their processes of meetings and claims-making.

The heavy cluster of activity surrounding the petitioning of Parliament was both a legacy of the Repeal campaign and motivated by the weavers' conceptions of citizens' rights.[9] As one weaver noted in a repartee to a critic of the weavers' practice, "We hold it as a peculiar privilege of our constitution to be allowed to petition Parliament for redress of any grievance under which we suffer or suppose ourselves to suffer" (*Trades' Free Press*, 15 March 1826). Because of their history, the weavers viewed trade protection as a laborer's right of citizenship, and therefore as a *political* issue, to be pursued through trade society meetings and petitions.

When directing claims against masters, the weavers developed an action repertoire that emphasized trade society meetings for the purposes of claims-making and negotiations, and (with less frequency) strikes.[10] Violence against property or person was used sparingly but strikingly. This was particularly true in the strike of 1829, when the weavers revived the practice of "cutting," the destruction of partially worked fabric in looms of manufacturers deemed particularly obnoxious or of weavers who ignored the strike call. Cutting had been a signature practice of the weavers' campaigns that led to the passage of the Spitalfields Acts but had not been resorted to since that time.[11]

The weavers thus had an action repertoire directed both at various branches of government and at manufacturers. Accompanying such actions was a discursive repertoire through which they articulated their claims, a moral economy of political and economic equity and entitlement, and an ideology of social justice. In the remaining sections below I demonstrate how this repertoire was constructed through struggle.

THE MANUFACTURERS' DISCURSIVE REPERTOIRE

Post-repeal contention occurred on a discursive level as well, and the repertoire of discourse served to mark the boundaries of legitimate debate and action. As I argued above, the development of a discursive repertoire is a dialogic process. The silk weavers reworked their moral economy in relation to the discourse of their adversaries. The warehousers and free traders in Parliament developed a discursive repertoire derived from the texts of political economy and bourgeois evangelicalism. Their particular repertoire was partly derivative of discursive conflicts between the moral economy of labor and the political economy of capital that had evolved over the previous 15 years. By the time of the repeal debate, political economy had gained hegemony, in that it critically shaped both Parliamentary discussions and those in the stamped press (Berg 1980; Claeys 1985, 1987; Dean 1991; Hilton 1988; Randall 1986, 1990, 1991; Smail 1987, 1991; N. W. Thompson 1984).[12]

Through the discourses of political economy, manufacturers and their allies depicted protected trade as precluding the full rewards of industry by interfering in labor relations, artificially structuring wages, and inhibiting the free use of capital. As one observer argued, trade protection was a fraud perpetrated against the worker to rob him of the full value of his labor. In constructing a case for natural rights, their discourse individuated the worker as a single and equal male actor in a marketplace and sought to undermine conceptions of collective rights commonly articulated through a moral economy.

> I have no hesitation in calling it barbarous, oppressive and unjust, for the weaver has the same natural right to the value of his labor, as the Nobleman has to the rent of his estates, the fundholder to his dividends. . . . To deprive the labourer of the full value of his work, is under any circumstances, an act of *Oppression and Robbery*; but to do this by means of a measure which affects to protect him, is indeed to add hypocrisy to injustice (*Observations*, 1822: 76).

Through this discourse weavers' fortunes were not only individuated but hierarchically tied to the fortunes of the manufacturers, rather than being a negotiated order between the two parties: "The great objects of the manufacturer are or ought to be, to extend the market for his commodities and increase the amount and productiveness of his capital; and the real interests of the labourer are secured exactly in proportion as these objects are accomplished" (ibid.: 23).

Finally, warehousers contested the weavers' notion of the status of the poor. The manufacturers' power and influence on the trade did not cause the weavers' dearth. Rather, his penury stemmed from his own lack of resources that would enable both alternatives and bargaining power in an impersonal market.

> All men who have not property, whatever be their rank, profession, or pretensions, are obliged in order to live to dispose of their commodity, be it what it may, at the market

price. . . . The labourer is obliged to dispose of his labour "instantly" *not because he is a labourer*, but *because he is poor.* . . . His helplessness, *so far as it consists in the necessity of constantly bringing his labour to the existing market*, is not *caused* by them. It is part of that higher legislation which has decreed that "the poor shall always be with us." (ibid.: 54–55; emphasis in the original)

In the last sentence we find a theme of quiet Christian resignation often tied to the logic of political economy. Spitalfields was patrolled by bourgeois benevolent societies from the first decades of the nineteenth century. Their members made tens of thousands of site visits, bearing a message of spiritual quiescence (McCann 1977; Steinberg 1989: 1: 187–96). "All success," noted the Spitalfields Benevolent Society, "must depend on the blessing of God. Many discouragements and disappointments must be expected; but, when Christians have done their duty, they will leave events to God" (*First Report* 1812: 21). An evangelical propagandist, seeking to provide the plebeians of Spitalfields with the proper self-image, equated working-class piety with such resignation:

> We are poor and industrious men, and cannot be expected to be conversant in politics or the science of government. We are Christians, and are instructed to fear God, be subject to the higher powers, and not meddle with them who are given to chance. It does not become us to agitate a subject of which we are entirely ignorant. (Brock 1817: 9)

In the discourse by which manufacturers and free traders structured notions of trade and industry, the course of the silk industry was determined as much by Providence as the market. This is articulated in Harriet Martineau's didactic novel *The Loom Lugger*, written for the silk weavers to instill the proper principles of political economy.

> When will men learn that the plan of Divine Providence indicates the scheme of human providence; that man should distribute his possessions as God scatters his gifts; that, as man is created for kindliness and for social ease, he should be governed so as to secure them; that as all interests naturally harmonize under a law of impartial love, it is an impiety to

institute a law of partiality, by which interests are arbitrarily opposed. (Martineau 1833: 110)

Another theme that dominated the hegemonic discourse, countering notions of interventionism, was the destructiveness of governmental protection. Manufacturers and their allies constantly emphasized that it stultified expansion and improvement, impoverishing weaver, manufacturer, and consumer. "The very essence of manufacturing and commercial industry," remarked the free-trader M.P. Poulett-Thompson in a debate on trade restrictions, "is freedom from legislative interefeference" (*Hansards*, n.s., 1829, v. 21, c. 843). Protection in this discourse was the disruption of the "perfect liberty" of exchange which "for the sake of benefiting any particular class or classes, is a sacrifice of a larger interest to a smaller,—that is, a sin of government" (Martineau 1833: 143). As the *Westminster Review* commented, protection actually instigated conflict:

> Prohibitions and protections, restrictions, and monopolies, are in truth nothing but Toryism applied to the daily concerns of life. They are part and parcel of the great delusions by which strong multitudes are made tools of a handful of leaders, prompted and led astray by those who are interested in increasing the causes of national distress. (1833: 18: 5)

The state thus guarded both the rights of citizens and economic vibrancy by maintaining a clear separation between polity and economy.

Through this discourse manufacturers and free traders constructed a moral and political context within which any argument for protection was prima face illegitimate. Proper self-interested action on the part of the weavers was individualistic and responsive to market demands. This discourse defined collective action to secure wage or trade protection as impolitic, exploitative of trade and market, and ultimately fruitless. Moreover, free traders structured an ideological vision of the economy cleansed of morality. As one warehouser half-jokingly declared during a spring meeting in 1829, "For his part, he did not know that it was always safe to introduce morality when they were discussing a return on capital and commercial transactions" (Place Coll., set 16, v. 2, fol. 118). In pursuing either wage protection from the government or stable list prices from manufacturers, the weavers developed a counter-hegemonic discursive repertoire which contested this dominant framing.

THE WEAVERS' DISCURSIVE REPERTOIRE

As I noted in the discussion of discursive repertoires, their development by challengers is in part a process of counter-hegemony. Challengers actively appropriate and subvert hegemonic discourse in ongoing dialogue. From the start of the repeal debate through the end of the decade the weavers refashioned their moral economy in just this way. Through both processes their grammar of motives emphasized their positive collective rights as productive citizens, the political legitimacy of protection, and the moral righteousness of their claims.

The actual mix through which weavers responded depended on context and the target of claims, but by the later 1820s several reasonably stable themes emerged in response to the dominant discourses. Foremost amongst their themes was a moral claim of positive rights as productive members of the polity. In their numerous actions directed at the state, the weavers wove together several moral motivations for trade and wage protection under "the great principle contended for, namely, that of *equal justice*" (*Trades' Free Press*, 3 May 1828, p. 322). In these cases the weavers depicted themselves as aggrieved citizens, productive members of the community whose welfare merited state intervention. Within the theme of equity the weavers argued that they sought the same protection for their only property, their labor, as other classes received for theirs.[13] The petition of 1 May 1828 is emblematic of this claim.

> The petitioners are convinced from the long experience they have had under the late Spitalfields Acts, that they are confident, if their wages were again regulated and protected by a general law, much of their sufferings would be alleviated; for having no other property than their labour, and it being of that nature they cannot withhold it from the market, are consequently compelled, by the unfeeling dictum of their employers, to yield to what price they think proper to give, or literally starve. This species of property is, therefore the

> weakest, and more exposed than any other; not so with per-
> sons whose incomes are derived from landed property, the
> funds, tithes, law fees, salaries, & c. and from monopolies
> of every kind. Their incomes are subjected to and protected
> by legislative or conventional regulations; but labour, and
> labourers alone, are left prey to the depredations of rapa-
> cious, needy, speculating contractors and employers, and to
> enable them to make a profit at the expense of labourers,
> the parishes are alternately called upon to make up a portion
> of their just wages. It is therefore irreconcilable with every
> principle of justice, or of right, that the incomes and prop-
> erty of all other classes should be protected, and his alone
> plundered by unprincipled men. (*Trades' Free Press*, 31 May
> 1828, p. 354; see also Powell 1824).

Within this discourse the weavers attempted both to extend concepts from political economy and explicitly to repoliticize them.
They did not deny the operation of markets, but rather argued
that other groups were able to take advantage of them because of
political protection. A dominant theme of the weavers' discourse
(as well as that of many other working-class groups) was that labor
was a form of property that deserved the same protection as the
property of all other classes.

The theme of equitable justice recurs in many of the weavers'
petitions to Parliament and in meeting oratory from the mid 1820s
into the 1830s. Opposing the minimalist concept of the state
offered by the free traders, the weavers argued that government
should be an active guardian of workers' welfare. This is clearly
spelled out in a treatise on protection accompanying a petition in
February 1828. "The great end of all government," they argued,

> and that alone which renders a government necessary, is
> to prevent one man from taking advantage of another, by
> withholding or abstracting from him the fruits of his indus-
> try, and is most fully accomplished when every man has
> secured to him the greatest amount of the products of his
> labour. . . . There can be no profitable commerce,—no
> national prosperity,—no security to property,—no stability
> to institutions,—and all that machinery must accelerate their
> dissolution,—unless measures are speedily adopted tending

to reinstate artizans and labourers in their just sphere of influence and reward, by securing them, with a moderate portion of exertion to command, not only necessaries, but even the comforts of life. Wages being the grand pivotal point round which all interests of society turn, unless they are raised to a level above subsistence, and a declaratory law adopted, recognizing the maxim, that MAN SHALL LIVE BY HIS LABOUR,—all other remedies will be of no avail. (*Report* 1828: 12–14, 22; see also "Coventry Freeman" 1824).

At times, these conceptions of protection and welfare were accompanied by a political critique of "Old Corruption" as a means of highlighting the state's insensitivity to workers' interests. Popular among period radicals, the critique claimed that the productive classes of society were prey to the machinations of profligate politicians and aristocrats. A corrupt Parliament's excessive taxation supported the former's idleness (Hollis 1970; Hone 1982; Rubenstein 1988; Stedman Jones 1983). On several occasions in the post-repeal period, when radical politics was experiencing a resurgence in the push for Parliamentary reform, the weavers drew upon an Old Corruption analysis, as in their petition of May 1827:

While the voracious system of excessive taxation, and its unjust and profligate expenditure, together with the ruinous paper currency, cruel and oppressive Corn Laws, and that unnatural and monsterous overgrown debt, called National, continue to exist, they devour, with unrelenting rapacity, the greatest portion of the produce of the petitioners' paltry but hard-earned labour. The distress which the petitioners suffer and which they continue to suffer, is unexampled in the history of this country; and it must be apparent to the House, that it is rapidly involving the industrious classes of the community in immediate and irretrievable ruin. The petitioners are well aware that the misery of the times in which they live is not caused by any visitation of Providence, nor has it been occasioned by any accidental combination of circumstances, physical or moral; it is the result, the natural result of laws emanating from the House, such having arisen solely from the want of fair and equal representation of the people in the House. (Place Coll., set 16, v. 2, fol. 78)

A second distinctive, though less frequent, theme pronounced a moral economy of trade to counter political economy. Weavers opposed a trade community to a soulless market. They did not repudiate capitalism per se, nor did they advocate cooperative socialism which was gaining increasing currency in London. Rather, they focused on the weavers' collective rights as trade members and articulated the legitimate boundaries of master-servant relationships. Ideally these relations were based in reciprocity, albeit one that was hierarchically organized. William Hunter, a weavers' leader, articulated this idea during the strike of 1829. He argued that both groups could prosper, even in the face of French competition, if they recognized each other's trade rights.

> The Frenchmen was in their own market, and it required a cordial co-operation of both to beat them out; and he well knew that, with the protecting duty afforded by the Government, the masters could, with safety to themselves, return to the book prices, and afterwards beat the foreigner. It was, no doubt, the duty of the masters to protect the property of their journeymen, as it was the bounden duty of the journeymen to protect the property of their masters. (*London Morning Chronicle*, 7 May 1829)

An emphasis on the economic vitality of the entire trade community led to a premium on trade stability, rejecting ideas of unbridled markets. Mutuality was counterposed to hierarchical dependence. The recognition of the bounded autonomy of workers within the production process legitimated the silk weavers' claims to their position as honorable artisans and to a living wage.[14] It also provided clear motivation for taking action when these were violated. By articulating their understanding of labor's independence, the weavers explicitly rejected the idea of the "freedom" of the market as it was posed by political economy. Such freedom insured an imbalance between worker and manufacturer which "renders the labouring classes a ready prey to the capitalists, who have the means of acquiring authority over others, in proportion to the quantity of objects of desire which they are able to possess, by whatever means those objects are attained" (*Report* 1828: 25–26). The weavers' Macclesfield brethren echoed this idea in their support of a reenactment of the Spitalfields Acts in 1826:

Can the workmen themselves fix a minimum price? Not without acting in opposition to the will of the employers; and does it not almost amount to a moral impossibility for men who are unable to live by their labour, and support their families by their industry, to withstand the rich capitalist who has thousands of pounds to back his cause? . . . Is labour free?—Yes—for the rich capitalist to command it at his will and pleasure, and generally speaking for what price he chooses. . . . Is labour free for the operative to fix the value of his labour?—We answer, no; for though he is not compelled by the law of the land to work for what is not a living price, yet he is compelled by necessity—his poverty renders him dependent—his masters' will is his law, and he has no alternative but to work or absolutely perish (*Trades' Newspaper*, 9 July 1826).

Here poverty was the inevitable outcome of the manufacturers' unmitigated power. Opposing the idea of wages finding their level in the market, the weavers argued for a just price. In so doing they reframed their expectations in terms not of citizens' but of workers' rights. As the secretaries of the weavers' committee asserted in an address of June 1826,

no Journeyman Mechanic (who is willing to work for his living) should be paid a less rate for labour than what will enable him to provide for the wants of his family, is a truth which the enemies of fair remuneration for labour cannot successfully disprove; and, when innovations are made by avaricious and unprincipled employers, it is a duty incumbent upon us, the working classes, to resist such innovations to the utmost in our power." (*Trades' Free Press*, 2 July 1826)

The weavers also countered the production-centered economic discourse of the warehousers and free traders with a consumption-centered model of economic prosperity. Appropriating Smith's labor theory of value, they argued that fair remuneration was in the end also sound economic policy.

An equitable return for labour is best adapted, and is indeed indispensable to secure the greatest quantity of wealth in any country, and to promote the legitimate interests of all classes in society.

1st. Because it is labour which gives value to the land and raw material for manufactures. "The labour of the country is the wealth of the country" (Adam Smith), and in proportion as the wages are high or low, the value of wealth in such country is increased or diminished. (*Report* 1828: 14).[15]

Finally, the weavers also answered the evangelicals' call for Christian resignation with their own populist use of the Bible. Drawing upon God's blessings of the poor and weak, they argued that such resignation was fostered by divine guarantees of security and subsistence. Within their own understanding of Christian charity and divine guidance, God commanded the equitable distribution of wealth among all of his faithful. As the weavers proclaimed in a circular disseminated to M.P.s, "It may be said of the weaving business, what Solomon said of husbandry—'the profits of the earth are for all' " (*An Account* 1823: 25). Moreover, avaricious manufacturers could expect divine retribution if they did not follow God's tenets. As the weavers' leader John Poynton warned,

The Lord will pour out vengeance on the oppressors of the poor and needy, that keep back the hire of the labourer by fraud and violence, which (by the by) is entered into the ears of the Lord of the Sabaoth, whose voice is "go now, ye rich men, howl and weep, for the miseries that come upon you. Your riches are corrupted; your gold and silver is cankered; and the rust of them shall be witness against you, and shall eat your flesh like fire, and be as burning metal in your bowels." (*An Account* 1823: 62)

The weavers thus dialogically developed a coherent discursive repertoire in their struggles with manufacturers and free traders. Through this repertoire they sought to structure a counter-hegemony, delegitimizing the tenets of the powerholders in part through appropriating the very discourses by which the latter justified their actions. The repertoire offered a grammar of motives for collective actions to defend their rights as citizens and workers. Moreover, in refashioning their moral economy, the weavers did not fundamentally question the foundations of the polity or economy. Rather, they critically shifted meanings within these discourses to create an ideological vision focused upon community, equity, and stability. Over the course of their struggles with state actors and manufacturers, these themes stabilized to become the foundations of an enduring discursive repertoire. In the final section I turn to the ways in which the discursive and instrumental repertoires mutually reinforced each other.

THE MEDIATION OF CONSCIOUSNESS AND ACTION

The stability of the weavers' action repertoire requires explanation, for despite repeated failures and the gradual transformation of such repertoires in other trades, theirs remained remarkably stable. In this section I argue that both the weavers' material and social circumstances and the relationship between the action and discursive repertoires led to a continued emphasis on claims against the state.

The pattern of continued claims against the Parliament, the Board of Trade, and the royal family, despite the paucity of redress, is not easily explicable within the assumptions of rational collective interest. Despite the intransigence of Parliament and the building of more permanent unions in other trades, the weavers persisted with their repertoire.[16] The short-lived but clear successes of the strikes also raise the question of why the weavers did not opt for more permanent union activity.

The weavers' action repertoire seems to be somewhat at variance with that of other London trades. As Prothero observes, the silk weavers' relatively diverse action repertoire had features typical of those of many trades under threat of degradation and unemployment (1979: 212). Several trades—including the silk weavers, printers, bookbinders, and sawyers—joined working-class leaders such as John Gast in seeking legislative protection for wages and against machinery during the later 1820s. Moreover, general strikes by trades were not frequent in these years of depression; those that did occur were largely in reaction to piece rate reductions.

However, few if any of the other London trades seem to have devoted as much effort to trade or wage protection. In addition, the silk weavers were latecomers to or lesser participants in other working-class actions of these years. They were derided by the

Trades' Newspaper in early 1826 for their continued support of the Corn Laws, with the paper claiming they had engaged in "desertion" of their class in the hopes of receiving a reenactment of the Spitalfields Acts in return (*Trades' Newspaper*, 26 Feb. and 5 March 1826).[17] More generally, their support for radical working-class political causes often developed more slowly, or was viewed with suspicions by others, though by 1830 there is evidence that disaffection among the weavers had led to increasing radicalism.[18] Additionally, the weavers seem to have been less involved in cooperation than other metropolitan trade groups, even though they were the subject of some attention by pundits within the movement (*The Co-Operative Magazine and Monthly Herald*, v. 1, no. 11, Nov. 1826, pp. 333–37; and n.s., no. 5, May 1827, p. 227; *The Lancashire Co-Operator*, no. 6, 20 Aug. 1831, p. 5; Place Coll., set 16, v. 2, fol. 70).[19] Finally, while the more prosperous 1830s brought increased trade action, even among degraded trades such as the tailors, the silk weavers do not seem to have engaged in a single strike during these years.

In all, three linked explanations may be offered for the stability of the weavers' actions. First, and most simply, petitioning required the mobilization of fewer resources than the alternatives. The destitution of the weavers during these years was severe. An inmate of the Bethnal Green workhouse reported to the radical William Lovett in 1831 that the weavers in that facility were "dying off like rotten sheep." Even the staunch free-trade manufacturer Ambrose Moore willingly admitted to Parliament the following year that the weavers "in fact, possess nothing, if I may so speak, really beyond the extent of their own skins" (Lovett 1967, 2: 57; P.P. 1832, XIX, p. 770).

Second, the weavers' appeals for protection were by no means chimerical given similar actions by other trades. Third, if experience is the fount of consciousness, then the weavers had ample reason to look toward trade protection. For a half-century they had maintained a trade community in peace and comparative prosperity under the aegis of the Acts, and time had not erased the memory of that reality.

There were thus sound experiential and material circumstances for the silk weavers to anchor their instrumental repertoire in claims against the state. Yet it is not sufficient to argue that the weavers pursued protection simply because it was expedient; the moral economy that they developed during their struggles provided compelling motives to seek state intervention, even in the face of repeated failure. A veteran weaver neatly summed up this persistent moral economy as he testified before a select committee in 1832.

> When I was bound apprentice, the government of the country had protected the trade, and I considered was bound to protect it; I thought I had done the same as purchased an annuity for life, as something by which I should be able to get a living for my family; I considered the government ought to have protected the same as every other species of property, but I am sorry to my cost, and the cost of those in Spitalfields, that they have not kept good faith. (P.P. 1832, XIX, p. 734)

Through their continuing struggles with both the City warehousers and governmental proponents of political economy, the weavers had developed counter-hegemonic discourse that framed legitimate courses of action. The history of the Spitalfields Acts maintained its cogency long after the Parliamentary battle of 1823–24, in part because of the dialogic struggles it had fostered. The notion of productive citizens' just entitlement to a living wage, coupled with the weavers' dire poverty, became mutually reinforcing rationales. In the past, threats to livelihood augured intervention, both on the national level in the creation and extension of the Acts and in the continuing support of local authorities in applying them.

Moreover, the theater of petitioning reinforced the process as a "peculiar privilege" of the constitution, for at no time did the government seek to delegitimize the weavers' state-oriented actions. Indeed, such activity as the political maneuvering in the Commons, leading to the extensive special committee hearings in 1832, only validated the weavers' grievances as political. Authorities participated in a standard set of interactions specified by the weavers' discourse, giving the process of petitioning credibility. The organs of government, through their denials of the weavers' claims, sanctified their rights as claimants. In doing so they also reinforced the saliency of the discursive repertoire.

The repeal debates thus set in motion a process through which the weavers constructed discursive and instrumental repertoires focused upon the state. In the response to their continuing campaigns the weavers found sufficient affirmation of both repertoires, so that the two remained mutually reinforcing. This process, coupled with the weighty history of the Acts and their present poverty, suggested a steady course despite the poor results and the gradual changes among other metropolitan trades.

CONCLUSION

The case of the silk weavers shows that to understand the dynamics of collective action repertoires we must analyze their discursive as well as their instrumental dimensions. The moral bases of both grievances and targets are collectively constructed through discourses of contention, which are developed dialogically in struggle. Through a process of counter-hegemony, contenders develop a discursive repertoire, attempting to expose the partiality of the dominant ideology through which justifications for power are constructed. These discursive repertoires can be reinforced through the validation of their instrumental counterparts, creating a stability in each even in the face of persistent failure. To understand stasis and change in repertoires thus requires an analysis of patterns of both discourse and collective action and their temporal relations. In sum, to wholly understand the drama, we need to pay more careful attention to the roar of the crowd.

NOTES

1   The term *discourse* is currently used to connote a variety of actions and ideas. I take it in the Bakhtinian sense as the flow of verbal communication between actors which creates scenarios for relationships and events (Todorov 1984: 47, 52). Discourse in this sense is used in a narrower context than in some forms of poststructural analysis in which all activity, and indeed reality itself, is viewed as a semiotic meaning. I refer to it as largely expressive action because I wish to emphasize that it is not simply epiphenomenal. To paraphrase Austin (1962), people do things with words, and the doing has palpable consequences just as other forms of largely instrumental action (e.g., demonstrations, strikes, and riots).

2   See, for example, the essays by Gamson, Snow and Benford, Klandermans, and Tarrow in Morris and Mueller 1992. Klandermans draws attention to three specific levels of the social construction of meaning in collective action: "(1) the level of public discourse and the formation and transformation of collective identities; (2) the level of persuasive communication during mobilization campaigns by movement organizations, their opponents, and

countermovement organizations; and (3) the level of consciousness raising during episodes of collective action" (1992: 82).

3   This analysis draws heavily on the work of the Bakhtinian school of literary analysis. For original key texts upon which this theory has developed, see Bakhtin 1981 and 1986 and Volosinov 1986 and 1983. For recent work on the dialogic perspective see Clark and Holquist 1984, Hirschkop 1986 and 1989, Holquist 1990, and Todorov 1984.

4   As Volosinov argues, "Each period and each social group has its own repertoire of speech forms for ideological communication" (1986: 20). Bakhtin captures this idea of a repertoire of discourse in his notions of heterology and speech genres. Every group in every epoch has a limited number of forms of expression through which it can produce meaning (see Bakhtin 1986; Todorov 1984, esp. 56–59).

5   In part because the production of meanings within the sign is a *relational* process, the meaning of particular words or phrases is dependent on their use within the utterance and its context. A range of semantic practices such as metaphor, metonomy, euphemization, implicature, tropes, etc. are available to accentuate and partly shape the meaning of signs (Gastil 1992; Lackoff and Johnson 1979; J. B. Thompson 1990).

6   An act of 1792 extended these provisions to mixed fabrics. In 1811 they were legally extended to women as well, providing some indication of the significance of women in the trade (Clapham 1916: 462; Hammonds 1967: 209).

7   My use of the term *moral economy* here follows the concept as recently rearticulated by E. P. Thompson and also by Charles Tilly. Tilly argues that "the term 'moral economy' makes sense when claimants to a commodity can invoke non-monetary rights to that commodity, and third parties will support *these* claims—when, for example, community membership supersedes price as a basis for entitlement" (quoted in E. P. Thompson 1991: 338). Thompson argues that class relations can be analyzed in terms of a moral economy when they are negotiated through a series of community practices that recognize mutual obligations, when market practices are thus publicly acknowledged to have normative underpinnings, and when the ideological bases of these practices are articulated in plebeian discourses (ibid.: 271, 343, 350).

8   For a detailed listing of the weavers' actions for 1825–30 see Steinberg 1993.

9   The local parishes also conducted meetings to petition various arms of government; no doubt these too were heavily attended by the weavers (*Trades' Newspaper*, 22 Jan. 1826, 3 June 1827, 14 Feb. 1829). These meetings are indicative of the symbiotic relationship between the weavers and parish officers described above. Because they were led by parish officers in the name of the vestry, however, they are not included in the weavers' repertoire.

10   During the post-repeal years both manufacturers and weavers brought conflicts concerning wages and disciplinary actions to the local magistrates for adjudication. The actions brought by the weavers cannot in any straightforward sense be termed part of a collective action repertoire, because they involved individual claimants. However, weavers on occasion were repre-

sented before the bench by the secretary of the weavers' society (see for example, *Trades' Free Press*, 16 Sept. and 16 Dec. 1827). Whether there was any collective deliberation to the process of bringing claims against particular manufacturers is impossible to say.

11   For an analysis of cutting during the spring 1829 strike see Steinberg 1989, 1: 261–73. On rare occasions the weavers resorted to attacks against people and personal property (Place Coll., set 16, v. 2, fol. 128; *Trades' Free Press*, 16 June 1829).

12   In claiming that political economy was hegemonic, I follow Richard Terdiman's notion of dominance. He argues that "the dominant discourse is the discourse whose presence is defined by the *social impossibility of its absence*" (1986: 61). From the early nineteenth century it was impossible to conduct a public debate on major economic and social policy without reacting to political economy. As the historian Gregory Claeys notes in an analysis of the development of radical politics, "Though the direct and immediate impact of *laissez-faire* ideals upon contemporary legislation has probably been exaggerated, the rapid ascendancy of political economy as a social and political philosophy remains undisputed. For much of the nineteenth century, political economy successfully dictated the terms of the debate about such vital issues as the poor laws, trades' unions, hours and conditions of labour, emigration, the morals of the poor, and the extension of the factory system" (1989: 144).

13   The weavers, as in the case of many other trade groups, were fond of quoting Adam Smith that "the labour of the country is the wealth of the country" (*Report* 1828: 14). This is one example of how discursive appropriation was used in the process of constructing a counter-hegemony.

14   In his study of the woolen workers of the West Country and West Riding, Adrian Randall (1988, 1991) details a similar moral economy of trade relations (see particularly, 1991, ch. 8). As he notes in the case of the woolen workers, "The origins of the moral economy therefore have to be found within a capitalist economy, not outside or in opposition to one" (1991: 255).

15   This argument is continued in a footnote by quoting Locke on the impartation of value to land through labour (p. 14).

16   Whether the weavers were entirely unsuccessful is open to debate. They never achieved any success in their claims for wage control, increased tariff protection, or assistance with emigration. However, it is possible to argue that their actions during 1826 were partly responsible for the creation of the Spitalfields Relief Society by the City establishment, to which the king did make two substantial donations (see Place Coll., set 16, v. 2, for accounts of the Relief Society; *Trades' Newspaper*, 4 Apr. 1826; *Weekly Free Press*, 22 Apr. 1829). Moreover, the king and queen did patronize the Spitalfields trade with orders in response to their pleas for assistance (*Trades' Free Press*, 29 Oct. 1826, *Weekly Free Press*, 23 Oct. 1830).

    The evidence on unions is reasonably clear. As Frank Warner noted, no attempt to maintain a permanent union during these years was ever successful (1921: 514). Rather, the pattern seems to have been one of pub-based trade societies temporarily coalescing under the umbrella of a general trades' committee for purposes of coordination (Jordan 1931: 147, 149–51, 194; Prothero 1979: 212; P.P. 1818, IX, pp. 55, 188, 194–96; B.L., Add. MSS. 27799).

17 By 1827 the weavers had changed their stance, perhaps realizing that they could not effect a deal with agricultural interests for the mutual support of protective trade legislation. The *Trades' Newspaper* was also critical of the weavers' memorials to the royal family for patronage, claiming that they were acting as a "slave kissing the feet of his oppressors" (29 Oct. 1926).

18 Witnesses substantiated the loyalty of the weavers in the their testimony before Parliament well into the 1830s (P.P. 1832, XIX, p. 230; P.P. 1834, X, p. 320). However, the weavers seem to be more active in radical associations and politics, though even their participation in the National Union of the Working Classes was viewed by some as a self-interested maneuver to seek a renewal of trade protection (Hollis 1970: 265; see Prothero 1979, passim; H.O. 40/25 fols. 274–75).

19 Both Prothero and Goodway suggest that the weavers were relatively enthusiastic about cooperation (Prothero 1979: 251, 253; Goodway 1984: 188). However, there is little evidence to support wide, sustained participation. The National Silk Weavers' Society, which was inaugurated on 25 June 1827 with grandiose claims for employment and the education of children, quickly lapsed into obscurity (Place Coll., set 16, v. 2, fols. 74–76; *Trades' Free Press*, 3 Dec. 1826). The *Weekly Free Press* was urging the weavers to foster a cooperative society once again in 1829 to alleviate their unemployment. Phillip Skeene, in a letter to the *Weekly Free Press* in August on donations to facilitate such production, notes that cooperative societies in Bethnal Green were inexperienced and when combined would not contain more than 150 members (22 Aug. 1829).

REFERENCES

Archives

British Library, London
  Francis Place Collection of Newspaper Clippings and Pamphlets.
British Public Record Office (Kew Gardens), Home Office Papers.
  H.O. 40/23–27. Correspondence, Civil Disturbances.
  H.O. 62/1–7. Metropolitan Police Reports.

British Parliamentary Debates, Papers, and Reports

Hansards Parliamentary Debates, New Series
  House of Commons
    P.P. 1818 (134) IX. Report of the Committee on Silk Weavers' Petitions.
    P.P. 1818 (211) IX. Second Report of the Committee on Silk Weavers' Petitions.

P.P. 1832 (678) XIX. Report of the Select Committee on the Silk Trade.

P.P. 1834 (465) VII. Report from the Select Committee on Education in England and Wales.

P.P. 1834 (556) X. Report from the Select Committee on Handloom Weavers' Petitions.

P.P. 1834 (44) XXIX. Report from the Assistant Poor Law Commissioners, Pt. III.

P.P. 1834 (36) XXXV. Appendices to the Report of the Poor Law Commissioners. Appendix B.2. Answers to Questions Circulated by the Commissioners in Towns.

P.P. 1834 (556) Report of the Select Committee on Handloom Weavers' Petitions.

P.P. 1835 (572) VII. Report from the Select Committee on the State of Education in England and Wales.

House of Lords

L.S.P. 1823 (57) CLVI. Report of the Lords' Committee on the Bill to repeal certain Acts . . . relating to the Wages of Person employed in the Manufacture of Silk.

Newspapers and Periodicals

The Co-operative Magazine and Monthly Herald.

Lancashire and Yorkshire Cooperator.

London Morning Chronicle.

Times of London.

Trades' Newspaper and Mechanics' Weekly Journal.

Trades' Free Press.

Voice of the People.

Weekly Free Press.

Westminister Review.

Contemporary Literature

An Account of the Proceedings of the Committees of the Journeymen Silk Weavers of Spitalfields; in the Legal Defence of the Acts of Parliament, Granted to their Trade, in the 13th, 32nd, and 51st Years of the Reign of his late Majesty, King George the Third (1823) London: E. Justins.

Badnall, Richard (1828) A View of the Silk Trade; With Remarks on the Recent Measures of Government in Regard to the Branch of Manufacture. London: John Miller.

Brock, Irving (1817) A Letter to the Inhabitants of Spital-Fields, On the Character and Views of Modern Reformers. London: F. C. and J. Rivington.

Hale, William (1822) An Appeal to the Public, in Defence of the Spitalfields Act: with Remarks on the Causes Which Have Led to the Miseries and Moral Deterioration of the Poor. London: E. Justins.

Letters, Taken from Various Newspapers, Tending to Injure the Journeymen

Silk Weavers of Spitalfields, with an Attack against the Acts of Parliament, Regulating the Prices of Their Work . . . Also, the Answers, by the Journeymen and Their Friends (1818) London:. E. Justins.

Lovett, William (1967 [1867]) The Life and Struggles of William Lovett, vol. 1. London: MacGibbon and Kee.

Martineau, Harriet (1833) Illustrations of Political Economy. No. 17, The Loom Lugger, Part 1. London: Charles Fox.

—— (1819b) The Contented Spital-Fields Weaver; Jeremiah Nott, His Address to His Brother Artificers, Respecting the Smithfield Meeting, and Other Matters. 8th ed. London: Howard.

Observations on the Ruinous Effects of the Spitalfields Acts to the Silk Manufacture of London: to Which is Added a Reply to Mr. Hale's Appeal to the Public in Defence of the Acts (1822). London: John and Arthur Arch.

Porter, G. R. (1831) Treatise on the Origin, Progressive Improvement, and Present State of the Silk Trade. London:

Pymlot, J. (1826) Strictures on the Wisdom and Policy of the Present Measures Relative to the Importation of Silk. Macclesfield: Philip Hall.

Report Adopted at a General Meeting of the Journeymen Broad Silk Weavers, held in Saint John Street Chapel, Brick-lane, Spitalfields, On Wednesday, the 20th of February, 1828, to take into their Consideration the Necessity of Petitioning the Legislature for a Wage Protection Bill and such other purposes as may arise out of the same. To which is Appended, The Petition. London: W. C. Mantz.

Spitalfields Benevolent Society (1812) First Report of the Spitalfields Benevolent Society, Instituted in the Year MDCCCXI for Visiting and Relieving Cases of Great Distress, Chiefly among the Numerous Poor of Spitalfields and its Vicinity. London: Ellerton and Henderson.

"Verax" (1822) Review of the Statements in Hale's Appeal to the Public on the Spitalfields Acts. London: J. Hudson.

Data Sets

Great Britain Study. New School for Social Research. Charles Tilly, Principal Investigator.

Secondary Literature

Alexander, Sally (1976) "Women's work in nineteenth-century London. A study of the years 1820–50," in Juliet Mitchell and Ann Oakley (eds.) The Rights and Wrongs of Women. Harmondsworth: Penguin: 59–111.

Austin, J. L. (1962) How to Do Things with Words. Cambridge, MA: Harvard University Press.

Bakhtin, Mikhail M. (1981) The Dialogic Imagination: Four Essays. Translated by Caryl Emerson and Michael Holquist and edited by Michael Holquist. Austin: University of Texas Press.

—— (1986) Speech Genres and Other Late Essays. Translated by Vern W.

McGee and edited by Caryl Emerson and Michael Holquist. Austin: University of Texas Press.

Belchem, John (1981) "Republicanism, popular constitutionalism, and the radical platform in nineteenth-century England." Social History 6: 1–32.

Berg, Maxine (1980) The Machinery Question and the Making of Political Economy, 1815–1848. Cambridge: Cambridge University Press.

Bland, A. E., P. A. Brown, and R. H. Tawney, eds. (1919) English Economic History: Select Documents. New York: Macmillan.

Claeys, Gregory (1989) Citizens and Saints: Politics and Anti-Politics in Early British Socialism. Cambridge: Cambridge University Press.

——— (1987) Machinery, Money, and the Millennium: From Moral Economy to Socialism, 1815–1850. Cambridge: Polity.

——— (1985) "The reaction to political radicalism and the popularisation of political economy in early nineteenth-century England," in Terry Shinn and Richard Whitley (eds.) Expository Science: Forms and Functions of Popularisation. Dordrecht: D. Reidel: 119–36.

Clapham, J. H. (1916) "The Spitalfields Acts, 1773–1824." Economic Journal 26: 459–71.

Clark, Katrina, and Michael Holquist (1984) Mikhail Bakhtin. Cambridge, MA: Harvard University Press.

Dean, Mitchell (1991) The Constitution of Poverty: Toward a Genealogy of Liberal Governance. London: Routledge.

Gamson, William A. (1992a) Talking Politics. Cambridge: Cambridge University Press.

——— (1992b) "The social psychology of collective action," in Aldon Morris and Carol McClurg Mueller (eds.) Frontiers in Social Movement Theory. New Haven: Yale University Press: 53–76.

——— (1988) "Political discourse and collective action." International Social Movement Research 1: 219–44.

Gamson, William A., Bruce Fireman, and Steve Rytina (1982) Encounters with Unjust Authority. Homewood: Dorsey Press.

Gastil, John (1992) "Undemocratic discourse: A review of theory and research on political discourse." Discourse and Society 3: 469–500.

George, M. Dorothy (1925) London Life in the Eighteenth Century. London: K. Paul, Trench, and Trubner.

Goodway, David (1984) London Chartism, 1838–1848. Cambridge: Cambridge University Press.

Hammond, J. L., and Barbara Hammond (1967 [1919]) The Skilled Labourer, 1780–1832. New York: August M. Kelley.

Hilton, Boyd (1988) The Age of Atonement: The Influence of Evangelicalism on Social and Economic Thought, 1795–1865. Oxford: Clarendon Press.

Hirschkop, Ken, and David Shepard (eds.) (1989) Bakhtin and Cultural Theory. Manchester: Manchester University Press.

——— (1986) "Bakhtin, discourse, and democracy." New Left Review 160: 91–111.

Hollis, Patricia (1970) The Pauper Press: A Study of Working-Class Radicalism of the 1830s. Oxford: Oxford University Press.

Holquist, Michael (1990) Dialogism: Bakhtin and His World. London: Routledge.

Hone, J. Ann (1982) For the Cause of Truth: Radicalism in London, 1796–1821. Oxford: Clarendon Press.

Hunt, Alan (1990) "Rights and social movements: Counter-hegemonic strategies." Journal of Law and Society 17: 309–28.

Jordan, W. M. (1931) The silk industry in London, 1760–1830, with special reference to the conditions of the wage-earners and the policy of the Spitalfields Acts. M.A. thesis, University of London.

Klandermans, Bert (1992) "The social construction of protest and multiorganizational fields," in Aldon Morris and Carol McClurg Mueller (eds.) Frontiers in Social Movement Theory. New Haven: Yale University Press: 77–103.

Lackoff, George, and Mark Johnson (1979) Metaphors We Live By. Chicago: University of Chicago Press.

Lown, Judy (1990) Women and Industrialization: Gender at Work in Nineteenth-Century England. Minneapolis: University of Minnesota Press.

McCann, Phillip (1977) "Popular education, socialization, and social control: Spitalfields 1812–1824," in Phillip McCann (ed.) Popular Education and Socialization in the Nineteenth Century. London: Methuen: 1–40.

Mouffe, Chantal (1979) "Hegemony and ideology in Gramsci," in Chantal Mouffe (ed.) Gramsci and Marxist Theory. London: Routledge and Kegan Paul: 168–204.

Parssinen, T. (1972) "Association, convention, and anti-Parliament in British radical politics, 1771–1848." English Historical Review 86: 504–33.

Pinchbeck, Ivy (1969) Women Workers and the Industrial Revolution, 1750–1850. London: Virago.

Plummer, Alfred (1972) The London Weavers' Company, 1600–1970. London: Routledge and Kegan Paul.

Prothero, Iowerth (1979) Artisans and Politics in Early Nineteenth-Century London: John Gast and His Times. London: Methuen.

Randall, Adrian (1986) "The philosophy of Luddism: The case of the west of England woolen workers, ca. 1790–1809." Technology and Culture 27: 1–17.

——— (1990) "New languages or old? Labour, capital, and discourse in the Industrial Revolution." Social History 15: 195–216.

——— (1991) Before the Luddites: Custom, Community, and Machinery in the English Woollen Industry, 1776–1809. Cambridge: Cambridge University Press.

Rothstein, Natalie (1977) "The introduction of the jacquard loom to Great Britain," in Veronica Gervers (ed.) Studies in Textile History. Toronto: Royal Ontario Museum: 281–304.

Rubenstein, W. D. (1987) "The end of 'old corruption' in Britain," in Elites and the Wealthy in Modern British History. Brighton: The Harvester Press: 265–303.

Rude, George (1962) Wilkes and Liberty. Oxford: Oxford University Press.

Rule, John (1988) "The property of skill in the period of manufacture," in

Patrick Joyce (ed.) The Historical Meaning of Work. Cambridge: Cambridge University Press: 99–118.

Scott, James (1990) Domination and the Arts of Resistance: Hidden Transcripts. New Haven: Yale University Press.

Shelton, Walter J. (1972) English Hunger and Industrial Disorders. Toronto: University of Toronto Press.

Smail, John (1987) "New languages for labour and capital: The transformation of discourse in the early years of the Industrial Revolution." Social History 12: 49–72.

——— (1991) "New languages? Yes indeed: A reply to Adrian Randall." Social History 16: 217–22.

Snow, David A., and Robert Benford (1992) "Master frames and cycles of protest" in Aldon Morris and Carol McClurg Mueller (eds.) Frontiers in Social Movement Theory. New Haven: Yale University Press: 133–55.

Snow, David A., E. Burke Rochford, Jr., Steven K. Worden, and Robert Benford (1986) "Frame alignment processes, micromobilization, and movement participation." American Sociological Review 51: 464–81.

Stedman Jones, Gareth (1983) Languages of Class: Studies in English Working-Class History, 1832–1982. Cambridge: Cambridge University Press.

Steinberg, Marc W. (1989) "Worthy of hire: Discourse, ideology, and collective action among English working-class trade groups," v. 1. Ph.D. dissertation, University of Michigan.

——— (1993) "New canons or loose cannons?: The post-Marxist challenge to neo-Marxism as represented in the work of Calhoun and Reddy," Political Power and Social Theory.

Tarrow, Sidney (1992) "Mentalities, political cultures, and collective action frames: Constructing meanings through action," in Aldon Morris and Carol McClurg Mueller (eds.) Frontiers in Social Movement Theory. New Haven: Yale University Press: 74–201.

Taylor, Barbara (1983) Eve and the New Jerusalem: Socialism and Feminism in the Nineteenth Century. New York: Pantheon.

Terdiman, Richard (1986) Discourse/Counter-Discourse: The Theory and Practice of Symbolic Resistance in Nineteenth-Century France. Ithaca: Cornell University Press.

Thompson, Edward P. (1966) The Making of the English Working Class. New York: Vintage.

——— (1971) "The moral economy of the crowd in the eighteenth century." Past and Present 50: 76–136.

——— (1991) Customs in Common: Studies in Traditional Popular Culture. New York: New Press.

Thompson, John B. (1990) Ideology and Modern Culture: Critical Social Theory in the Era of Mass Communication. Stanford: Stanford University Press.

Thompson, Noel W. (1984) The People's Science: The Popular Political Economy of Exploitation and Crisis, 1816–34. Cambridge: Cambridge University Press.

Tilly, Charles (1992) "Contentious repertoires in Great Britain, 1758–1834." Center for Studies of Social Change Working Paper Series, no. 141.

———— (1986) The Contentious French. Cambridge, MA: Harvard University Press.
———— (1982) "Britain creates the social movement," in James Cronin and Jonathan Schneer (eds.) Social Conflict and Political Order in Modern Britain. New Brunswick: Rutgers University Press: 21–51.
Todorov, Tzvetan (1984) Mikhail Bakhtin: The Dialogic Principle. Minneapolis: University of Minnesota Press.
Volosinov, V. N. (1986 [1929]) Marxism and the Philosophy of Language. Cambridge, MA: Harvard University Press.
———— (1983) "Literary stylistics," in Ann Shukman (ed.) Bakhtin School Poetics. Oxford: RPT Publications: 93–152.
Warner, Frank (1921) The Silk Industry in the United Kingdom: Its Origin and Development. London: Drane's.

Cycles of Collective Action: Between Moments of Madness and the Repertoire of Contention

SIDNEY TARROW

MOMENTS OF MADNESS—when "all is possible"—recur persistently in the history of social movements. In such turbulent points of history, writes Aristide Zolberg, "the wall between the instrumental and the expressive collapses." "Politics bursts its bounds to invade all of life" and "political animals somehow transcend their fate" (1972: 183). Such moments are unsettling and often leave even participants disillusioned—not to mention elites and political authorities. But they may be "necessary for the political transformation of societies," writes Zolberg, for they are the source of the new actors, the audiences and the force to break through the crust of convention (1972: 206). In Kafka's parable: "Leopards break into the temple and drink to the dregs what is in the sacrificial pitchers; this is repeated over and over again;

Sidney Tarrow is Maxwell M. Upson Professor of Government at Cornell University. The author of three books on social movements, *Peasant Communism in Southern Italy*, *Democracy and Disorder*, and *Struggle, Politics and Reform*, he is currently completing a book-length study, *Power in Movement: Collective Action, Social Movements, and Politics in the Modern World*. I am grateful to David Apter, Craig Jenkins, Peter Lange, Diarmuid Maguire, Arthur L. Stinchcombe, Charles Tilly, Mark Traugott, David Weakliem, and Aristide Zolberg for helpful reactions to an earlier version of the argument advanced in this essay, which was presented at the 1987 annual meeting of the American Political Science Association. The current version was written with the assistance of an Interpretive Research Grant from the National Endowment for the Humanities.

finally it can be calculated in advance, and it becomes a part of the ceremony." [1]

With de Tocqueville, look at the 1848 Revolution, when "a thousand strange systems issued impetuously from the minds of innovators and spread through the troubled mind of the crowd. Everything was still standing except the monarchy and parliament, and yet it appeared as if society itself had crumbled into dust under the shock of revolution" (1942; quoted in Zolberg 1972: 195). Or look with Edgar Morin at May 1968 in France. It "was carried away by 'the great festival of youthful solidarity,' the 'permanent game' which was also a serious strategy, in which revolutionary incantations achieved a 'genuine socialization' " (1968; in Zolberg 1972: 184). In such moments, the impossible becomes real— at least in the minds of participants.

But an important question about such moments is often overlooked: their relation to the historical development of the repertoire of contention. Some observers think that such moments create totally new forms of collective life.[2] But when we confront the creative aspects of moments of madness with the historical development of the repertoire of collective action, we find a puzzle. For as Tilly has shown, the repertoire developed slowly and haltingly and no faster than the development of states and capitalism. If moments of madness produce as rich a tapestry of collective action as we think, why has the repertoire developed as slowly as it has? Is it because the forms of contention that explode during such exceptional moments are not as exceptional as they seem at the time? Or is it because—precisely because they are so exceptional—they are rejected and repressed when order returns? Or rather, is the incremental pace of the repertoire's change due to the fact that the absorption of new forms of contention is mediated by institutional processes?

THE REPERTOIRE OF CONTENTION

The question can be posed in more analytical terms if we return to the concept of the repertoire as it was developed by Charles Tilly in the 1970s and 1980s.[3] Tilly sees the repertoire as the whole set of means that a group has for making claims of different kinds on different individuals or groups (1986: 4). Because different groups in similar circumstances have similar repertoires, he speaks more loosely of a general repertoire that is available to the population as a whole. At any point in time, he writes, the repertoire available to a given population is limited, despite the possibility of using virtually any form of contention against any opponent. The repertoire is therefore not only what people *do* when they make a claim; it is what they *know how to do* and what society has come to expect them to choose to do from within a culturally sanctioned and empirically limited set of options (Tilly 1978: 151).

It follows from this definition that the repertoire of contention changes very slowly, constrained by overarching configurations of economics and state-building and by the slow pace of cultural change. As Arthur L. Stinchcombe writes in a perceptive review of Tilly's *The Contentious French*:

> The elements of the repertoire are . . . simultaneously the skills of population members and the cultural forms of the population. . . . Only rarely is a new type of collective action invented in the heat of the moment. Repertoires instead change by long run evolutionary processes. The viability of one of the elements of a repertoire depends on what sorts of things work in a given social or political structure, on what forms of protest have been invented and disseminated in a population and on what grievances a given form is appropriate to express. (1987: 1248, 1249)

But if Stinchcombe is right, what then is the effect of Zolberg's "moments of madness," in which men and women not only "choose their parts from the available repertoire" but "forge new ones in an act of creation" (1972: 196)? Are the newly forged acts no more than chimeric explosions against the slowly evolving drama of the history of contention, doomed to disappear as participants tire, supporters melt away, and the forces of order regroup and repress their challenges? Or are they related in some way to longer-term changes in collective action? How do history's moments of madness relate to the long, slow progress of the repertoire of contention?

This essay proposes a solution to that problem through the concept of systemic cycles of protest. I will argue that moments of madness do not transform the repertoire of contention all at once and out of whole cloth, but contribute to its evolution through the dynamic evolution of larger cycles of mobilization in which the innovations in collective action that they produce are diffused, tested, and refined in adumbrated form and eventually become part of the accepted repertoire. It is within these larger cycles that new forms of contention combine with old ones, the expressive encounters the instrumental, traditional social actors adopt tactics from new arrivals, and newly invented forms of collective action become what I call "modular." Cycles of protest are the crucibles in which moments of madness are tempered into the permanent tools of a society's repertoire of contention. Let us begin with the concept of the protest cycle.

CYCLES OF PROTEST

That there are regular variations in political or social phenomena is scarcely a new or surprising idea. Wilhelm Buerklin, for example, writes that "virtually all time series describing and explaining social and political change display deviations or fluctuations of one sort or another" (1987: 1). Students of history recognize cycles in various forms: reform cycles, electoral cycles, generational cycles, economic cycles.[4] Yet empirical studies of political cycles rarely go beyond these generic classifications and seldom escape their putative dependence on economic fluctuations.

Elements of Cyclicity

Although protest waves do not have a regular frequency or extend uniformly to entire populations, a number of features have characterized such waves in recent history. These features include heightened conflict, broad sectoral and geographic extension, the appearance of new social movement organizations and the empowerment of old ones, the creation of new "master frames" of meaning, and the invention of new forms of collective action. Since these elements provide the skeleton for the rest of this analysis, I will briefly outline them here.

1. Heightened conflict: Protest cycles are characterized by heightened conflict across the social system: not only in industrial relations, but in the streets; not only in the streets, but in the villages or in the schools. For example, in their time-series data on France, Shorter and Tilly correlated the rate of violence per year with other forms of collective action. They reported that "since the 1890s, the times of extensive collective violence in France have also been the times of hostile demonstrations, mass meetings, explicitly political strikes and calls for revolution" (1974: 81). Similar findings emerged from my study on the Italian wave of protest in the late 1960s and early 1970s. It is this co-occurrence of turbulence across the social sector that brings it to the attention of elites and sets in motion a process of institutional adaptation or collapse (Tarrow 1989: chap. 3).

2. *Geographic and sectoral diffusion*: Cycles of protest also have traceable paths of diffusion from center to periphery, as was discovered by Rudé in the grain seizures he studied in France from the 1770s; by Shorter and Tilly in the nineteenth- and twentieth-century French strikes that they analyzed; and by Beccalli in her study of Italian strikes. Such cycles also spread from heavy industrial areas to adjacent areas of light industry and farming, as Beccalli found in Italy in the 1970s. Particular groups recur with regularity in the vanguard of waves of social protest (e.g., miners, students), but they are frequently joined during the peak of the wave by groups that are not generally known for their insurgent tendencies (e.g., peasants, workers in small industry, white-collar workers).[5]

3. *Social movement organizations*: Protest cycles are often touched off by unpredictable events, and they almost never are under the control of a single movement organization. The high point of the wave is often marked by the appearance of supposedly spontaneous collective action, but in fact both previous traditions of organization and new forms of organization structure their strategies and outcomes. Nor do existing organizations necessarily give way to new movements in the course of the wave. From the wave of industrial unrest in Western Europe in the 1968–72 period we have evidence that—while organized groups were taken by surprise—many of them quickly recouped their positions and adapted to the new forms of collective action created at the peak of the strike wave (Dubois 1978: 5; Klandermans 1990).

The importance of movement organizations in cycles of protest is that they have a vested interest in contentious collective action because protest is their major—and often their only—resource. To the extent that these organizations become the major carriers of a protest wave, contention will not cease just because a particular group has been satisfied, repressed, or becomes tired of life in the streets. A major reason for the acceleration in the appearance of protest cycles in the past 150 years is the invention of these organized actors with their stake in contentious collective action.

4. *New frames of meaning*: Protest cycles characteristically produce new or transformed symbols, frames of meaning and ideologies that justify and dignify collective action and around which a following can be mobilized.[6] These frames typically arise among insurgent groups and spread outward, which is how the traditional concept of "rights" expanded in the United States in the 1960s. The rights frame eventually spread to women, gays, Native Americans and advocates of the rights of children and animals (Snow and Benford 1988). These new cultural constructs are born, tested, and refined within the cycle and may then enter the political culture in more diffuse and less militant form, serving as a source of the symbols mobilized by future movement entrepreneurs.

5. *Expanding repertoires of contention*: A final characteristic of protest cycles is perhaps their most distinctive trait: they are crucibles within which new weapons of social protest are fashioned. The barricades in the French revolutions of the nineteenth century; the factory occupations of 1919–20; the sitdown strikes of the French Popular Front period; the direct actions of the 1968–72 period in Italy—new forms of collective action develop within the experimental context of cycles of protest. The most successful—and the most transferable—become part of the future repertoire of collective action even during quieter times.

In a number of cases, forms of collective action are not merely the instrumental means that people use to demand new rights and privileges; rather, they themselves express the rights and privileges that protesters are demanding and are diffused as general expressions of their claims and similar ones. For example, the 1960 lunch counter sit-ins in the American South were not simply a way of gaining attention or opposing racism; by sitting-in at lunch counters, African American college students were actually practicing the objective they sought. Honed, tested, and refined into known and adaptable forms, this new form of collective action was then applied in bus stations, movie theaters, and welfare agencies. Surviving beyond the end of the cycle as a permanent form of popular politics, it contributed to the evolution of the entire repertoire of contention.

To summarize: A cycle of protest will be operationalized in this essay as an increasing and then decreasing wave of inter-related collective actions and reactions to them whose aggregate frequency, intensity, and forms increase and then decline in rough chronological proximity. This leads to three related questions:

First, what is the balance within a cycle of protest be-tween the institutionalized forms of collective action from the inherited repertoire and the less institutionalized ones that reflect something like Zolberg's moments of madness?

Second, what kinds of activities does the moment of mad-ness contain? Is it predominantly made up of violence? Of conventional forms of action used in greater magnitude? Or of a combination of violent, confrontational, and conventional forms of participation?

Third, how are these forms of collective action translated into permanent changes in the repertoire of contention?

These questions will be examined in the case of a ten-year period of mass mobilization and protest in Italy from 1965 through 1974.

Assumptions and Data

A few simplifying assumptions will have to be accepted in order to fit Zolberg's intuitive concept of moments of madness into an empirical and historical framework. We will identify moments of madness with the sudden onset of collective action near the be-ginning of a protest cycle. We will operationalize new social and ideological actors with the presence and frequency of unorganized protest. And we will reduce Zolberg's complex question of "last-ing political accomplishments" to the character of collective action observable at the close of the cycle.

The data that will be used to illustrate the incidence and im-pact of moments of madness come from both machine-readable and qualitative newspaper data collected in Italy for the 1965–74 period from a daily reading and coding of *Corriere della Sera* that have been presented in greater detail elsewhere (della Porta and Tarrow 1986; Tarrow 1989). For each protest event identified, information was recorded on the forms of action used, the partici-pants, the groups targeted, the claims made, and the outcomes that could be observed. The newspaper data were supplemented by archival research, interviews with former participants, and documentary sources.[7] Secondary data from other studies supplemented the primary Italian data.

THE ITALIAN PROTEST CYCLE

Historical memory always foreshortens histories of collective action into long, shallow valleys and short, pointed peaks that punctuate them. But when we reconstruct cycles of protest from both public records and private memories, the peaks that leave indelible impressions in public consciousness are really only the high ground of broader swells of mobilization that rise and fall from the doldrums of compliance to waves of mobilization more gradually than popular memory recognizes.[8]

For example, although the year 1789 had world-historical importance beyond most others, it could probably not have occurred if not for the "pre-revolution" of 1787–88 and the campaign of public assemblies that preceded the taking of the Bastille. Similarly, the 1848 revolution was presaged by food riots, land seizures, and public demonstrations in the guise of public banquets. As for the explosive year 1968, the subtitle of Todd Gitlin's book says it all: *Years of Hope, Days of Rage* (1987).

In Italy the public record shows a rise and fall in contentious collective actions beginning in the mid-1960s and continuing in large numbers into the early 1970s. Figure 1 presents the number of codeable events recorded from our reading of the *Corriere* data for each half year from the beginning of 1965 through the end of 1974. The curve is based on the total number of conflictual events found in the daily newspaper record, from routine petitions, delegations, and strikes to public marches and demonstrations, occupations, and traffic obstructions to violent clashes and organized attacks on others.[9] It shows that Italy in the mid-1960s was entering a period of extensive social and political conflict.

There is a puzzle in Figure 1 that can help us understand the relationship between the cycle's most memorable moment and its long-term dynamic: 1968 has been remembered as the peak of the cycle, yet the evidence in Figure 1 shows that collective action continued to rise in quantity until after the turn of the decade.[10] Was 1968 a false spring, a mere reflection of what was happening across the French Alps during the same time? Or did it have special characteristics that distinguish it from the larger, quantita-

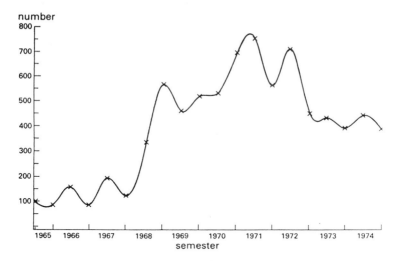

Figure 1   Number of conflictual events, Italy, 1965–74.

tive peak of collective action later on? Unraveling the puzzle will require us to turn from the quantitative data to their changing character in the course of the cycle. We can do so first by distinguishing the institutional from the noninstitutional aspects of collective action and then by looking at the appearance of new social actors.

Convention and Contention

The most important contribution of Tilly's concept of the repertoire is to help us disaggregate the popular notion of protest into its conventional and less conventional components. In each period of history some forms of collective action are sanctioned by habit, expectations, and even legality, while others are unfamiliar, unexpected, and are rejected as illegitimate by elites and the mass public alike. Consider the strike. As late as the 1870s it was barely known, poorly understood, and widely rejected as a legitimate form of collective action. By the 1960s, however, the strike can be considered as an accepted part of collective bargaining practice.

Looking again at the Italian data from the 1960s and 1970s, we find routine and conventional forms alongside confrontational

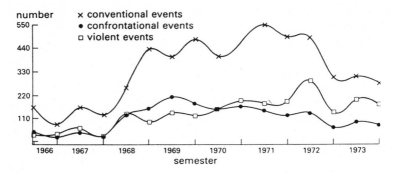

Figure 2   Incidence of conventional, confrontational, and violent
events, Italy, 1966–73.

and violent ones. As "confrontation," we shall operationalize
forms such as occupations, obstructions, forced entries, and radical strikes, and as "violence" attacks on property, on antagonists
and on authorities, and clashes with police. "Conventional" forms
contain petitions, audiences, and legal actions,[11] marches and
public meetings and strikes and assemblies. We consider the inherited repertoire as the presence and relative frequency of the
conventional forms of collective action as opposed to the use of
both confrontation and violence. The question here is, within a
generalized period of contentious collective action, do the conventional forms give way to disorder and violence, or do they rise in
magnitude along with more unruly and contentious actions?

Figure 2 shows that the answer to the question is unambiguous:
just as confrontational and violent forms of collective action rose
during the period, so did routine and conventional ones. Italians at
the peak of their protest cycle were fighting, raiding, obstructing,
and occupying premises far more often than they had in the recent past. But they were also—and predominantly, in quantitative
terms—engaging in well-known routines of collective action inherited from the conventional repertoire. The most common forms
of collective action enumerated from the newspaper data in Italy
between 1966 and 1973 were strikes, marches, and public meetings (see Table 1). Just behind these were the confrontational forms
of occupations and obstructions, with the conventional forms of

assemblies and petitions close behind them. Only then do we find the four main forms of violent conflict.[12] The numerical predominance of the conventional repertoire is not surprising when we take into account the fact that the late 1960s were a period of *mass* collective action. When we consider the difficulties in mobilizing large numbers of people into any form of collective action, it becomes clear that it must be particularly hard to get them to participate in high-risk confrontational and violent protest. When movement organizers think of how best to mobilize large numbers of people against superior forces, they therefore most naturally turn to the inherited repertoire. What is most interesting is that moments of madness and institutional forms of collective action co-occurred all through the cycle.[13]

But note the differences in the employment of the different types of collective action over time. In Figure 2 the numerous types of collective action from Table 1 have been aggregated into three main curves (conventional events, confrontational events, and violent events) and their numerical appearance traced over the eight-year period for which we have detailed data. As the figure shows, while all three major types increased during the upward slope of the cycle, their respective curves differed. While violent forms of attack increased mainly toward the end of the cycle,[14] the much larger conventional curve peaked in 1971. As for confrontational forms of collective action, these reached their height in 1968–69—the years celebrated in popular memory as the peak of contestation. This contrast between the peaks of conventional and confrontational collective action will help us to understand the internal dynamic of the cycle and the role of the moment of madness of 1968–69 within it.

New Social Actors and Identities

Something else occurred during the 1968–69 period: the appearance of new social actors and collective identities, operationalized here as the relative absence in the protests of known movement organizations and parties. Throughout the Italian cycle, both organized and nonorganized protests were found in great numbers. At times, however, organized actors were more prominent than at others.[15]

Table I   Incidence of all forms of collective action as percentages of
total forms of action, Italian newspaper data, 1966–73

Action form	% of all forms	Incidence
Strike	20.3	1,974
March	12.4	1,206
Public meeting	9.8	955
Occupation	8.3	812
Obstruction	8.2	797
Assembly	7.3	709
Petition	6.6	639
Violent attack	6.0	589
Attack on property	6.0	584
Violent clash	5.1	497
Clash with police	3.9	382
Forced entry	1.0	100
Hunger strike	.7	70
Rampage	.6	58
Direct action	.4	48
Leafleting	.3	33
Symbolic protest	.3	33
Legal action	.2	18
Random violence	.1	15
Theft	.1	11
Campout in public place	.1	7
Miscellaneous other	1.6	154
Unclassified	.4	48
Total	99.7	9,739

Source: Tarrow (1989): 68.

The years 1968–69 produced the largest percentage of protest
events with no known organizations. Two-thirds of the protests
in the mid-1960s had involved known organizations, and half of
these were organized by the trade unions. Even the 1966 bombings
in Alto Adige were carried out by known nationalist organizations
and—as for protests against the war in Vietnam—the majority
were mounted by the institutional left-wing parties or their youth
affiliates (Tarrow 1989: chap. 9). But by 1968 the proportion of
protests in which known organizations could be identified fell
to less than half of the total, and only one-quarter involved the
unions.[16]

The "Hot Autumn"

The trend continued in 1969 and expanded from the university to the factory. In the autumn of that year a wave of factory-level strikes, often sparked by grass-roots committees outside the unions, began. This "hot autumn," which stretched through the winter of 1970, was largely propelled by younger, unskilled "mass workers," many of them of southern parentage, who lacked the discipline and respect for work of their northern elders. Many workers adopted the forms of collective action experimented with by the student movement in 1968 and added new twists to conventional strikes (see below). This tactical flexibility was a major challenge to industrialists, but it also was a challenge for the trade unions, which were forced to respond by absorbing the new forms of organization that had been invented at the base (Regalia 1979).

Organizing Disruption

By 1971 the trend had begun to reverse itself in both factories and universities. Two major organizational developments changed the nature and extent of collective action during this period. First, the trade unions integrated many of the younger workers into their base-level structures; and second, the student movement was increasingly absorbed by the Leninist-type organizations that had emerged from the mass movement of 1968 (Lumley 1983). By 1973 more than half of the events studied were led by either the unions or by these new extraparliamentary groups. Although the two trends were different in many ways—for example, in the degree of violence they produced—they were united in helping to bring collective action back within an organizational framework after the moment of madness of 1968–69.[17] Disruption was being increasingly organized.

THE MOMENT OF MADNESS

Thus, the years 1968–69 brought a wave of confrontational collective action to Italy that placed workers and students in unprecedented confrontation with authority in the absence of the traditional mediating leadership of unions and parties. Yet the capacity of these social actors for organizing protest did not seem to

be impaired. This can be seen first in their level of tactical flexibility. It also can be seen, for the workers, in the radicalization of
the strike, and, for the students, in the form of collective action
that most dramatically marked their protests—the occupation of
university premises.

Tactical Flexibility

To some, in order to be effective, social protests must be well-
organized (Hobsbawm 1978), but to others, disruptiveness is actually dependent on the emergent quality of the movement, which
implies a lack of stable leadership and organization (Piven and
Cloward 1977). As protest intensified, did the decline in the presence of known organizations imply a loss in tactical ability? Quite
the contrary. During this period the degree of tactical flexibility
increased, as evidenced by the increase in the average number of
forms of action used in each protest event.

Figure 3 presents the average number of tactical forms observed
per event in the protest events. It shows a rapid increase in organizational capacity in 1967–68, just as the confrontational forms of
collective action we saw earlier were peaking and as the presence
of known organizations declined. If the ability to array a variety
of forms of collective action in the absence of known organizations and of confrontations with authorities is a sign of a moment
of madness, then the academic year 1967–68 was just such a
moment.

Radicalizing the Strike

Strike behavior—especially during periods of contract negotiation—follows a national and sectoral logic in Italy that is both
regular and predictable (Franzosi 1981), and strikes were the most
common and most conventional form of collective action we found
during the period studied.[18] As we saw in Table 1, strikes appeared
in 40 percent of the events and made up more than 20 percent of
the forms of action that were recorded. Strikers almost always put
forward instrumental demands, although some of these—like the
demand for equal pay increases for all classes of workers—had
strongly expressive elements (Pizzorno 1978).

The largely conventional role of striking can be seen in the

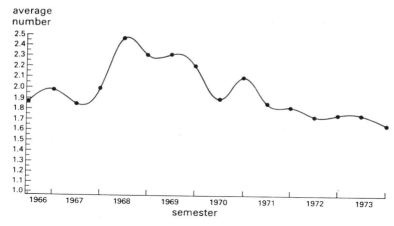

Figure 3   Action forms per event, Italy, 1966–73.

rhythm of the strike rate during periods of national and sectoral contract renewal.[19] These conflicts often followed an almost ritualistic sequence. First, the unions would hold conferences at which platforms were elaborated and voted on; then brief strikes would be called in key firms or industries—usually those in which the unions were strongest; then, building on the momentum that had been demonstrated in these strongholds, national strikes would be called; finally, contract negotiations would begin (Golden 1988).

But toward the end of the 1960s a new phase was added to the sequence; plant committees began to regard contract agreements reached at the national level, not as a ceiling, but as a floor on which to construct more ambitious plant-level agreements. This meant that industrial conflict extended beyond contract renewal periods into the trough between them and that the center of gravity of the strike fell from the national level to the plant or local level.

The dramatic rise of plant-level disputes that this change signified can be seen in Figure 4, which breaks down the strike data into those that were observed only at the local level and those that were organized nationally. The curves show a sharp proportional increase in local strikes from the middle of 1968, when the first plant-level wildcat strikes broke out. The number of national strikes—although they included many more workers—expanded much more slowly throughout the period.

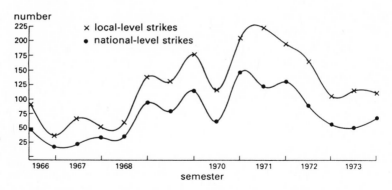

Figure 4   Incidence of national and local-level strikes, Italy, 1966–73.

The extension of the strike to the plant level was more than quantitative; it reflected a flowering of new strike forms, some inherited from past cycles of industrial conflict, but others invented on the spot (Dubois, 1978). A whole new vocabulary of strike forms rapidly developed, from the *sciopero bianco* (go-slow) to the *sciopero a singhiozzo* (literally, hiccup strikes) to the *sciopero a scacchiera* (chessboard strikes) to the *corteo interno* (marches around the factory grounds to carry along undecided workers) to the *presidio al cancello* (blocking factory gates to prevent goods from entering or leaving the plant). The logic of these innovations in the strike repertoire was to attempt to produce the maximum amount of disruption with the minimum expenditure of resources.

In addition to these permutations within the strike, workers learned to combine distinctly different forms of collective action with striking. In the factory, occupations, obstructions, and forced entries challenged assembly-line rhythms and the authority of foremen. Collective action extended outside the factory as workers adopted public forms of display, expressive forms of action, and traffic blockages to publicize their demands. These public demonstrations often contained symbolic military elements (e.g., mechanics would frequently bang on milk cans with pipes as they marched), but they also contained important elements of play and theater and bore a resemblance to the traditional carnival.[20]

Both the expansion in the forms of conflict within the workplace and its extension into the public sphere can be seen in Table 2, which analyzes the strikes in our newspaper data for their combination with other forms of collective action. As the table shows, the ratio of other forms of action to strikes was much higher in 1968 and 1969 than either earlier or later in the period. During their moment of madness, workers were simultaneously going public and intensifying disruption in the workplace.

The Occupation as Collective Life

As in the United States during the 1960s, occupying institutional premises was the form of collective action most frequently used by Italian students, and it owed much to the American example. At first, such occupations were enthusiastic and joyful activities, especially in the takeovers of university faculties carried out during the 1967–68 academic year (Ortoleva 1988). Lumley writes of one the first important university sit-ins—that of the architecture faculty in Milan—that "an environment was created which was functional to collective living, debate and shared work; all major decisions were taken by the general meetings" (1983: 164).

But although some faculties were almost continuously occupied from early in the 1967–68 academic year until the spring of 1969, the magic of shared participation and achievement could

Table 2   Strike events: Use of Nonstrike forms by strikers; aggregated protest forms by year (number of events)

Forms of action	1966	1967	1968	1969	1970	1971	1972	1973
Public display	31	28	78	107	97	110	78	74
Assembly	10	15	40	69	84	59	43	33
Routine action	13	15	37	59	88	77	87	14
Confrontation	32	15	52	118	72	70	31	33
Violent encounter	20	5	33	18	23	34	16	15
Attack on property	12	4	13	28	19	12	3	8
Attack on persons	2	3	4	19	9	10	4	6
Total other forms	120	85	257	418	392	372	262	183
Total strike events [a]	127	117	196	306	319	416	269	224
Ratio other/total	.94	.73	1.31	1.37	1.23	.89	.97	.82

[a]Strike events are defined nominally as all events in which a strike took place.
Source: Tarrow (1989): 189.

not endure. Not only did vacations and ever more frequent roust-ings by the police prevent the occupations from achieving their goal of creating "free spaces" in the universities, but such actions became institutionalized, as "commissions were set up to exam-ine political and educational issues with the participation of some lecturers" (ibid.), and factional groupings formed their own orga-nizations that attempted to gain control of the various assemblies and commissions.

By 1969–70 the university occupations had taken on a ritualis-tic character, with standard banners and posters that reflected the ideological line of this or that movement organization, a *servizio d'ordine* of security guards—some of whom would later appear as the military cadres of the extraparliamentary groups—and almost as ritualistic police roustings and counterdemonstrations. By the early 1970s the main force of the occupations had moved to the secondary schools, where far less sophisticated leaders turned them into staging grounds for battles over turf.

THE DIFFUSION AND MODULARIZATION OF PROTEST

Thus, the most innovative and confrontational forms of collec-tive action that arose in the Italian moment of madness declined after 1969. Unions—never absent from the factory—had regained control of the strike movement by 1970. In the universities, extra-parliamentary groups turned student protests into set piece pro-ductions that soon took on a routine character. When participation flagged, the extraparliamentary groups moved into the secondary schools. In those instances where the police moved in, clashes ensued, providing an opportunity for the groups' armed *servizi d'ordine* to gain prominence and inducing much of the mass base to vanish.[21]

What was the impact of the moment of madness on Italian society and on its continuing repertoire of protest? To answer that question, we will have to ask what parts of the new repertoire survived the collapse of the movements of 1968–69. As we saw in Figure 2, while the sharpest decline in institutionalization and the greatest increases in confrontation and tactical innovation oc-curred in 1968 and 1969, conventional collective action continued to grow in magnitude until 1971. That such mobilization increased after tactical creativity declined suggests that the period legiti-

reduction of rents in public housing projects and in the mass refusal to pay gas and electricity bills and transit fares (Perlmutter, 1987; 1988). Between 1968, when it was invented in the Pirelli factory, and the mid-1970s, when it was turned into a weapon of urban struggle, *autoriduzione* became modular—that is, a model of collective action that was diffused across a wide range of social and territorial space and adapted to a variety of social and political conflicts.

As it was diffused, the practice became more routinized, with professional movement organizers teaching their supporters how it was done. As this occurred, *autoriduzione* became stylized and modular, permitting it to be employed with a minimum of organizational effort in a variety of social and economic settings—much as the sit-in had been diffused to a variety of protest groups in the United States. But repetition and modularization had another effect; unlike its first employment at Pirelli, where it caught management off-guard, elites and authorities soon learned how to respond.

If workers could self-reduce their assembly lines, piecework rates could be adjusted to penalize them for it; if rate-payers refused to pay their utility bills, their gas or electricity could be cut off; and if commuters failed to pay their bus or tram fares, the fare itself could be canceled, as occurred in one Italian city, with the cost transferred to general revenue collection. Modularization of the new forms of collective action made them easier to diffuse to new sectors and social actors, but it also facilitated social control.[23]

The Assembly in the Place of Work

Not all of the innovations in collective action that first appeared in the moment of madness were as easily defeated as *autoriduzione* was. Before 1969, union organizers had been unable to gain access to factories to meet with workers. They were forced to waylay them at the factory gates after a hard day's work or organize meetings after hours. Some of the most dramatic moments in the Hot Autumn of 1969 occurred when insurgent workers triumphantly carried their leaders onto factory grounds, where tumultuous assemblies were organized and strike votes taken.

mated protest in sectors of Italian society that otherwise would not have engaged in it.

Most of the effects were less than creative—and some were often violent. But this does not negate the significance of the diffusion and legitimation of protest throughout Italian society. Social groups and regions that had not participated in the first wave of mobilization began to strike, demonstrate, and—in a few cases— loot and burn in the early 1970s.[22] Collective action frames that the students developed in the context of university occupations— such as the theme of *autonomia*—spread to the workers and other groups and became a key slogan (albeit with different implications) during the conflicts of the early 1970s. And forms of protest that were first experimented with in university faculties and the large factories of the north became general models for collective action in other settings and other regions—for example, the practice of self-reduction, which can serve as an archetypical example of the modularization of protest.

Autoriduzione

Production and institutional routines do not have to be attacked by straightforward striking; they can be disrupted by simple non-cooperation, as was the case for the prison revolts that broke out in 1968, or by setting one's own schedule, as was the case for the *autoriduzione* campaigns that began in the Pirelli factory near Milan in the same year. The skilled Pirelli workers sensed that the increase in factory orders in the context of a labor shortage gave them an unusual degree of leverage vis-à-vis management. As the practice spread, workers would simply decide on their production rate, ignoring piecework schedules in coordinated passive resistance. According to Lumley, *autoriduzione* "captured the imagination of a wide section of activists on the shopfloor, in the Left, within the trade unions, and in the social movements more generally" (1983: 329–39).

Observers of the period thought they saw spontaneity here; but it took enormous coordination for a technically advanced productive process to be deliberately slowed down in a self-reduction campaign. By the early 1970s the technique had been extended to urban movements by well-organized national extraparliamentary organizations like *Lotta Continua*—for example in the self-

As the cycle wound down and the unions reasserted their control, workers returned to more conventional and institutionalized forms of collective action. Of course, the factory councils that organized factory assemblies soon lost their tumultuous character, and their elected delegates often felt "elected and abandoned" by their unions (Regalia 1985). But the assembly in the place of work remained a permanent conquest for the workers and an institutionalized accretion to the repertoire of collective action.

MOMENTS, CYCLES, AGES OF CONTENTION

In his intuitive and perceptive article Zolberg concludes of moments of madness that they bring about significant transformations in three distinct ways:

> First of all, the "torrent of words" involves a sort of intensive learning experience whereby new ideas, formulated initially in coteries, sects, etc., emerge as widely shared beliefs among much larger publics. . . .
> Secondly, these new beliefs expressed in new language are anchored in new networks of relationships which are rapidly constituted during such periods of intense activity. . . .
> Thirdly, from the point of view of policy . . . the instant formulations become irreversible goals which are often institutionalized in the not-very-distant future. (206)

Each of Zolberg's themes implies an indirect and a mediated— rather than a direct and unmediated—effect on political culture, which is why we need to look beyond great events and crises to the cycles of protest they trigger in order to observe their effects. Let us turn from the discourse of the movements that preoccupied Zolberg to their effects on the repertoire of collective action to ask if there is a similar logic.

In the first case, just as new ideas filter down from their originators to those who vulgarize and domesticate them, the new forms of collective action invented in the enthusiasm of the moment of madness become modular. One thinks of the practice of *autoriduzione* as it spread from Pirelli to other factories, then to urban protests for rent and rate reductions, and finally (and in its most farcical version) as a teenager's justification for breaking into rock concerts without a ticket. Not the new invention itself, but its distilled, refined, and often routinized products become part of a more lasting practice of collective action.

In the second case, just as networks of people that form in the heat of a moment of madness diffuse new ideas, they also spread out across society—to the cities, the factories, the schools—and induce others to take up tactics that they have found successful. College students who go home for the weekend teach younger brothers and sisters how to organize an occupation; arrested militants who are shifted from troublesome urban prisons to more remote ones teach common criminals how to politicize their discontent; radicalized workers who become union organizers bring their militant practice to smaller and less politicized factories.

In the third case, through changes in public policy (in which Zolberg includes the creation of new political institutions as well as new programs), society absorbs a portion of the message of moments of madness. This can be as true for the practice of collective action as it is for ideas and substantive policies. For example, one thinks of the factory councils that became the grass-roots institutions of the Italian trade unions after being created in shop floor conflicts or of the practice of decisions made through assemblies that affected life in Italian universities for years to come.

Each of these hypothetical effects requires separate—and much more qualitative—investigation than we have been able to give them here. (And, needless to say, they should be examined in countries other than Italy as well.) If true, these effects imply an intervening and dynamic process connecting the utopian dreams, the intoxicating solidarity and the violent rhetoric of the moment of madness, and the glacially changing, culturally constrained, and socially resisted pace of change. I have proposed such a mediation in the concept of cycles of protest.

Few people dare to break the crust of convention. When they do so during moments of madness, they create the opportunities and provide the models for others. Moments of madness—seldom widely shared, usually rapidly suppressed, and soon condemned even by their participants—appear as sharp peaks on the long curve of history. New forms of contention flare up briefly within them and disappear, and their rate of absorption into the ongoing repertoire is slow and partial. But the cycles they trigger last much longer and have broader influence than the moments of madness themselves; they are, in Zolberg's words, "like a flood tide which loosens up much of the soil but leaves alluvial deposits in its wake" (206).

NOTES

1 From Franz Kafka, *Parables and Paradoxes* (1937): 92–93.
2 Listen to Henri Lefebvre as he speaks of the Paris Commune: "In this movement prompted by the negative, and therefore creative, elements of existing society—the proletariat—social action wills itself and makes itself free, disengaged of constraints" (1965; quoted in Zolberg: 190).
3 The discussion here is based on Tilly (1978, 1986). For a more detailed examination of Tilly's concept in a historical context, see Tarrow (1993).
4 The discussion below is a summary from two more developed versions of my argument about the structure and dynamics of protest cycles in Tarrow (1991a and 1991b). For a formal model of revolutionary violence that emphasizes the importance of the dynamics of conflict, see Tsebelis and Sprague (1989).
5 The best evidence on how grain seizures spread comes from Rudé (1964: chap. 1). On the spread of strikes from areas of large to small industry in France, see Shorter and Tilly (1974: 106); in Italy, see Beccalli (1971).
6 My argument here owes much to the work of David Snow and Robert Benford. See, in particular, Snow and Benford (1988). Also see Gamson (1988) and Klandermans (1988) for related discussions of the importance of framing discourses in the social construction of collective action.
7 The data collection strategy owes much to Tilly's monumental work on British contentious events. For a brief discussion of the British project, see Horn and Tilly (1986). A similar discussion of the Italian project can be found in Project on Social Protest and Policy Innovation, Project Manual, Cornell University, Ithaca, New York (1985), available from the author on request. Many of these data summarized below were presented in different form in my final report (Tarrow 1989).
8 For example, see the excellent example of the development of the themes and networks of the future women's movement in the doldrums of the 1940s and 1950s in the United States in Rupp and Taylor (1987).
9 Two points: first, the figure includes both coded events and those for which a defining grievance, a starting date, or a disruptive form of collective action could not be identified; therefore, they were not coded further. The analysis in the remainder of this essay is based on only the first type, for which these basic data could be gathered. Second, for the years 1965 and 1974 a one-month-in-four sampling procedure has been used, while for the remaining eight years in the series, the entire population of codable events was used. For further details on sampling and enumeration of the protest events, see Tarrow (1989: Appendixes A and B), and Project Manual (1985).
10 The puzzle was reinforced by the memories of participants, many of whom remembered 1968 as the cathartic moment of the cycle, even in the face of

the quantitative record of increasing collective action in later years. For the interview evidence, see Tarrow (1989: chap. 9).

11   Strictly speaking, the Italian study focused only on contentious collective action, which was operationalized as actions that disrupted the lives of someone else and did not enumerate "audiences, petitions and legal actions." These appear in the data only when they accompanied at least one disruptive form of collective action in the same protest event. Thus, the overall use of these conventional forms is probably grossly underestimated in the data, which makes their magnitude here even more striking.

12   Notice that the table calculates the forms that were used as a proportion of the total forms of collective action, since several forms of action were often employed in the same event. Calculating the presence of each form as a proportion of events (N = 4,980) changes the weight of each only slightly.

13   I am grateful to Arthur Stinchcombe for putting clearly, in his comments on an earlier version of this essay, what had been only implicit in an earlier discussion. For a fascinating historical parallel from the Russian Revolution, see his "Milieu and Structure Updated" in *Theory and Society* (1986: 909–11) on the relationship between elite and mass parts of the movement.

14   On this point, see della Porta and Tarrow (1986) and Tarrow (1989: chap. 12). For the most careful analysis of the left-wing terrorism that followed, see della Porta (1991).

15   There is a risk here of mistaking journalistic ignorance for spontaneity. But it is interesting that detailed inspection of some portions of the data showed that the absence of known organizations in a protest correlates closely with expressive modes and the formation of new collective identities, as suggested by Pizzorno (1978).

16   For evidence that the replacement of party or interest group leadership by new actors and groups using confrontational forms of collective action occurs elsewhere than Italy, see Diarmuid Maguire's Ph.D. thesis, "Parties into Movements," Cornell University, Department of Government, 1990.

17   In a personal correspondence to the author, J. Craig Jenkins points out that something similar happened in the United States, where "unnamed groups launched the protest, then national social movement organizations and coalitions of SMOs (social movement organizations) took over by the late 1960s." I am grateful to Jenkins, whose excellent work on this question has been published in a joint article with Craig Eckert (1986).

18   Strikes are defined as the withdrawal of labor or (in the case of nonproducing institutions like schools) noncooperation in the institution's functioning. We shall see that strikes were frequently accompanied by more public and more confrontational forms of action.

19   A large technical literature exists on the fluctuation in the strike rate during this period (see Franzosi 1981; Bordogna and Provasi 1984, and the sources cited in those works).

20   The finest evocation of this aspect of the movement will be found in Lumley (1983). Some, but not all, of his rich and evocative analysis is carried forward in his book, *States of Emergency: Cultures of Revolt in Italy from 1968 to 1978* (1990).

21   The appearance of violence—even in its early, disorganized stages—seems

to have been an important motive in the defection of many young women from the movement, as could be seen from a number of interviews carried out in the study. For a particularly significant case of violence and the resulting defection of women from an important extraparliamentary group, see Tarrow (1989: 327–28).

22 The notorious case of the "Revolt of Reggio Calabria," in which a city was paralyzed by right-wing mobs, and thousands of police ringed the city for months, is a prime example. (See Tarrow 1989: chap. 9, for a brief discussion.)

23 In a similar way, Diarmuid Maguire recounts how CND (Committee for Nuclear Disarmament) activists tried to encourage the use of nonviolent direct action among British printmakers and miners, both of whom went on strike in the mid-1980s. But there were legal and cultural obstacles to diffusion in both cases, and the attempt to apply this successful peace movement tactic to another sector failed miserably. In contrast, CND was able to use NVDA (non-violent direct action) successfully in protesting local antinuclear waste dumping, even in conservative constituencies. (Personal communication to the author. See Maguire (1990) for the relationship between conventional and unconventional protest in the British peace movement.)

REFERENCES

Aron, Raymond (1968) La revolution introuvable: Reflexions sur la revolution de mai. Paris: Fayard.

Beccalli [Salvati], Bianca (1971) "Scioperi e organizzazione sindacale: Milano 1950–1970." Rassegna Italiana di sociologia 12: 83–120.

Bordogna, Lorenzo, and Giancarlo Provasi (1979) "Il movimento degli scioperi in Italia, 1881–1973," in Gian Primo Cella (ed.) Il movimento degli scioperi nel XX secolo. Bologna: Il Mulino: 169–304.

Buerklin, Wilhelm (1987) "Why study political cycles: An introduction." European Journal of Political Research 15: 131–43.

Della Porta, Donatella (1991) Il terrorismo di sinistra in Italia. Bologna: Il Mulino.

Della Porta, Donatella, and Sidney Tarrow (1987) "Unwanted children: Political violence and the cycle of Protest in Italy, 1966–1973." European Journal of Political Research 14: 607–32.

Dubois, Pierre (1978) "New forms of industrial conflict, 1960–74," in Colin Crouch and Alessandro Pizzorno (eds.) The Resurgence of Class Conflict in Europe since 1968, vol. 2. London: Macmillan: 1–34.

Franzosi, Roberto (1981) "Strikes in Italy in the postwar period." Unpublished Ph.D. dissertation, Johns Hopkins University.

Gamson, William (1988) "Political discourse and collective action," in Bert Klandermans, Hanspeter Kriesi, and Sidney Tarrow (eds.) From Structure to Action: Social Movement Participation Across Cultures, International Social Movement Research I. Greenwich, CT: JAI Press: 219–46.

Gitlin, Todd (1987) The Sixties: Years of Hope, Days of Rage. New York: Bantam.

Golden, Miriam (1988) Labor Divided: Austerity and Working-Class Politics in Contemporary Italy. Ithaca, NY: Cornell University Press.

Hobsbawm, Eric (1978) "The left and the crisis of organization." New Society 44 (13 April): 63–66.

Horn, Nancy, and Charles Tilly (1986) "Catalogs of contention in Britain, 1758–1834." Center for the Study of Social Change Working Paper No. 32, New School for Social Research.

Jenkins, J. Craig, and Craig Eckert (1986) "Channeling black insurgency: Elite patronage and professional social movement organizations in the development of the black movement." American Sociological Review 51: 812–29.

Kafka, Franz (1937) Parables and Paradoxes, translated by Ernst Kaiser et al. New York: Schocken.

Klandermans, Bert (1988) "The formation and mobilization of consensus," in Bert Klandermans, Hanspeter Kriesi, and Sidney Tarrow (eds.) From Structure to Action: Social Movement Participation Across Cultures, International Social Movement Research I. Greenwich, CT: JAI Press: 173–96.

——— (1990) "Linking the 'old' and the 'new': Movement networks in the Netherlands," in Russell Dalton and Manfred Kuechler (eds.) Challenging the Political Order. New York: Oxford University Press: 123–36.

Lefebvre, Henri (1965) La Proclamation de la Commune, 26 mars 1871. Paris: Gallimard.

Lumley, Bob (1983) "Social movements in Italy, 1968–78." Unpublished Ph.D. dissertation, University of Birmingham, Centre for Contemporary Cultural Studies.

——— (1990) States of Emergency: Cultures of Revolt in Italy from 1968 to 1978. London: Verso.

Maguire, Diarmuid (1990) "Parties into movements." Unpublished Ph.D. thesis, Cornell University.

Morin, Edgar, Claude Lefort, and Jean-Marc Coudray (1968) La Brèche: Premières réflexions sur les événements. Paris: Fayard.

Ortoleva, Peppino (1988) Saggio sui movimenti del 1968 in Europa e in America. Rome: Editori Riuniti.

Perlmutter, Edward (1987) "Modelling the polity: Autoriduzione in Turin." Unpublished paper.

——— (1988) "Intellectuals and urban protest: Extraparliamentary politics in Turin, Italy, 1968–1976." Unpublished Ph.D. thesis, Harvard University.

Piven, Frances Fox, and Richard Cloward (1977) Poor People's Movements: How They Succeed and Why They Fail. New York: Vintage.

Pizzorno, Alessandro (1978) "Political exchange and collective identity in industrial conflict," in Colin C. Crouch and Alessandro Pizzorno (eds.) The Resurgence of Class Conflict in Western Europe since 1968, vol. 2. London: Macmillan: 277–98.

Project on Social Protest and Policy Innovation (1985) Project Manual. Ithaca, NY: Cornell University.

Regalia, Ida (1979) "Delegati e consigli di fabbrica nelle ricerche degli anni Settanta," in Annali della Fondazione Luigi Einaudi, vol. 13. Turin: Fondazione Einaudi.

—— (1985) Eletti e abbandonati: Modelli e stili di rappresentanza in fabbrica. Bologna: Il Mulino.

Rudé, George (1964) The Crowd in History: A Study of Popular Disturbances in France and England, 1730–1848. New York: Wiley.

Rupp, Leila J., and Verta Taylor (1987) The American Women's Rights Movement from 1945 to the 1960s. New York: Oxford University Press.

Shorter, Edward, and Charles Tilly (1974) Strikes in France. Cambridge, MA: Harvard University Press.

Snow, David, and Robert Benford (1988) "Ideology, frame resonance and participant mobilization," in Bert Klandermans, Hanspeter Kriesi, and Sidney Tarrow (eds.) From Structure to Action: Social Movement Participation Across Cultures, International Social Movement Research I. Greenwich, CT: JAI Press: 197–218.

Stinchcombe, Arthur L. (1986) "Milieu and structure updated." Theory and Society 15: 901–13.

—— (1987) Review of The Contentious French. American Journal of Sociology 93: 1248–49.

Tarrow, Sidney (1989) Democracy and Disorder: Protest and Politics in Italy, 1965–1975. Oxford: Oxford University Press.

—— (1991a) "Kollektives handeln und politische gelegenheitsstruktur." Kölner Zeitschrift für Soziologie und Sozialpsychologie 43: 647–70.

—— (1991b) Struggle, Politics and Reform: Collective Action, Social Movements and Cycles of Protest. Ithaca, NY: Western Societies Occasional Paper No. 21.

—— (1993) "Collective action and the rise of the social movement: Why the French Revolution was not enough." Politics and Society 22: 69–90.

Tilly, Charles (1978) From Mobilization to Revolution. Reading, MA: Addison-Wesley.

—— (1986) The Contentious French: Four Centuries of Popular Struggle. Cambridge, MA: Harvard University Press.

Tocqueville, Alexis de (1942) Souvenirs d'Alexis de Tocqueville. Paris: Gallimard.

Tsebelis, George, and John Sprague (1989) "Coercion and revolution: Variations on a predator-prey model." Mathematical Computer Modelling 12: 547–59.

Zolberg, Aristide R. (1972) "Moments of madness." Politics and Society 2 (Winter): 183–207.

A Protest-Cycle Resolution of the Repression/Popular-Protest Paradox

CHARLES D. BROCKETT

Many people [in Guatemala] did begin to join the guerrillas, while many more were sympathetic or quietly supportive. The guerrillas are the only remaining source of defense left to a community or family. I know of villages that experienced actual massacres against innocent campesinos, *who were not even members of coops. The survivors of these massacres would often turn to the guerrillas. With all their anger about the murders of their kin and neighbors, there was nowhere else to turn.*

—quoted in S. Davis and J. Hodson, *Witnesses to Political Violence in Guatemala*

CENTRAL AMERICAN EVENTS of recent decades show human behavior at both its most courageous and its most barbaric. The opposing phenomena of popular mobilization and state terrorism

Charles D. Brockett is professor of political science at the University of the South in Sewanee, Tennessee. The author of *Land, Power, and Poverty: Agrarian Transformation and Political Conflict in Central America*, his most recent work has appeared in *American Political Science Review* and *Comparative Politics*. This chapter is a revision of a paper presented at the annual meeting of the Social Science History Association, New Orleans, 31 October–3 November 1991. The author is grateful to panel participants for their comments, especially Sidney Tarrow, as well as Alfred Cuzán, Kenneth Sharpe, and *Social Science History*'s anonymous reviewers. He is further indebted to Sidney Tarrow for the original suggestion that he attempt this type of solution to the repression/popular-protest paradox.

pose some of the most profound questions that can be asked by social science. How can we explain the willingness of political elites and their agents to slay thousands—tens of thousands—of their fellow human beings, even when their victims are unarmed? Conversely, how do we account for ordinary people undertaking collective action under circumstances so dangerous that even their lives are at risk?

The specific focus of this article is the often-noted paradox that regime violence smothers popular mobilization under some circumstances, but at other times similar (or even greater) levels of violence will provoke mass collective action rather than pacify the target population. This paradox remains even when the usual explanatory variables, such as the level of socioeconomic grievances or political regime type, are held constant.

The consequences of governmental repression for mass protest and rebellion have been the subject of much scholarly attention. Theories have been advanced for linear relationships, but in both negative and positive directions. Curvilinear relationships have also been proposed, again with the curves running in both directions. Each of these four models has found some empirical support—but also contradiction—from a variety of cross-national aggregate data studies.[1] Zimmerman's review (1980: 191) of the relevant literature states the point well: "There are two contradictory expectations about the effects of governmental coercion on protest and rebellion: coercion either will deter them or will instigate people to higher levels of conflict behavior. . . . Thus there are theoretical arguments for all conceivable basic relations between governmental coercion and group protest and rebellion except for no relationship."[2]

Given that empirical support is available for each of these models, Opp and Roehl (1990: 523) wisely note that our task is not to continue the attempt to establish whether repression has a radicalizing or deterring effect on collective action, but rather to determine "which effect is to be expected under what conditions." As a first step in this direction, we should distinguish between high and low levels of repression. For the empirical test of their model, Opp and Roehl utilize a survey of opponents of nuclear power in West Germany, which is certainly a condition of low repression in a comparative context. However, much of the theoretical literature about the repression/protest paradox concerns high levels of repression, such as the indiscriminate murder of citizens by the state. Although it is possible that a model for the high-repression situation could incorporate the variables necessary to explain the paradox in a low-repression situation, it is improbable that the converse would be true.[3]

The scholar who has made the most thorough and rigorous attempt to resolve the repression/protest paradox under high levels of repression is T. David Mason, both alone (1989a, 1989b) and with Dale A. Krane (1985, 1989). Although this work has much to be praised, I argue here that in the end it is unsuccessful. This effort falls short both because it bases too much of its argument on individual motivation and because of the shortcomings of the motivational theory that it uses. In contrast, I argue that rational-choice theory, especially narrowly construed individualist approaches, gives an incomplete account of mass political behavior and, therefore, a faulty resolution of the paradox at hand. Furthermore, and more critically, the relationship between regime repression and individual choice must be placed in its broader political context.[4] The most significant argument of this essay is that the repression/protest relationship is mediated by its temporal location in what Sidney Tarrow has conceptualized as "the cycle of protest." I will demonstrate that the key to the resolution of the repression/protest paradox is its location within the protest cycle.

The case material for this article comes from Central America, especially the recent histories of El Salvador and Guatemala through the first third of the 1980s, which is when their protest cycles were brought to an end. The subject matter of this article has not been an abstract question for the people of these countries: a repressive response to popular mobilization has been probable throughout their histories. Indeed, tens of thousands of people innocent of any crime have been slain in recent years by the agents of state terrorism in both countries.[5] This tragic story will be utilized to demonstrate that a protest-cycle model resolves the paradoxical relationship between repression and mobilization, whereas the Mason and Krane model is at odds with the Central American reality.

THE RATIONAL INDIVIDUALIST EXPLANATION

Mason and Krane, unlike most scholars of revolution and rebellion, look beyond the decision making of contending elites to give serious consideration to the motivation of nonelites.[6] In doing so, they give "explicit attention to the ways in which differing mixes of benefits and sanctions [from both the government and its opposition] affect the political preferences and behavioral choices" of the masses (1989: 177). As a result, they are able to shed considerable light on certain aspects of the paradoxical relationship between repression and mass collective action. In the end, though, their model is both theoretically incomplete and empirically falsifiable.

Mason and Krane employ a rational-choice perspective to model nonelite responses to regime repression.[7] As they point out, the distribution of mass support, opposition, and apathy toward the regime will vary depending on the targeting strategy employed in a regime's repressive activities. This regime violence might be directed (1) just against leaders of opposition organizations, (2) against the rank and file membership of opposing organizations, or (3) indiscriminately at the mass public, regardless of its involvement with the opposition.

Violence targeted against just the opposition leadership is postulated to reduce the willingness of nonelites actively to support the opposition, not so much out of fear as out of futility.[8] As opposition leaders are murdered, "nonelites begin to doubt whether opposition organizations can deliver collective benefits" (ibid.: 180). The more effective the regime's violence, the more rational these doubts and, consequently, the lower the probability that inactive nonelites would join the opposition struggle against the regime.[9]

Similar outcomes are to be expected if the regime targets not only leaders but also rank and file supporters of the opposition. Now the inactive masses are all the more likely to remain uninvolved because fear has been added to futility. To support or join the opposition under this condition is to become a possible victim of the violence. Therefore, Mason and Krane claim that if the regime can confine its violence successfully to known opponents then "it may temporarily preempt any expansion in the base of overt support for the opposition" (ibid.: 181).[10]

However, they argue that this targeting strategy will have the opposite effect on nonelites who already support the opposition. Mason (1989b: 482) develops the argument further, pointing out that it would be logical for this group to presume that they are already "on the government's 'hit list.'" Becoming inactive would probably not remove them from being at risk. With their very self-preservation at stake, "they are likely to calculate that a victory by the opposition is now even more urgent." As a result, past supporters are "likely to shift to more extreme and perhaps violent forms of support, especially if what is now being repressed is nonelite support for non-violent activities."

The third targeting strategy leads to a different set of rational calculations that are especially relevant to contemporary Central America. Indiscriminate regime violence victimizes politically neutral masses as well as regime opponents. Consequently, simply refraining from support for the opposition no longer protects inactive nonelites from the repression. As regime violence grows more widespread and more arbitrary, self-preservation for previously indifferent nonelites might lead to support for the opposition, especially if the opposition can offer protection.[11] At this point in their analysis, Mason and Krane believe that they can now resolve the paradox with which we are concerned: "In this manner, indiscriminate repressive violence ceases to deter and, indeed, stimulates a shift in nonelite support to the insurgents" (1989: 181).

Mason and Krane's model helps to clarify the responses by nonelites to different levels of regime violence. However, this explanation in turn creates two new sets of questions. First, if regime violence that targets opposition leaders deters further mass opposition, then how do we explain why popular opposition sometimes continues to grow to the level where the regime believes it is necessary to expand its targeting strategy? Similarly, if regime violence that expands to target the rank and file of the opposition deters further mass opposition, then how do even more threatening levels of mass opposition develop? Second, if indiscriminate regime violence intensifies, rather than deters, popular opposition, then why are there not more successful popular rebellions and revolutions when regime violence escalates to this level? If regime violence is unsuccessful as a deterrent at this level but is successful at the lower levels, then why would the regime ever escalate violence to this self-defeating point in the first place?

Mason and Krane acknowledge these questions, but their responses are brief and uncompelling. Furthermore, their explanation is at odds with the Central American reality, as I demonstrate in the following section. Indeed, I argue that a successful answer cannot be found without grounding individual choice within the broader social and political contexts. This broader perspective will be elaborated in the third section and then applied to the Central American experience to resolve more successfully the paradoxical relationship between repression and popular protest.

The discussion in the following two sections will apply primarily to the third targeting strategy, that is, indiscriminate violence. Before moving to that discussion, I must address decision making by individual nonelites under any of the three targeting strategies. Recall that Mason and Krane postulate that when a regime pursues either of the more limited strategies of targeting its violence, politically passive nonelites will rationally calculate that their interest is best served by continuing not to support the opposition. The logic of their argument is perhaps sound when the actor is conceptualized as an autonomous individual. However, real individuals are usually enmeshed in social networks, which might lead them to different perceptions, calculations, and behavior.

This brings us to the edge of the substantial and significant debates catalyzed by Mancur Olson's (1965) work on the relationships between public goods, free riding, and selective incentives in motivating collective action. Without dipping too far into these controversies, I argue that when the relevant actor is conceived more as a social being and less as an autonomous individual, then efforts to model the individual's response to any of the regime's targeting strategies will have been greatly complicated. This argument will be briefly developed along three lines, each proceeding to a more fundamental critique of the individualist rational-choice position.

First, individual rationality should be distinguished from collective rationality, as has been stressed by Muller and Opp and their associates.[12] As they contend, nonelites can recognize and do act on the basis of this distinction. Opp (1989: 77) states the point well: "Average citizens may adopt a collectivist conception of rationality because they recognize that what is individually rational is collectively irrational—that if people like themselves were individually rational free riders, the likelihood of success of protest action would be very small, and that, therefore, it is collectively rational for all to protest despite the fact that the objective probability of a single individual influencing the outcome is negligible." The thrust of this work is to posit a second type of rational choice model: the Public Goods model. At least in their work, it fares better empirically than the conventional Private Interest model (for example, Muller et al. 1991).

Second, the community-based existence of both rural and urban masses dissolves much of the free-rider problem. It will be remembered that the risk-avoiding free riders, who enjoy collective goods with no input of their own, present a problem for collective action when it involves large potential groups. Although "the masses" are certainly a large potential group, popular mobilization usually takes place within discrete communities, which often means, then, relatively small groups. For example, Moore (1989) finds in his assessment of the peasant mobilization literature that peasant rebellion is a two-step process. Even the large-scale rebellions tie together much smaller movements where "people are mobilized in the context of the social networks in which they live their daily lives" (ibid.: 16).[13] Within these networks, "micromobilization processes" (Opp and Roehl 1990) unfold involving a variety of nonmaterial incentives and sanctions. These processes can facilitate individual participation in oppositional activities that might appear irrational from an individualist private-interest perspective. Calhoun (1988: 150) makes the point particularly well for inhabitants of traditional communities, observing that these processes "give people the 'interests' for which they will risk their lives—families, friends, customary crafts, and ways of life." [14]

The essential point, then, is this: solidarity and principle are motivational forces just as important under certain conditions as private self-interest (Fireman and Gamson 1979: 21). Individuals are related through familial and friendship ties as well as through membership in groups. These relationships can "generate a sense of common identity, shared fate, and a general commitment to defend the group" (ibid.). Such bonds of solidarity can be important motivators for collective action, especially when shared understandings of principles such as "justice, equity, or right" (ibid.: 26) lend legitimacy to that action.[15]

How far rational-choice theories can be stretched to encompass important motivational forces beyond private interest is a controversy that cannot be settled here.[16] Certainly, though, a third critique goes beyond the widest boundaries. The role of emotion in motivating collective action is greatly downplayed in the contemporary literature, probably as a reaction to the earlier literature, which portrayed mass collective action as irrational (the "mob").

Honoring the rationality of mass behavior is important but should not be achieved at the expense of a more complete account of human (elite and mass) behavior.[17] To be concrete, a violent attack by the state on a member of the group (such as a parent, a close friend, a village elder) could provoke antiregime activity from other group members, not necessarily out of self-defense but out of outrage and a desire for revenge (as well as justice). This could be true even if the attack were part of a regime strategy of targeting so carefully that the politically neutral are given no serious cause for fear for themselves. As Miller and Vidmar (1981: 156) point out, "The response to a crime like murder involves far more than just the perception that the act has challenged the group's values; it confronts essential belief systems—an impersonal objective order has been disturbed. The affective reaction in these instances is strong, and a compelling need to see the moral order set right is aroused." [18]

In summary, and to combine these three related critiques more tightly, when a "collectivist conception of rationality" is joined with the shared principles and the solidarity that grow from living together within social networks, then it is quite possible that people will behave in ways not predicted by private-interest models, especially under emotionally charged conditions.[19] In terms of the repression/protest paradox, this means that nontargeted politically neutral nonelites might join oppositional activities, even under the conditions of Mason and Krane's first two targeting strategies. The likelihood that they would do so will be all the greater if the larger political context is one of escalating popular mobilization throughout society, as will be shown in the third section.

THE CENTRAL AMERICAN REALITY

It is generally agreed that in the 1970s popular challenges to elite rule reached unparalleled levels in Central America.[20] Tragically, this mass mobilization was matched by extraordinary levels of state terrorism. This contradiction was most intense in El Salvador and Guatemala, both of which are utilized as examples in Mason and Krane's first application of their model (1985), while only El Salvador is utilized in the published version (1989). Both countries will be examined here (with limited comparisons to Nicaragua in the following section). I argue that predictions about popular mobilization based on Mason and Krane's model are contradicted in several crucial respects by what actually did occur in these two countries.

Salvadoran society in the early 1970s was aptly characterized as a "culture of repression" by one scholar with substantial experience in the country (Huizer 1972: 52–61). The lack of popular opposition to the regime was not because of the lack of grievances or because of support for the government. Instead, the paramount factor was the high level of coercion built into the system and the intermittent use of violence by public and private elites to maintain quiescence. This description applied to Guatemala as well. Although there are important differences in the histories of the two countries, these repressive structures had evolved in both across the centuries to ensure elite control of the land and labor necessary for the enrichment of the elite.

Socioeconomic grievances intensified during the 1960s and 1970s in both countries as the economic security of many people deteriorated, especially in rural areas. At the same time, new opportunities for acting on their discontent opened for nonelites, beginning in El Salvador in the late 1960s and then in Guatemala in the mid-1970s when a more moderate government came to power. Mass political activity was facilitated by the sustained efforts of outside "catalysts for change" (Pearce 1986: 108), such as church workers, some of whom brought a new biblical message of liberation here on earth.[21] As the 1970s progressed, new forms of popular political activity appeared and new levels of popular opposition to the regimes were reached. Most important were the popular organizations with their large mass memberships and their use of nonviolent but confrontational actions, such as demonstrations, strikes, occupations of buildings, and land seizures. In response to this growing popular challenge, violence from the entrenched security forces escalated, essentially progressing through the three targeting strategies identified by Mason and Krane.[22] From a strategy of targeted and intermittent killings in the mid-1970s, by early 1980 the violence became widespread and indiscriminate in its scope.[23] Recall that their model predicts that indiscriminate violence will provoke mass opposition "because the likelihood of becoming a victim is no longer related to one's support or non-support of the insurgents" (Mason and Krane 1989:

188). This happened in both countries, but only for awhile. Then the violence succeeded in its objective: it terrorized much of the population back into passivity, saving the regimes from overthrow by their citizenry.

Concerning Guatemala, Mason and Krane's model misses this central fact about contemporary events. Indiscriminate and widespread political violence crushed a popular mobilization involving many different interests, organizations, and strategies that drew on substantial support across many sectors of society. Some of these groups were mainly seeking progress toward political democracy and respect for civil liberties. The last fairly elected president had been the leftist Jacobo Arbenz, who was covertly overthrown by the United States in 1954. Since then, the military had tightened its control of the country, with military candidates winning the presidency in each election since 1970. Other groups stressed the need to reform Guatemala's grossly unequal socioeconomic structures and exploitive labor practices. Most significantly, for the first time there were groups representing the interests and needs of the country's Mayan population, still about one-half of the entire population and concentrated primarily in the rugged highlands of the west.

In its early stages the indiscriminate violence of the late 1970s and into the early 1980s did bolster active support for the opposition and especially the armed revolutionary movements operating among Indian communities, particularly in the isolated back reaches of the western highlands. But as the military violence intensified and continued virtually without restraint in the Mayan countryside, where even the young and the elderly were murdered in large numbers, and as it continued relentlessly month after month and year after year, the guerrillas were thrown on the defensive and then isolated. The military destroyed some 440 villages with the "scorched earth" tactics of 1980–84 and left up to one million Guatemalans displaced from their homes (Black 1985: 16).[24] In the face of this unrelenting brutality, it became clear that the revolutionaries would not win and then that they could not protect their supporters. Exile to Mexico or the United States was often the only rational choice. The military's recourse to massive indiscriminate violence against innocent civilians not only won the war against the people but also created structures of control that penetrated the Indian highlands of western Guatemala far beyond that which had existed previously.

The Salvadoran case is more complex, both in itself and in Mason and Krane's account. Ideally, competing models and descriptions are tested with appropriate empirical data. Regrettably, such a data set does not exist for Central America. The most impressive data set, and the one invariably used to test hypotheses such as those with which this study is concerned, is provided by the *World Handbook of Political and Social Indicators* (Taylor and Jodice 1983). At least for Central America, though, the data is wildly inaccurate, the result of gross and systematic errors in data collection (Brockett 1992).[25] Because the appropriate quantitative data are not available (except for one variable), rival explanations can only be assessed by reference to the nonquantitative scholarship and journalistic accounts that are available.

The military had directly ruled El Salvador since 1932. When civilian centrist forces looked like they might win in the elections of both 1972 and 1977, the military relied on fraud and intimidation to maintain its power. As the 1970s progressed, Salvadoran society became increasingly mobilized through a multitude of organizations representing peasants and workers, students and professionals. With the electoral path blocked, regime opponents turned to strikes, demonstrations, and occupations. In the face of this growing popular challenge, the Salvadoran regime increasingly turned to violence. A coup by junior military officers brought a reformist government to office in October 1979 and the hope of a peaceful resolution to the crisis. The new government, however, was divided, was distrusted by the militant left, and most importantly, had no control over the security forces. As confrontational activities of the left (especially occupations of buildings and mass demonstrations) increased, regime violence escalated even further. Civilian deaths at the hands of the regime averaged over 300 a month for the remainder of the year, more than double the rate of the preceding period (Morales Velado et al. 1988: 190).[26] In March 1980, following two virtually complete changes in the new government, an agrarian reform was promulgated. It is at this point that informed observers identify the beginning of the civil war (for example, Baloyra 1982: 137; Dunkerley 1982: 162). Regime violence accelerated again, with civilian deaths doubling to 584 during March and then more than doubling in May to 1,424 (Morales Velado et al. 1988: 195). By the end of the year virtually all political space for nonviolent opposition to the regime had been eliminated (ibid.: 73), the key symbol being the November kidnapping and execution of six leaders of the nonviolent left. The remaining leadership then either went into exile or underground. Over 10,000 civilians were murdered by the security forces and their allied death squads in El Salvador in both 1980 and 1981, with 6,000 more killed in 1982 (Brown, 1985: 122).[27]

The relationship between popular opposition and regime violence during these years in El Salvador was multifaceted.[28] Generally, as regime violence grew through the late 1970s into 1980, collective actions against the regime increased in number, intensity, and militancy. During this period, the guerrilla forces remained relatively small and comparatively limited in their activities. Instead, the major vehicles for popular opposition were the popular organizations (which had semi-covert ties to the guerrilla movements)[29] and their (largely) nonviolent confrontational tactics. As the regime violence became increasingly widespread in early 1980, many of the leaders and the rank and file of the popular organizations were killed, and the space for their forms of collective action disappeared. It was at this point that the guerrilla forces rapidly grew in size, popular support, and ability to oppose the regime.[30] This growth in the size and actions of what became later in the year the Faribundo Marti National Liberation Front (FMLN), however, coincided with a *decline* in the total number of people who were actively engaged in all forms of oppositional activities. The civil war intensified until about early 1984. Although the war continued through 1991, the FMLN never was able to reachieve the level of threat to the regime that it represented at that time.[31] Vital to the ability of the Salvadoran military to contain the threat from the FMLN, of course, was the tremendous financial support it received from the United States, which totaled $6 billion (Gugliotta and Farah 1993: 6), peaking in 1985 at $115 per resident of El Salvador (Congressional Research Service 1989: 25–27).

Mason and Krane acknowledge both this decline in regime opposition and that the decline could be taken as a contradiction of their model and its central prediction that regime violence that indiscriminately strikes politically neutral nonelites is counterproductive because it makes oppositional activities rational. Their explanation for this declining opposition is the "positive effects of the reform program"[32] and, most importantly, "the dramatic decline in the level and arbitrariness of death squad violence." They add that as "repression has become less pervasive and arbitrary, the option of remaining uninvolved in the conflict has been restored" (1989: 191). This interpretation does preserve their model's accuracy, but it does not agree with the usual interpretation of Salvadoran events.

The issue here is that of causality. Did popular opposition to the regime decline because regime violence declined first? Or did regime violence eventually decline because it had successfully eliminated most overt popular opposition, with the exception of the guerrilla armies, and even with the armed opposition had stemmed the growth of its support?[33] If the latter, then the indiscriminate violence was successful, not counterproductive, from the viewpoint of the regime, just as it was in Guatemala.

In reality, nonelites have another alternative besides supporting either the regime or the guerrillas as regime violence escalates. They can also flee: about one-quarter of the entire population of El Salvador were refugees by mid-1984.[34] Close to 750,000 people had fled the country in the preceding five years (Brown 1985: 135). If nonelites believe that the opposition has a chance of winning, then active support might be rational in the face of indiscriminate violence that might strike them. If they find the program and/or the tactics of that opposition also objectionable, however, then exile might be the more rational alternative. Furthermore, when regime violence continues and intensifies to the point where victory by the opposition is doubtful, then exile might be the more likely response, regardless of agreement with the program of the guerrillas.

When calculating the probable consequences of a recourse to systematic state terrorism in response to escalating popular opposition, elites in El Salvador and Guatemala only needed to contemplate their own histories. Elites in El Salvador could look back to *la mantanza* of 1932, when 10,000 to 30,000 peasants were massacred, as "a model response to the threat of rebellion," as well as to the four decades of "peace" that the massacre brought (McClintock 1985a: 99–100; Anderson 1971). Guatemalan elites considering violence only needed to refer to 1966–72 when over 10,000 innocents were murdered[35] or to the 22-year reign of terror of Manuel Estrada Cabrera early in the century. Going further back in time, elites in both countries evaluating violence as an instrument of control could recall the coercion employed in converting peasant food-crop land to elite-owned coffee land beginning in the latter third of the nineteenth century, or they could go all the way back to the massive violence of the Conquest itself and the consequent coercion utilized to maintain colonial society. The fundamental point has been aptly stated by Gurr (1986: 66): "Historical traditions of state terror . . . probably encourage elites to use terror irrespective of . . . structural factors." Although morally abhorrent, the historic reliance on violence by Guatemalan and Salvadoran elites has not been counterproductive to their interests. Violence-as-necessary has allowed a small group to maintain its privileged position to the severe disadvantage of the vast majority. From the viewpoint of those in charge, state terrorism has been a success.

Summarizing this section, I argue in partial agreement with Mason and Krane that in its early stages indiscriminate violence targeted against neutral nonelites can increase mass involvement in and support for oppositional collective action, including revolutionary activities. However, state terrorism when sustained has often had the opposite effect in Central America, smashing overt popular opposition to the terrorist regime.[36] In the following section a superior model will be proposed for differentiating which effect regime violence will have, regardless of whether it be violence from an indiscriminate targeting strategy or from the two more limited strategies.

THE POLITICAL CYCLE EXPLANATION

Social movement scholars writing from the political-process perspective provide the critical insight that collective action is as much a function of "the political realities confronting members and challengers at any given time" (McAdam 1988: 245) as it is of grievances, group organization, availability of resources, or underlying socioeconomic change. When joined together, these political realities can best be conceptualized as "the structure of political opportunity." As the political opportunity structure shifts to the advantage of challengers, the power discrepancy between them and elites diminishes, increasing the challengers' political leverage and improving the possibility of outcomes in their interest (McAdam 1982: 43).[37]

Socioeconomic grievances did escalate throughout Central America in the 1970s. Equally critical to the development of the mass movements of the decade, though, was the development of a more favorable opportunity structure. Mass mobilization was catalyzed and sustained by assistance from support groups and allies, such as religious groups, revolutionary organizers, political party activists, and international development workers. Also crucial was the opening of political space for oppositional activities in El Salvador and Guatemala, as well as in Nicaragua and Honduras.[38] Repression lightened, lowering the risks of organization and action. With the possibilities for winning beneficial changes improving, mass organizations and oppositional activities proliferated.

Tarrow has demonstrated in a number of his works (for example, 1983, 1989a, 1989b) that such mass collective action sometimes occurs in the larger context of a protest cycle, a temporal location with significant implications for challengers. Protest cycles begin when the structure of political opportunity turns more favorable, encouraging groups to act on long-standing grievances and/or newly created ones. The activities of these early mobilizers then encourage other groups and movements to activate as well. As a result, conflict diffuses throughout society at higher than normal levels of frequency and intensity. This activity builds, peaks, and then declines to more normal levels (Tarrow 1983: 38–39). For example, in his detailed study of the Italian protest cycle of the late 1960s and early 1970s, Tarrow (1989a: 62) records an average of less than 150 protest events for each half-year during 1965–67 but an average of over 500 for the twelve half-year points beginning with late 1968 (and peaking at about 750 events for the last half of 1971).

A challenger asserting claims on the upswing of the protest cycle generally will fare better than challengers late in the cycle or outside its duration. During the upswing of a cycle, many groups and movements will be asserting claims, placing greater pressure on the system than could any group individually. Systems and their elites, though, adapt only so far; short of revolutionary transformations, responsiveness eventually declines and repressive measures become more likely. Challenges made late in the cycle or afterward face a less favorable opportunity structure.

When the concept of the protest cycle is wedded to government violence, the essential argument is this: indiscriminate repression is likely to provoke further popular mobilization only during the ascendant phase of the protest cycle. In contrast, indiscriminate repression deters popular collective action before the initiation of a cycle, and it can (and does) bring protest cycles to an abrupt end. For example, the widespread and arbitrary murders of thousands of noncombatant peasants in Guatemala in the mid-1960s and in Nicaragua in the mid-1970s did not provoke mass mobilization among the survivors (see Brockett 1990). The revolutionary guerrilla organizations in their midst (which were the "justifications" for the campaigns of terror) were small and isolated from other political forces. Indeed, society itself was largely demobilized, as certainly the peasantry was even prior to the counterinsurgency campaigns. Under these circumstances, survivors in the targeted regions, no matter how sharp their pain nor how strong their rage, had no opportunities for collective action. The structure of political opportunity offered no hope for justice, no possibility for revenge.

Later, though, the political context changed. Political space for organizing and action opened for a variety of reasons in each country: in urban El Salvador in the late 1960s, slowly spreading to its rural areas; in Guatemala in the mid-1970s; and to a lesser extent in Nicaragua in the last third of the 1970s. Collective action was greatly assisted by the appearance of numerous support groups. In this more supportive context, intermittent regime violence provoked anger, determination, and resistance in each country. Popular organizations grew in number, in size, and in assertiveness. Vigorous protest cycles were initiated in El Salvador and Guatemala and to a lesser extent in Nicaragua.

Faced with this sustained threat from below, the regimes of each country turned to even more violence. Although this violence became increasingly widespread, brutal, and arbitrary, initially it did not deter popular mobilization but provoked even greater mass opposition. Opponents who were already active redoubled their efforts, and some turned to violence. Increasing numbers of nonelites gave their support to the growing revolutionary armies, many becoming participants themselves. Previously passive regime opponents were activated, and new opponents were created as the indiscriminate violence delegitimized regimes, on the one hand, and created incentives for opposition, such as protection, revenge, and justice, on the other.

The desires for justice and for revenge can find an outlet through collective action in this ascendant phase of the protest cycle (and violence as self-protection can appear rational) for at least two reasons. First, there is hope of winning. Despite the brutality of the regime's indiscriminate violence, the active opposition of large numbers of people and of many organizations from many different sectors of society sustains the belief that the regime will be defeated. This belief was widespread among the popular forces in Nicaragua during the insurrections of 1978–79 and, shortly thereafter, in El Salvador and Guatemala for a brief time at the peak of their popular mobilizations.

The second reason goes beyond rational calculation of the probability of victory to include both emotional response and location in the protest cycle. Assume two sets of regime opponents where the first set is already engaged in collective action against the regime but the second set is not. When indiscriminate repression is directed against the population, the people who are already mobilized are more likely to continue their opposition than the people who are unmobilized are likely to act on their rage by initiating oppositional activities. For the first set, although the indiscriminate violence increases the dangers of further collective action (and might even diminish the probability of success), the rage engendered by that violence provides additional motivation for action, perhaps more than enough to offset the increased danger.[39] Since these opponents are already active, the momentum of that activity can carry them into clandestine and violent forms of resistance and retaliation as the regime closes nonviolent channels of protest. For the second set, however, the configuration of grievances and risks will be different. They had not been active before the violence, which now increases the dangers of opposition while further restricting the opportunities for action.

Furthermore, the active individuals are not isolated. The fact that they have already been involved in oppositional activities means that they are integrated, at least to some extent, into groups and organizations. These social networks provide the leadership and opportunities for continuing activity, as well as the solidarity bonds and obligations and the examples that encourage action.

As with individuals, we can posit two different situations concerning the social movement sector: organizations making demands on the political system are either numerous or few. The ascendant phase of the protest cycle is marked by the proliferation of organizations and their activities and by unusually large numbers of individuals involved in collective action. Under these circumstances (for example, Guatemala in the early 1980s), indiscriminate regime violence is likely to accelerate antiregime action, for the reasons identified above. However, prior to the initiation of a protest cycle (for example, Guatemala in the late 1960s) there are far fewer people in the active category and far fewer organizations to give direction to their grievances. Therefore, indiscriminate regime violence outside the protest cycle deters popular collective action.[40]

The popular mobilizations in El Salvador and Guatemala during the 1970s and early 1980s, however, were met by ever more vicious repression, abruptly ending their protest cycles. The tens of thousands of murders in each country in the early 1980s were sufficient to destroy most popular organizations or drive them underground, to restore fear and passivity to much of the countryside, and to contain the revolutionary forces.[41] The fact is, successful rebellions and revolutions are rare. Although indiscriminate violence might escalate regime opposition under some circumstances, there are limitations to a people's ability to withstand ferocious regime violence. The difference in the outcomes between these two countries and Nicaragua, where the popular forces succeeded in overthrowing the murderous Somoza regime in 1979, was the result of more than the fact that the opposition to Somoza was more widespread across classes. In addition, Somoza did not have nearly the same capacity for state terrorism as his neighbors,[42] and the Guatemalan and Salvadoran regimes had the willingness to use their greater capacity to the extent necessary to ensure their survival.[43]

CONCLUSION

The central issue dealt with in this article is the paradoxical relationship between regime violence and popular protest. In attempting to explain why sometimes regime violence deters mass oppositional activities but at other times it provokes further opposition, I claim here that the most important determinant is the temporal location in the protest cycle. The targeting strategy pursued by the regime is, of course, a critical variable. However, the evidence from Central America indicates that during "normal conditions," that is, prior to the onset of a protest cycle, escalating repression will deter popular mobilization against the regime.

In contrast, in the ascendant phase of the protest cycle the same repression is likely to provoke increased mass oppositional activities. Nonetheless, if elites are willing and are capable of instituting widespread indiscriminate killing on a sustained basis, then they have often been successful in ending the protest cycle and terrorizing the population back into political passivity. That is to say, if the level of regime violence is the independent variable, then location in the protest cycle is a control variable exercising greater influence over mass protest behavior, the dependent variable.

In addition, I have argued that rational-choice theory—especially in its narrower versions—can take us only so far in understanding the protest behavior of nonelites. Certainly nonelites rationally calculate the expected utility of the probable mix of the provision of goods and services and the application of sanctions that would result from supporting the government, supporting the opposition, maintaining neutrality, or migrating, perhaps into exile. However, violence activates human responses that are usually not involved in deciding, for example, the firm from which to purchase some consumer good.[44] When agents of the state rape members of one's village or torture some of its elders, ties of solidarity and shared principles concerning, for example, obligation and justice will undoubtedly influence the nature of one's response. If those agents of state terror strike against one's own family, murdering perhaps a daughter or a father, then the resulting rage and anguish certainly would be an important determinant of the choice one makes as to how to respond to this escalating regime violence.

The following is the testimony of Rigoberta Menchú, a Quiché Indian from Guatemala and recipient of the 1992 Nobel Peace Prize. In September 1979 her sixteen-year-old brother was kidnapped by the army. He was then subjected to two weeks of extraordinary torture and then, with others in the same condition, was burned alive in front of their families.

> When we got home Father . . . started to talk to us. He said, rightly, that if so many people were brave enough to give their lives, their last moments, their last drop of blood, then wouldn't we be brave enough to do the same? And my mother, too, said: "It's not possible that other mothers should suffer as I have suffered. The people cannot endure that, their children being killed. I've decided too to abandon

everything. I shall go away." And we all said the same: there was nothing else you could say. . . . We concluded that the most important thing was to organise the people so that they wouldn't have to suffer the way we had, see that horror film that was my brother's death. [Burgos-Debray 1984: 181] [45]

NOTES

1 The validity of many of these empirical studies is questionable, though, because of the dataset used. This point is discussed further below.
2 Also see Mason 1989b: 468–70 for a good, concise review of this literature.
3 For example, much of Opp and Roehl's complex and compelling model for explaining the paradox under conditions of low repression is also of value for high-repression conditions. However, I show below that such models are incomplete for explaining important aspects of the relationship between repression and collective action under conditions of high repression.
4 Lichbach (1987) also attempts to resolve the paradox using rational-choice theory. His effort, although elaborate, is devoted to elites and their decision making in a manner abstracted from much of the relevant political context.
5 For the three decades after 1954, the death toll in Guatemala climbed to over 100,000 killed and 38,000 disappeared, according to the British Parliamentary Group on Human Rights (U.S. Congress 1985: 63); another one million were internal refugees (Bowen 1985: 106). In El Salvador, more than 40,000 civilian noncombatants were murdered through 1984 by government security forces and allied death squads (Brown 1985: 115), with the common figure of 75,000 cited for all deaths to the present. It is important to note that numerous murders outside of combat have also been committed by the revolutionary left in both countries, especially in El Salvador. Nonetheless, human rights observers agree that the killing by the governments overwhelms that by the left; while the left has killed selectively, the governments have murdered indiscriminately. For substantiation, see Americas Watch Committee 1991: 64–70.
6 The fullest explication of their model is in Mason and Krane (1989); accordingly, most attention will be given to this text, with occasional reference to the other works as appropriate.
7 Their discussion is framed in terms of "death squad violence." In the case of Central America, this is the same as "regime repression" and the latter, more general, terminology will be employed here. For substantiation, see Americas Watch Committee 1991: 21–27.
8 For a more elaborate discussion of the ramifications of this targeting strategy, see DeNardo 1984.
9 They also argue that latent support for the opposition should rise "as the loss of benefits from the opposition is not likely to be offset by a comparable increase in benefits from the regime" (Mason and Krane 1989: 180). This hypothesis does not seem as supportable since its two assumptions are subject to qualification by a number of other variables. Furthermore, a

withdrawal of regime support does not invariably lead to preference for the opposition; neutrality is a third possibility, as the authors recognize in other parts of their work. Mason (1989b: 475–76) gives more complete attention to this third possibility.

10 In its implementation, of course, this targeting strategy would be impossible to execute without striking some uninvolved bystanders. From the perspective of these victims, this strategy is no different from the third. Descriptively and analytically, however, there is an important distinction between a targeting strategy that attempts selectively to eliminate only known opponents and one that murders indiscriminately in order to terrorize a broader population.

11 Here the authors overstate their case, claiming that "the insurgents need only offer an individual the means to avoid state-sanctioned terror to win his or her support" (Mason and Krane 1989: 181).

12 See, for example, Muller and Opp 1986; Opp 1989; Finkel et al. 1989; Muller et al. 1991; and Opp and Roehl 1990.

13 This point is well portrayed, of course, by Popkin's (1979, 1988) work on Vietnam. Also see Wilson and Orum 1976: 198.

14 Along related lines, see the essay in the same edited volume by Taylor (1988), as well as Calhoun 1982: 136.

15 Sabia (1989) also stresses the importance of solidarity. Opp and Roehl (1990) include both social and moral incentives in their model, along with public-goods incentives. Some organizations, such as military units, make considerable efforts to forge solidarity bonds among their members. The importance of organizational (relational) factors to understanding the critical events of France in 1848, as opposed to the calculation of individual interest, is well documented by Traugott (1985).

16 For example, both Muller and Opp place themselves within a rational-choice framework, albeit a greatly expanded one. See, in particular, Opp 1989. In contrast, Fireman and Gamson (1979: 20) argue that such an expansion of the model "is to destroy the raison d'être of the selective incentive argument by reducing it to a useless tautology."

17 As Marcus et al. (1991: 4) point out, presumptions "that conscious awareness can monitor all senses, and that conscious awareness can control all human actions, are no longer supportable in light of the evidence of brain research and is no longer accepted by those who have studied cognitive function in humans." Therefore, as they add, "by understanding the role of feelings . . . we can gain a more comprehensive understanding of . . . under what circumstances . . . [people] will take action."

18 For further discussion, see the essay by Hogan and Emler (1981) in the same volume.

19 Suggestive in this context is the link Wickham-Crowley (1991: 38–40) finds between Weber's four ideal types of social action (calculating and value-based rationalities and affective and traditional orientations) with four different conditions underlying peasant support for revolutionary movements.

20 For an extensive bibliography on contemporary Central America, and for additional documentation for this section, see Brockett 1990.

21   For fuller treatments of the determinants of mass mobilization during this period in El Salvador and Guatemala, see Aguilera Peralta et al. 1981; Alas 1982; Brockett 1991b; Cabarrús 1983; and Morales Velado et al. 1988.

22   Mason and Krane make the important point that as violence eliminates the leadership of early opposing organizations, new leaders that emerge are likely to adopt different strategies and seek different types of supporters. They are also likely to be more militant and more violent (1989: 180, 188). However, why the regimes could not handle these new leaders with the same targeting strategy as before, that is, without recourse to indiscriminate violence, is not clear in the authors' account.

23   This targeting strategy actually has several dimensions. Its key feature is that it is arbitrary in its selection of victims. At the same time, the scope of that violence can vary, from regional to national in focus. Within that scope, the amount of violence could range from mild to massive. In the cases of El Salvador and Guatemala, at its peak the violence was massive and national, in addition to arbitrary.

24   For documentation on Guatemala, also see Americas Watch Committee 1982 and 1983; Bowen 1985 and 1987; Carmack 1988; and Krueger and Enge 1985.

25   These inaccuracies are undoubtedly a major reason for the contradictory findings in cross-national empirical studies of political violence.

26   This data set was compiled by Socorro Jurídico, an independent human rights organization once associated with the Roman Catholic archdiocese of San Salvador. For a good discussion of the controversies associated with this and other efforts to count the dead in El Salvador and assess responsibility, see Congressional Research Service 1989: 77–98.

27   Americas Watch (Brown 1985: 122) is the source for 1981 and 1982; Socorro Jurídico (Morales Velado et al. 1988: 195–96) lists 11,895 regime civilian murders for 1980 and 16,276 for 1981. Mason and Krane (1989: 190) have the violence increasing into 1982, but clearly the peak was 1980–81.

28   Support for the account provided here on El Salvador during this period can be found in the following: Alas 1982; AWC/ACLU 1982; Baloyra 1982; Berryman 1984; Cabarrús 1983; Diskin and Sharpe 1986; Dunkerley 1982; LeoGrande and Robbins 1980; Montgomery 1982; and Morales Velado et al. 1988.

29   The nature of the relationship between the guerrilla organizations and the popular organizations has been the subject of some controversy; compare, for example, Baloyra 1982: 67–69 to New York Times 15 Mar. 1982: A1. For further discussion of both types of organizations, see Leiken 1984 and, from a more friendly perspective, Alas 1982.

30   Mason and Krane (1989: 188) portray the guerrilla movements in 1979 as having reached a size that in reality was not achieved until sometime into the early 1980s. Their source is credible (Leiken 1984: 118); the problem is that the source is referring to the size and support of the FMLN in 1983 and not 1979. Indeed, as late as February 1980, the guerrillas were described as not yet "an effective military force" (Bonner 1984: 96), but instead needing several more months of preparation before they could undertake a challenge to the regime (New York Times 29 Feb. 1980: A10).

31   An offensive by the FMLN in late 1983 was so disastrous for the government
      that the country was "flooded with rumors of an impending coup" (*Chris-
      tian Science Monitor* 10 Nov. 1983). The *New York Times* correspondent who
      covered El Salvador during this period claimed that the guerrillas controlled
      more territory at the start of 1984, which is generally acknowledged to have
      been the peak of their threat to the regime (see, for example, Diskin and
      Sharpe 1986: 79), than at any prior time (Bonner 1984: 138). It should be
      noted, though, that at the end of the 1980s the Salvadoran revolutionaries
      still controlled about a sixth of the country, constituted a shadow govern-
      ment in a third (*New York Times* 30 July 1989), and had proven itself to
      be a force that the military could not defeat (Blachman and Sharpe 1988/
      89: 125).

32   For a good discussion of the problem of evaluating popular support, see
      Bonner 1984: 134–41, 290–307. There was indeed a reform program with
      some notable accomplishments that did generate some new public support.
      However, the land reform was also indistinguishable in implementation from
      the increase in indiscriminate repression, so it also generated opposition.
      For further discussion of this "reform with repression" and documentation,
      see Brockett 1990: 153–61.

33   Clearly there were other factors at work as well, including pressure from the
      United States government. Congress struggled with the Reagan administra-
      tion throughout the early 1980s over the provision of U.S. assistance to such
      a gross violator of human rights. Not until the end of 1983, however, did
      the Reagan administration apply any meaningful pressure on the Salvadoran
      government to clean up its abusive practices. Even then, the pressure was
      limited and undercut by other voices in the administration (Americas Watch
      Committee 1991: 119–32; Diskin and Sharpe 1986: 68).

34   Although this possibility is occasionally mentioned by Mason and Krane,
      it is hardly factored into their account of rational calculations by nonelites.
      Moore (1989: 15) also raises this objection to their model.

35   As discussed below, this widespread and indiscriminate violence should
      have provoked mass oppositional activities among the targeted population,
      according to the Mason/Krane model, but it did not. For documentation
      on the period, see Aguilera Peralta et al. 1981; Booth 1980; Bowen 1985;
      Johnson 1973; and McClintock 1985b.

36   Popular organizations did revive in the last half of the decade in both
      countries but in self-inhibited fashion: demands are now less radical and
      collective action less provocative. As Blachman and Sharpe (1988/89: 131)
      point out in reference to El Salvador, but equally well for Guatemala,
      "working against any insurrectionary impulse is the collective memory of
      a nation that has not forgotten the widespread government terror of the
      early 1980s. . . . While the government's continued repression may produce
      outrage and frustration and impel some to act, others are inhibited by fear."

37   The most complete discussions of the structure of political opportunity are
      those of Tarrow (1983, 1989b), Kitschelt (1986), and McAdam (1988). For
      a review of this literature, a more complete elaboration of the concept, and
      its application to the Central American case, see Brockett 1991b.

38   The reasons for this opening varied between countries. As Costa Rica is the

one institutionalized democracy in the region, its political dynamics do not feature the same radical fluctuations in access to the political system.

39   Gurr (1970: 259) argues that "aggression is self-satisfying for angered" people. If regime coercion "is massive and sanctions severe, retaliation may become more salient [to challengers] than the economic and participatory values for which" they originally acted.

40   A further implication here is that previously unmobilized individuals are more likely to become active during the ascendant phase of the protest cycle than at other times because they are more likely in this context to be tied through their social networks to already active individuals and their organizations.

41   Despite the level of this violence, it is important to remember that the armed revolutionary organizations were able to continue with armed opposition to the regimes, more successfully in El Salvador than in Guatemala.

42   The number of security force personnel per square mile in Guatemala in the late 1970s was more than three times greater than in Nicaragua; the comparable figure for El Salvador was more than twice as great as that of Guatemala. In addition, the Guatemalan and Salvadoran militaries were more effective professional institutions than was the Nicaraguan national guard (Brockett 1991a).

43   Another possible variable is the role of the United States. However, while important, its impact has not been unidirectional. Although the loss of U.S. support was critical to the collapse of Somoza, the ending of U.S. military assistance did not constrain the murderous mission of the Guatemalan military. The United States bankrolled El Salvador's repression, but after 1983 it also used that leverage to force the Salvadoran military to leave more space for a civilian opposition than the military undoubtedly would have preferred (Blachman and Sharpe 1988/89; Morales Velado et al. 1988: 110, 125). For a more complete comparative treatment of state terrorism in Central America, see Brockett 1991a.

44   Citing a number of prior studies, Mason (1989b: 470) claims that the model of the profit-maximizing firm "has simply been shown to be useful as a starting point from which to model the behavior of the state in its interactions with its constituents and its rivals." Although this model might be useful for understanding some state-citizen relationships, its utility for such emotionally charged relationships as those under consideration here is more limited. Similarly, Almond argues (1990: 135): "In situations where absolute values come into play, where habit and tradition are important, or where affect and emotion are controlling, hardly rare occurrences, a simple rational choice forecast is going to mislead us."

45   Rigoberta Menchú's father was among the protesters massacred in the January 1980 occupation of the Spanish embassy in Guatemala City. Her mother was kidnapped in April 1980 and subjected to incredible brutality prior to her murder. Rigoberta Menchú later went into exile, becoming a primary leader of the opposition to the Guatemalan regime.

REFERENCES

Aguilera Peralta, G., et al. (1981) Dialectica del terror en Guatemala. San José, Costa Rica: EDUCA.

Alas, H. (1982) El Salvador: Por qué la insurrección? San José, Costa Rica: Secretario Permanente de la Comisión para la Defensa de los Derechos Humanos en Centroamérica.

Almond, G. (1990) A Discipline Divided: Schools and Sects in Political Science. Newbury Park, CA: Sage.

Anderson, T. (1971) Matanza: El Salvador's Communist Revolt of 1932. Lincoln: University of Nebraska Press.

Arias, A. (1985) "El movimiento indígena en Guatemala: 1970–1983," in D. Camacho and R. Menjívar (eds.) Movimientos populares en centroamérica. San José, Costa Rica: EDUCA: 62–119.

Americas Watch Committee (1982) Human Rights in Guatemala: No Neutrals Allowed. New York: Americas Watch Committee.

——— (1983) Creating a Desolation and Calling It Peace. New York: Americas Watch Committee.

——— (1991) El Salvador's Decade of Terror: Human Rights since the Assassination of Archbishop Romero. New Haven, CT: Yale University Press.

AWC/ACLU (1982) Report on Human Rights in El Salvador. New York: Random House/Vintage Books.

Baloyra, E. (1982) El Salvador in Transition. Chapel Hill: University of North Carolina Press.

Berryman, P. (1984) The Religious Roots of Rebellion. Maryknoll, NY: Orbis.

Blachman, M., and K. Sharpe (1988/89) "Things fall apart in El Salvador." World Policy Journal 6: 107–39.

Black, G. (1985) "Under the gun." NACLA Report on the Americas xix, 6: 10–24.

Bonner, R. (1984) Weakness and Deceit: U.S. Policy and El Salvador. New York: Times Books.

Booth, J. (1980) "A Guatemalan nightmare: Levels of political violence, 1966–1972." Journal of Inter-American Studies and World Affairs 22: 195–220.

Bowen, G. (1985) "The political economy of state terrorism: Barrier to human rights in Guatemala," in G. Shepherd, Jr., and V. Nanda (eds.) Human Rights and Third World Development. Westport, CT: Greenwood: 83–124.

——— (1987) "Prospects for liberalization by way of democratization in Guatemala," in G. Lopez and M. Stohl (eds.) Liberalization and Redemocratization in Latin America. New York: Greenwood: 33–56.

Brockett, C. (1990) Land, Power, and Poverty: Agrarian Transformation and Political Conflict in Central America. Rev. ed. Boston: Unwin Hyman.

——— (1991a) "Sources of state terrorism in rural Central America," in P. Bushnell, V. Shlapentokh, C. Vanderpool, and J. Sundram (eds.) State Organized Terror: The Case of Violent Internal Repression. Boulder, CO: Westview: 59–76.

——— (1991b) "The structure of political opportunity and peasant mobilization in Central America." Comparative Politics 23: 253–74.

——— (1992) "Measuring political violence and rural inequality in Central America." American Political Science Review 86: 169–76.

Brown, C., ed. (1985) With Friends Like These: The Americas Watch Report on Human Rights & U.S. Policy in Latin America. New York: Pantheon.

Burgos-Debray, E., ed. (1984) I . . . Rigoberta Menchú: An Indian Woman in Guatemala. London: Verso.

Cabarrús, C. (1983) Génesis de una revolución: Análisis del surgimiento y desarrollo de la organización campesina en El Salvador. México, DF: Ediciones de la Casa Chata.

Calhoun, C. (1982) The Question of Class Struggle. Chicago: University of Chicago Press.

——— (1988) "The radicalism of tradition and the question of class struggle," in M. Taylor (ed.) Rationality and Revolution. New York: Cambridge University Press: 129–75.

Carmack, R., ed. (1988) Harvest of Violence: The Maya Indians and the Guatemalan Crisis. Norman: University of Oklahoma Press.

Congressional Research Service (1989) "El Salvador, 1979–1989: A briefing book on U.S. aid and the situation in El Salvador." Library of Congress CRS Report for Congress.

Davis, S., and J. Hodson (1982) Witnesses to Political Violence in Guatemala: The Suppression of a Rural Development Movement (Impact Audit 2). Boston: Oxfam America.

DeNardo, J. (1984) Power in Numbers: The Political Strategy of Protest and Rebellion. Princeton, NJ: Princeton University Press.

Diskin, M., and K. Sharpe (1986) "El Salvador," in M. Blachman, W. Leo-Grande, and K. Sharpe (eds.) Confronting Revolution: Security through Diplomacy in Central America. New York: Pantheon: 50–87.

Dunkerley, J. (1982) The Long War: Dictatorship and Revolution in El Salvador. London: Junction Books.

Finkel, S., E. Muller, and K. Opp (1989) "Selective incentives and collective political action." Paper presented at the annual meeting of the American Political Science Association, Atlanta, August 31–September 3.

Fireman, B., and W. Gamson (1979) "Utilitarian logic in the resource mobilization perspective," in M. Zald and J. McCarthy (eds.) The Dynamics of Social Movements. Cambridge: Winthrop: 8–44.

Gugliotta, G. and D. Farah (1993) "When the truth hurts: A U.N. report re-opens old wounds over civil rights abuses in El Salvador," Washington Post National Weekly Edition, March 29–April 4: 6–7.

Gurr, T. (1970) Why Men Rebel. Princeton, NJ: Princeton University Press.

——— (1986) "The political origins of state violence and terror: A theoretical analysis," in M. Stohl and G. Lopez (eds.). Government Violence and Repression: An Agenda for Research. New York: Greenwood: 45–71.

Hogan, R., and N. Emler (1981) "Retributive justice," in M. Lerner and S. Lerner (eds.) The Justice Motive in Social Behavior: Adapting to Times of Scarcity and Change. New York: Plenum: 125–44.

Huizer, G. (1972) The Revolutionary Potential of Peasants in Latin America. Lexington, MA: Lexington Books.

Johnson, K. (1973) "On the Guatemalan political violence." Politics & Society 4: 55–83.

Kitschelt, H. (1986) "Political opportunity structures and political protest:

Anti-nuclear movements in four democracies." British Journal of Political Science 16: 57–85.

Krueger, C., and K. Enge (1985) Security and Development Conditions in the Guatemalan Highlands. Washington, DC: Washington Office on Latin America.

Leiken, R. (1984) "The Salvadoran left," in R. Leiken (ed.) Central America: Anatomy of Conflict. New York: Pergamon: 111–30.

LeoGrande, W., and C. Robbins (1980) "Oligarchs and officers: The crisis in El Salvador." Foreign Affairs 58: 1084–1103.

Lichbach, M. (1987) "Deterrence or escalation? The puzzle of aggregate studies of repression and dissent." Journal of Conflict Resolution 31: 266–97.

McAdam, D. (1982) Political Process and the Development of Black Insurgency, 1930–1970. Chicago: University of Chicago Press.

——— (1988) "Micro-mobilization contexts and recruitment to activism," in B. Klandermans, H. Kriesi, and S. Tarrow (eds.) From Structure to Action: Comparing Movement Participation across Cultures. Greenwich, CT: JAI: 243–97.

McClintock, M. (1985a) The American Connection. Vol. 1, State Terror and Popular Resistance in El Salvador. London: Zed Books.

——— (1985b) The American Connection. Vol. 2, State Terror and Popular Resistance in Guatemala. London: Zed Books.

Marcus, G., M. MacKven, W. R. Neuman, and J. Sullivan (1991) "Dynamic models of emotional response: The role of affect in politics." Paper presented at the annual meeting of the American Political Science Association, Washington, DC, August 29–September 1.

Mason, T. (1989a) "The calculus of fear: Repression, revolution, and the rational peasant." Paper presented at the annual meeting of the American Political Science Association, Atlanta, August 31–September 3.

——— (1989b) "Nonelite response to state-sanctioned terror." Western Political Quarterly 42: 467–92.

Mason, T., and D. Krane (1985) "The political economy of death squads: Towards a theory of the impact of state-sanctioned terror." Paper presented at the annual meeting of the American Political Science Association, New Orleans, August 29–September 1.

——— (1989) "The political economy of death squads: Towards a theory of the impact of state-sanctioned terror." International Studies Quarterly 33: 175–98.

Miller, D., and N. Vidmar (1981) "The social psychology of punishment reactions," in M. Lerner and S. Lerner (eds.) The Justice Motive in Social Behavior: Adapting to Times of Scarcity and Change. New York: Plenum: 145–72.

Montgomery, T. (1982) Revolution in El Salvador. Boulder, CO: Westview.

Moore, W. (1989) "Rational rebels: Overcoming the free-rider problem." Paper presented at the annual meeting of the American Political Science Association, Atlanta, August 31–September 3.

Morales Velado, O., et al. (1988) La resistencia no violenta ante los regimenes salvadoreños que han utilizado el terror institucionalizado en el periodo 1972–1987. San Salvador: Universidad Centroamericanos J.S. Cañas.

Muller, E., S. Finkel, and H. Dietz (1991) "Discontent and the expected utility of rebellion: The case of Peru." American Political Science Review 85: 1261–83.

Muller, E., and K. Opp (1986) "Rational choice and rebellious collective action." American Political Science Review 80: 471–89.

Olson, M. (1965) The Logic of Collective Action. Cambridge, MA: Harvard University Press.

Opp, K. (1989) The Rationality of Political Protest: A Comparative Analysis of Rational Choice Theory. Boulder, CO: Westview.

Opp, K., and W. Roehl (1990) "Repression, micromobilization, and political protest." Social Forces 69: 521–47.

Pearce, J. (1986) Promised Land: Peasant Rebellion in Chalatenango El Salvador. London: Latin America Bureau.

Popkin, S. (1979) The Rational Peasant. Berkeley: University of California Press.

——— (1988) "Political entrepreneurs and peasant movements in Vietnam," in M. Taylor (ed.) Rationality and Revolution. New York: Cambridge University Press: 9–62.

Sabia, D. (1989) "The self and group solidarity." Paper presented at the annual meeting of the American Political Science Association, Atlanta, August 31–September 3.

Tarrow, S. (1983) Struggling to Reform: Social Movements and Policy Change during Cycles of Protest. Western Societies Paper no. 15. Ithaca, NY: Cornell University.

——— (1989a) Democracy and Disorder: Social Conflict, Protest and Politics in Italy, 1965–1975. New York: Oxford University Press.

——— (1989b) Struggle, Politics, and Reform: Collective Action, Social Movement, and Cycles of Protest. Western Societies Papers no. 21. Ithaca, NY: Cornell University.

Taylor, C., and D. Jodice (1983) World Handbook of Political and Social Indicators. 3d ed. Vol. 2, Political Protest and Government Change. New Haven, CT: Yale University Press.

Taylor, M. (1988) "Rationality and revolutionary collective action," in M. Taylor (ed.) Rationality and Revolution. New York: Cambridge University Press: 63–97.

Traugott, M. (1985) Armies of the Poor. Princeton, NJ: Princeton University Press.

U.S. Congress, House Committee on Foreign Affairs (1985) Developments in Guatemala and U.S. Options. Hearings before Subcommittee on Western Hemisphere Affairs. 99th Cong., 1st sess.

Wickham-Crowley, T. (1991) "The peasantry and insurgency in Latin America, 1956–1988: A Boolean approach." Paper presented at the 16th International Congress of the Latin American Studies Association, Washington, DC, April 4–6.

Wilson, L., and L. Orum (1976) "Mobilizing people for collective political action." Journal of Political and Military Sociology 4: 187–202.

Zimmerman, E. (1980) "Macro-comparative research on political protest," in T. Gurr (ed.) Handbook of Political Conflict: Theory and Research. New York: Free Press: 167–237.

Cycles and Repertoires of Popular Contention in Early Modern Japan

JAMES W. WHITE

THE CONCEPTS OF "repertoires" and "cycles" of collective action, as popularized in recent years in the works of Charles Tilly and Sidney Tarrow, respectively, are the focal point of this essay. I explore these concepts in the context of a set of data based on 7,664 incidents of social conflict and political protest occurring in Japan during the period 1590–1877,[1] in order to investigate their temporally and spatially comparative robustness.[2]

Repertoires of popular contention (see Tilly et al. 1975; Tilly 1978, 1986) are the more straightforward of the concepts of interest here, referring as they do to all the different ways in which people contend with each other and with the authorities and elites of the societies in which they live. Nevertheless, there are different ways to define repertoires. In this essay I differentiate between three: social and political conflict and political protest (defined below), actions of varying degrees of violence, and specific types of conflict and protest behavior with differing social, economic,

James W. White is professor of political science at the University of North Carolina at Chapel Hill. His major research interests are Japanese politics and mass political participation. This paper was originally prepared for delivery at the annual meeting of the Social Science History Association, New Orleans, 1–3 November 1991. The research on which it is based was supported by the National Science Foundation (SES 8308413), the Social Science Research Council, the Fulbright Commission, the Japan Foundation, the Carolina Population Center, and the UNC University Research Council.

and political implications. The concept of cycle, on the other hand (see Tarrow 1981, 1990, and 1989), travels less easily. Paraphrasing Tarrow, cycles of contention are phenomena caused more by the political opportunity structure that people face than by the grievances that drive them, and have the following features:

1. An increasing and then decreasing magnitude of disruptive direct action
2. An increasingly and then decreasingly broad spectrum of social sectors involved in disruptive direct action (that is, social diffusion)
3. Increasing spatial/geographical diffusion of contention
4. Increasing involvement of social movement organizations (relative to interest groups and ad hoc groups) as the cycle nears its peak
5. The broadening of grievances and demands from concrete, direct popular interests toward the reconstruction of society's overall concept of popular contention
6. Repertorial evolution from more institutional and patterned behavior to more confrontational and tactically versatile activities, and back

Moreover, Tarrow sees cycles as leaving behind three probable residues and one possible:

1. An expanded space in which people feel that they can effectively and/or legitimately express grievances
2. Expanded opportunities for collective action organizers and organizations
3. Expanded opportunities for social groups to increase their influence and achieve their goals, and perhaps
4. Policy reform, the likelihood of which depends on the presence within the elite of minorities whose own interests are served by reforms responsive to the wave of contention

Some of these characteristics appear intuitively to hold even in preindustrial societies, but it is well to keep in mind that they were all derived from the experiences of advanced industrial capitalist democracies. Even presuming that similar-appearing waves of contention also characterize early modern Japan, there are reasons to expect this model to fit uncomfortably in light of that society's much lower (and agrarian) level of economic development, the rudimentary nature of its communications networks, and the far lower level of politicization of the populace. Tarrow himself suggests that the autocratic nature of Tokugawa Japan will matter, since for him repertorial and tactical innovation presupposes a degree of freedom; at least initially I suspect Tarrow overestimates this constraint, since much repertorial innovation involves illegal or illegitimate behavior in any situation of mushrooming conflict. Beyond this, however, we shall provisionally accept his model and see how it stands up to the data. Specifically, we shall see if there were Tarrovian cycles in early modern Japan and if the relationship between cycles and repertoires is as posited, paying only brief attention to questions of reform and residue.

WAVES OF CONTENTION AND THEIR CORRELATES IN TOKUGAWA JAPAN

The first step is to see if the pattern of popular contention in early modern Japan reveals anything resembling waves; Figure 1 indicates that it does. The solid line (labeled "Total Magnitude of Contention") in Figure 1 represents the total annual magnitude of popular contention of all kinds, and three peaks are apparent, in the 1780s, the 1830s, and the 1860s. These three periods coincide, as indicated, with three of the four periods of major political reform during the era: the Temmei/Kansei Reforms (1787–93), the Tempo Reforms (1841–43), and the Keio Reforms (1864–67). Given this coincidence, and the role of reform in Tarrow's model, we shall look also at a fourth period, that of the Kyoho Reforms (1722–30), which saw a falling level of contention but were followed almost immediately by the highest peak of conflict in the era to date.

Based on a reading of the literature on Tokugawa-era contention, three other factors have been added to Figure 1.[3] The dotted line ("Four-City Mean Rice Price") represents the mean annual price of rice (the staple food and the basis of all government revenue accounting) in four major cities ranging across the country (western Hiroshima, central Osaka, eastern Edo, and northeastern Aizu); the line labeled "Builders' Wages" represents the wages in building trades in the city of Kyoto; and the "Cumulative Dis-

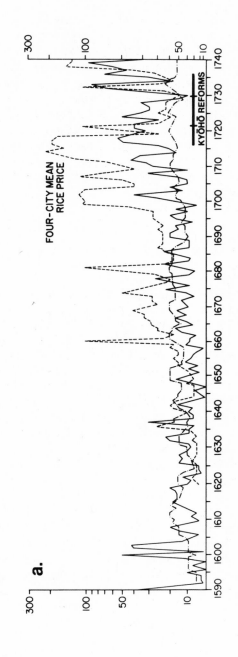

FOUR-CITY MEAN
RICE PRICE

KYŌHŌ REFORMS

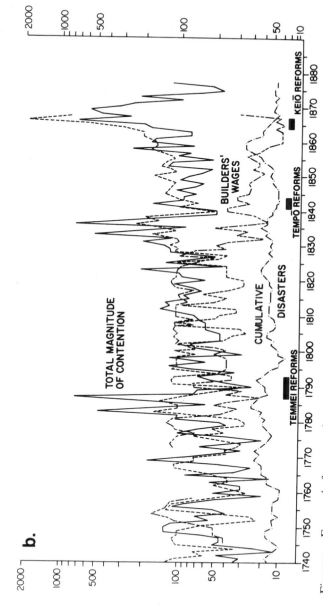

Figure 1   Economic factors and contention in early modern Japan

asters" line represents the total number of provinces affected by all forms of natural disasters in each year plus the previous four years. All curves are logarithmic, in order to dampen wide fluctuations; the left-margin scale is used for the contention and disaster curves (which are absolute magnitudes); the right-margin scale is used for the wage and price curves (which are index values, varying positively and negatively from 100 [1840–44 in the case of rice prices, 1801–10 for wages]).

The overall impression made by Figure 1 is of increasing levels of contention throughout the Tokugawa era and of increasingly close correspondence between economic factors and conflict. During the seventeenth century, conflict peaked independently during the years of regime establishment (ca. 1600), and rice prices peaked independently (ca. 1660 and 1680). Between 1700 and 1720, prices and conflict varied in tandem, but conflict levels were still much lower. By the nineteenth century, however, close congruence between the curves is seen, especially after the 1820s.

Separate examination of the four periods provides further insight. The Kyoho period seems to be less a cycle than a step-level change in contention, with the low levels of the seventeenth century never to be seen again. The reforms look as if they were quite successful (although clearly not prompted by contention) in bringing down the price of rice, although in an agrarian society the coincidental decline in disasters probably also contributed. Unfortunately, the reforms brought the price of rice so low that government revenues (denominated in rice) were threatened; a new price support program took hold just in time for a plague of locusts that hit western Japan. Together they drove rice prices up in 1732–33, and contention followed. Thus the contentious dimension of any cycle in this period seems to have followed reform, not preceded it.

The Temmei period perhaps exemplifies the contentious cycle: government profligacy in the 1770s combined with natural disaster in the 1780s, resulting in a great wave of conflict, wholesale personnel changes and policy reforms, and a fall in prices and contention that lasted for decades. The Tempo period was characterized more by disaster than by governmental factors, but the ensuing wave of conflict similarly led to reform; the reforms themselves, and their effects, were much more short lived this time. The Keio period was essentially one of extreme economic fluctuation and sharp inflation, exacerbated both by the full opening of Japan to foreign trade and by a poor harvest in 1866 (Totman 1980). This period is complicated, however, by the snowballing disintegration of the Tokugawa state, the growth of domestic elite-level challengers (to which the reforms were mainly a response), and the collapse of the regime in the Meiji Restoration of 1868.

Together, however, these four periods generate some impressions. First, the political variables emphasized by Tarrow may have shaped the pattern of contention. The interval between cycles went from 120 years (1600–1720) to 60 to 50 to 20 years as the system decayed (and the opportunities for contention opened, by inference); the cycles themselves became more compressed, and within each cycle conflict intensified as the successive peaks grew ever higher. Still, the clear parallels between prices, wages, disasters, and contention also suggest that in early modern Japan— and, we suspect, in early modern Europe—economic factors were more important than Tarrow found for contemporary Italy. Moreover, the geographical diffusion proposed by Tarrow does not accurately describe our phenomena: whereas the 74 years comprised by these four cycles and the 214 noncycle years (see below for periodization) saw almost equal numbers of contentious events (47% in the cycles, 53% in the noncycles), the events occurring in cycle years took place in only 397 of Japan's 631 counties, while contention in the noncycle years was spread over 521 counties. One suspects that cyclical conflict was concentrated where economic conditions were most severe *and* political responses— always highly variant in different units of a feudal system—least flexible. Thus, although with the exception of the Kyoho case our waves of contention look on the surface much like Tarrow's cycles, it is possible that they are very different creatures.

FOUR CYCLES OF CONTENTION

Figures 2–5 provide a more detailed look at the several waves of contention. They reinforce the above comments: the peak of conflict in 1732–33 possibly resulted from simple bad luck, since the reforms stemmed the falling rice price without driving contention above familiar levels; contention faded quickly after prices fell in 1733–34, unaccompanied by any policy response. In the Temmei and Tempo periods, conflict again seems economically driven. In

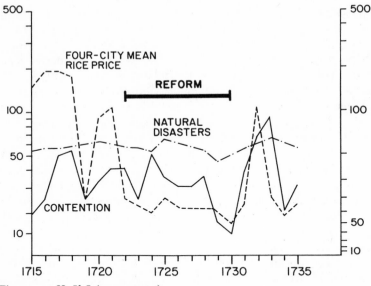

Figure 2   Kyōhō (1715–1735)

both cases reform got into gear only after the peak of conflict; the reforms themselves stimulated some conflict (especially in Tempo, when prices fell and conflict still rose in 1842) but were generally followed by (if not the cause of) the desired effect. The 1860s were marked by political and economic instability, and it is impossible to disentangle the two; after the restoration as well, as Figure 1 implies, the new regime both stabilized the economy and controlled contention far more effectively than its predecessor (see also Jansen 1989: chap. 6).

A more detailed look at contention reaffirms the notion that these periods were distinctive. As presented in Figures 2–5, the four cycles were periodized into 21, 21, 21, and 11 years, respectively, generating a total of 74 cycle years; the remaining 214 years of our data were then compared in the aggregate with the cycles. The cycle years saw *more* incidents (74 years, or 26% of the entire era, saw 47% of all events—42 incidents annually, as compared with 16 per noncycle year) and *bigger* incidents (the cycle years contained 55% of the total magnitude of contention, and the average magnitude of events during cycle years was 3.27, as opposed to 2.43 in noncycle years).

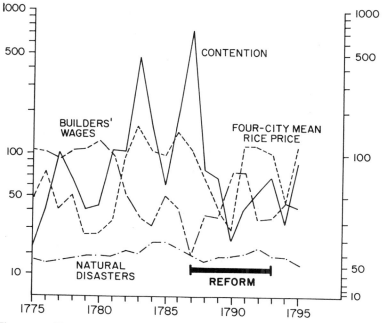

Figure 3   Temmei (1775–1795)

Looking at the cycles separately, the Kyoho period remains slightly anomalous. The average magnitude of events in that cycle was 2.33 (less than the average noncycle year), whereas that of Temmei events was 3.68; of Tempo, 2.90; and of Keio, 3.85. One must recall, however, that the Kyoho period ended a relative honeymoon for the state: in contrast with the 50 years before 1715, in which an average of 9 events occurred annually, 16 per year occurred in 1715–35.

Thus our four periods do appear exceptional, but our primary interest is not solely in their magnitude. Therefore I shift here to repertoires. In this essay I conceptualize repertoires of contention in three different ways, since the aim is to investigate the utility and implications of concepts, not simply to test hypotheses. The first type of repertoire is defined on the basis of actors and targets and has three components: social conflict (among members of the commoner class), political conflict (social conflict eventuating in overtures to the authorities for resolution or in attacks on the

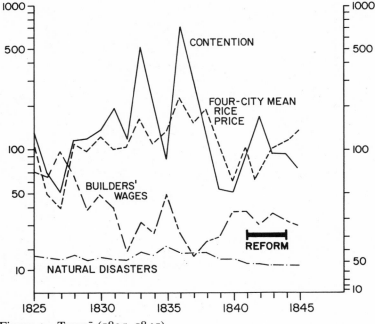

Figure 4   Tempō (1825–1845)

authorities for their treatment of the matter at hand or of one or
more of the contenders), and political protest (by commoners and
against the policies, incumbents, or structures of the state and its
formal or informal agencies).[4] When we look at the composition
of contention (the proportion of the total accounted for by each of
these three types), we again find support for the position that these
periods are indeed quite different from the norm (see Table 1).

First, and reinforcing our earlier suspicions about economic factors, the increased magnitude of conflict during cycle years seems
disproportionately due to an increase in social conflict, not political protest. This becomes increasingly clear when cycle years are
disaggregated: in the Temmei and Keio periods, social conflict
accounts for almost two-thirds of the total, and this is particularly
striking in light of the fact that the Keio period was one of extreme
political ferment. Even the Kyoho period represents a distinct depoliticization of contention compared with the previous century
(see Table 1, part B).

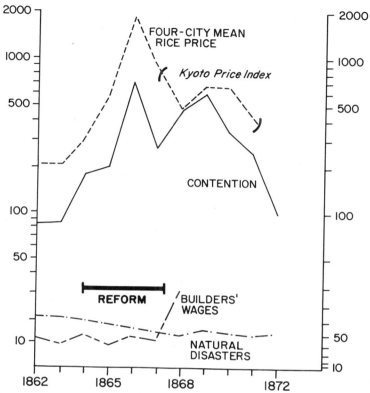

Figure 5 Keiō/Meiji (1862–1872)

Do the cycles represent eruptions of something different out of their temporal context, or are we looking simply at the glacial trends of the era, highlighted by cycles? Part B of Table I (simplified by the exclusion of the relatively invariant political conflict) suggests the former. During the seventeenth century, state consolidation and, consequently, a high volume of political protest took place; in the Kyoho period and every subsequent cycle, the proportion of total contention accounted for by political protest declined, and that of social conflict rose. Even during the Keio/Meiji period, only after the restoration in 1868 did the proportion of protest rise, to 27% in 1869, 43% in 1870, and 53% in the 1870s as, again, a new state was created and in many instances imposed over the opposition of the people. Thus waves of popular

Table 1   Repertoires of contention in early modern Japan:
The composition of conflict

A. Cycle and noncycle years

	Social conflict (%)	Political conflict (%)	Political protest (%)	Total contention (%)
214 noncycle years	48	12	41	101
74 cycle years	59	12	29	100
Kyoho period	35	12	54	101
Temmei period	64	9	26	99
Tempo period	57	16	27	100
Keio/Meiji period	63	11	26	100

B. Cycle and precycle years

	Social conflict (%)	Political protest (%)
1590–1714	24	61
Kyoho period	35	54
1736–74	48	41
Temmei period	64	26
1796–1824	54	35
Tempo period	57	27
1846–61	60	28
Keio/Meiji period	63	26
1873–77	40	53

contention in Tokugawa Japan not only coincide with distinctive patterns of economic fluctuation (and by implication nonpolitical stimulation); they also represent distinctive repertorial patterns in contrast to noncycle years in general and to the periods between cycles in each particular case. Perspective is crucial, however. On the basis of Figure 6 one might well argue that cycles are less important than glacial trends: high points to be sure, but really just points on an era-long, consistently rising curve of social contention. The other question raised by Tarrow's model—do these cycles witness repertorial innovation and creativity, or are they simply repetitive instances of response to repetitive stimuli?— remains to be answered, but the distinctiveness of these cycles seems clear.

Before we consider this question, however, we should address

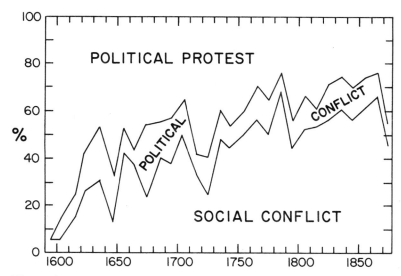

Figure 6   The composition of contention in Japan, 1590–1877

again Tarrow's assertion that cycles of contention come primarily in response to changes in the political opportunity structure. Our analysis thus far suggests that in relatively unpoliticized, relatively repressive agrarian states this does not hold, but corroboration is needed. An attempt at such precision can be seen in Table 2, which shows the results of a regression analysis for total magnitude of contention and for each of the three types of conflict, as explained by the variables included in Figures 1–5.[5] We are handicapped by the unavailability of data on political opportunity structure and catalytic events, but given the primitive nature of communications in early modern Japan it is far more likely that forces like dearth, felt by all (even if in mutual isolation), were likely short-term causes of contention. Even if such forces were not more powerful than political factors, Table 2 indicates that they certainly were powerful in their own right. Across the board the price of rice is the most influential independent variable, followed by the price-wage scissors and wage levels. Most strikingly, the price-wage scissors reaches maximum explanatory power vis-à-vis political protest, where we would expect it to be weakest. Also strikingly, contention during the cycle years appears to be more explicable in

Table 2 Correlates of sociopolitical contention in early modern Japan: A regression analysis

Independent variables	Total contention		Social conflict		Political conflict		Political protest	
	1590–1877	Cycle years[a]	1590–1877	Cycle years	1590–1877	Cycle years	1590–1877	Cycle years
Four-city mean rice price	.46*	.47*	.38*	.40*	.59*	.63*	.41*	.41*
Builders' wages	-.07	-.11	-.16	-.22	-.11	-.12	.25*	.33*
Disasters	.04	-.01	.05	.01	.04	.05	-.02	-.13
Price-wage scissors[b]	.20*	.22	.13	.09	.06	.16	.43*	.62*
R	.55	.58	.47	.49	.61	.69	.59	.73
R2 (corrected)	27%	27%	19%	17%	35%	43%	32%	49%

Note: all coefficients are betas, corrected for serial autocorrelation.
[a] n = 53 (1775–95, 1825–45, 1862–72).
[b] An interactive term combining rising rice prices and falling wages.
*p < .05.

terms of these factors than it does in noncycle years (the contrast is even sharper than it appears here, because 1590–1877 includes the cycle years). One cannot assess the relative weight of political and nonpolitical factors on the basis of these data, but if these four factors alone explain these proportions of contention (note especially protest), it seems likely that political opportunities play a smaller role in early modern societies, and conjuncture a larger role, than Tarrow's analysis indicates. Granted, in the Kyoho case the jump in rice prices resulted in large part from government price supports; in Keio/Meiji, prices rose partly due to inflation, apart from poor harvests, and the government was blamed accordingly. Perhaps we are dealing here with an extreme form of Ronald Inglehart's (1977, 1990) comparison of materialist and postmaterialist societies: agrarian, premodern societies in which a poor harvest could threaten physical survival might be "ultramaterialist," and economic issues consequently first and foremost. In such societies the state is far less likely than local merchants and landlords to be seen either as a cause of problems or as an avenue of remediation, and thus cyclical crises might result in more social and relatively less political contention.

The second dimension of repertoire of interest to us is defined on the basis of intensity. It is measured by a composite index including (1) whether or not an event involved one or more aggressive or violent acts against persons or property, (2) whether or not physical destruction of communal or personal buildings or property was involved, and (3) whether anyone was injured or killed by the commoner contenders (commoners killed or subsequently executed by the authorities are excluded).[6] This index, being purely behavioral, differs from the scale of magnitude of conflict, which combines intensity and size of event (measured in terms of duration and numbers of persons and villages involved; see White 1989). It also differs from the composition typology used above, in that neither actors nor targets are implied. It should be related to that typology, however, since social conflict tended to be more intense or violent than political protest.[7] A comparison of our cycle-of-contention years with noncycle years (see Table 3) both implies the relationship and emphasizes the distinctive nature of contention during the cycles.

The overall pattern of intense contention is first, and strikingly, characterized by extraordinarily deferential popular behav-

Table 3   Repertoires of intense contention in early modern Japan:
Aggression, destruction, and violence

	Percentage of events with no reported aggressive, destructive, or violent behavior	Average intensity of events
A. Cycle and noncycle years		
214 noncycle years	87	.14
74 cycle years	78	.25
B. Cycle and precycle years		
1590–1714	93	.08
Kyoho period	91	.10
1736–74	85	.16
Temmei period	71	.32
1796–1824	83	.18
Tempo period	81	.20
1846–61	86	.15
Keio/Meiji period	73	.30
1873–77	82	.21

ior: during noncycle years only 13% of all events included either
aggressive, destructive, or violent action, and the average event
scored only .14 on our 0–2 scale; even during the cycles only
22% of the events involved such behavior, although the intensity
of the average event rose to .25. When one compares the different cycles, the Kyoho period again seems to be less of a massive
eruption—aggressive behavior was slightly more common, and
events were slightly more intense, than in the previous 125 years—
than a period of transition to a more contentious age. It was a
sea change more than a rising and receding wave, as the data
for 1736–74 show. The other three cycles, however, rise in sharp
contrast to the years on either side, especially Temmei and Keio,
when almost 30% of the incidents included aggressive actions.
Moreover, these three cycles all represented increases in intensity
over prior years—by both of the measures included in part B of
Table 3—and were followed by a falloff in repertorial intensity
thereafter. Clearly, repertoires of conflict have distinctively violent
characteristics during major waves of conflict.

REPERTORIAL CHANGE IN POPULAR CONTENTION:
TRENDS OR CYCLES?

Two steps remain in this conceptual exercise. The first is to examine a third dimension of conflict repertoires, that is, specific types of contention that imply differing degrees of social cohesion, different physical loci of contention (and therefore levels of socioeconomic change), and different degrees of popular receptivity to violent contention. The second step is to pursue further the question of whether cycles are simply extraordinary waves of conflict that advance and then recede or whether, as Tarrow argues, they leave a culture changed durably if not permanently. Some of the data seen thus far cast light on these steps: the increased salience of social conflict during cycles suggests social disorganization and friction, and Table 3 suggests a gradually rising level of repertorial intensity during the Tokugawa era.

I focus on six types of contention in this analysis (see also Yokoyama 1977; Sugimoto 1978). The first two (combined for this analysis) are the "end-run" petition (*osso*) and absconding (*chikuden* or *chosan*). The end run was an (ordinarily quite deferential) overture by commoners to a level of government higher than that immediately above them. As violations of normal channels of dissent, such petitions were illegal—potentially a capital crime—and they were most often carried out by village officials in their capacities as responsible representatives of their constituents. Indeed, they presupposed a high degree of community cohesion. Flight presupposed the same, since it was almost always collective and carried out under the leadership of village headmen, and was similarly nonconfrontational, seeking respite from rapacious or corrupt rule by simple exit.

The third type of action was the "coercive appeal" (*goso*), similar to the *osso* but much more confrontational; leadership tended more often to come from sub-elite elements among the commoners, and such appeals imply both the inability of officials to represent the whole community (due largely to the socioeconomic differentiation that accompanied protoindustrialization) and a decline in popular awe of government and its objectively decaying coercive powers.

The fourth type of action was the destructive riot (*uchikowashi*), most often urban and most often over the price of rice. Moneylen-

Table 4   Repertoires of contention in cycle and noncycle years

	Noncycle years (%) (n = 214)	Cycle years (%) (n = 74)
End run and flight	15	7
Coercive appeal	11	13
Destructive riot	6	14
Insurrection	1	1
Intravillage dispute	48	44
Percentage of all contentions	75	77

ders, pawnbrokers, large landowners (whose holdings often grew through foreclosure of debtors), and other merchants were also targets of riots—which closely resembled their seventeenth- and eighteenth-century European counterparts—and the riots thus further indicated the growth of nonagricultural populations and the declining homogeneity of the commoner class. The fifth form of action was the insurrection (*hoki*), or widespread and sometimes armed rebellion of large numbers of commoners in direct challenge to the government. The sixth was the inter- or intravillage dispute (*murakata sodo*), which could take any number of levels of intensity but is significant here because it is a barometer of conflict within the (ideally harmonious) peasantry.

Table 4 shows the basic comparison between cycle and noncycle years in respect of these five action types—which together account for roughly three-fourths of all contention during the era—and cycle years appear to be considerably more urban, more "popular," and more aggressive. The proportion of end runs falls by half during cycles, signifying a diminished role for local elites. Coercive appeals increase slightly, representing a similar popular autonomy and also a less deferential outlook. The relative frequency of riots more than doubles. Village disputes decline slightly, but the riot, end run, and coercive appeal data nevertheless indicate considerable social turbulence during the cycles. Overall the contentious repertoires of cycle years do appear to indicate distinctive conditions of social coherence, aggressiveness, and physical location.

As decisive events in the evolution of a national culture of contention, however, the cycles do not appear so dramatic. Table 5 shows data on the five components of the contentious repertoire, and the long-term, glacial trends in Tokugawa society and policy seem to count for as much as the transformative impact of cycles of contention. In some instances cycles have consistent effects on conflict: all four cycles represent drops in end runs and abscondings from the previous period, and increases in riots. On the other hand, coercive appeals increase twice and decrease twice as precycle periods give way to cycles, and both insurrections and intravillage disputes seem to be responding to glacial trends: high during both polar periods of regime transition for the former, and high during the mid-era years of relative depoliticization for the latter.[8] Even the data on end runs could be interpreted as an almost monotonic trend irrespective of cycles. Did the cycles drive this trend? From these data we cannot tell.

Looking at the different cycles, those of Kyoho and Keio/Meiji appear most influential. The former saw a drop in end runs and insurrection and a rise in coercive appeals and riots; the latter, a drop in end runs and increases in coercive appeals, riots, and insurrections. The Temmei cycle, like the Kyoho, saw a drop in end runs and an increase in riots; the Tempo period, for all its turbulence, does not seem to matter very much in the repertorial evolution of contention. Taken together the influence of the cycles is consistent with the argument that they contributed to a lasting change in the social coherence, homogeneity, and aggressiveness of contention, but a more nuanced analysis will be necessary before one can disentangle the effects of cyclical upheaval from those of glacial change.

SUMMARY AND CONCLUSIONS

The above analysis, while hardly authoritative, permits some observations regarding Tarrow's generalizations about cycles and repertoires of popular contention that began this essay.

First, regarding causes, it appears that in societies where the economy has not yet been industrialized, where society has not been fully politicized, and where politics has not been nationalized, apparent cycles of popular contention occur more in response to economic/conjunctural than political factors and reflect sudden changes in levels of popular grievances rather than in the political opportunity structure.[9] In a sense the causation of conflict cycles in preindustrial societies is more "external" to the world of conten-

Table 5 Cycles and precycles in the repertoire of contention

	End run, flight (%)	Coercive appeal (%)	Riot (%)	Insurrection (%)	Intravillage dispute (%)	Total (%)
1590–1714	30	7	0	3	38	78
Kyoho period	18	18	2	1	43	82
1736–74	15	16	8	2	39	80
Temmei period	7	15	18	1	38	79
1796–1824	9	11	8	1	56	85
Tempo period	7	10	11	1	52	81
1846–61	8	8	6	0	63	85
Keio/Meiji period	3	13	20	2	37	75
1873–77	0	21	9	5	22	57

tion, whereas Tarrow found that causation was largely "internal," involving competition between movement organizations and the interaction of contentious groups with a popular audience and with the mass media.

Second, the characteristics of the conflict cycles apparent in Tokugawa Japan differ in some ways from those in, for example, contemporary Italy. The cycles seen here do consist of increasing and then decreasing magnitudes of disruptive action and do seem to involve a wider spectrum of social elements (particularly lower strata) than does contention at other times. On the other hand, contention does not appear to diffuse geographically. Indeed, the situation seems quite the opposite: localized—not national or central—causes appear key, and there is probably much less of an epidemiological or imitative spread because the communications media that facilitate such a spread were absent.

Tarrow's emphasis on specialized movement organizations does not really apply here since such organizations are peculiar to modern society; however, cycles—in that they contain relatively less contention by established groups like cohesive, coherently led communities—do imply the emergence of some sort of different organizational basis for action, presumably of a more fluid and socially heterogeneous type. As organization seems to change, so does repertoire, becoming more populist, more violent, and more urban during cycles. At the same time, however, the distinctive contribution of cycles to these changes is difficult to assess: patterns of change in the salience of social conflict as opposed to political protest, and in the relative frequency of insurrection and intravillage disputes, suggest that cycles are simply "more of the same," distinctive points along glacial curves. Tarrow's assertion of increased tactical versatility may not apply either. The five (actually six) types of action specified above account for roughly the same proportion of total contention in both cycle and noncycle years (see Table 4), and although three of the four cycles see a drop in this proportion from the previous period (that is, there are more other types of contention occurring; see Table 5), the overall trend is one of decreasing and then increasing tactical variety across the entire era, regardless of cycles. Finally, we cannot comment on change in the interests driving contention or in popular notions of contention per se with these data.

We are similarly frustrated in assessing the residue of conflict cycles. Did the cycles expand the space within which the people contended, expand opportunities for contentious organizers and organizations, and/or expand the opportunities for groups to contend for influence? We cannot say. The rising curve of contention throughout the era suggests positive answers to all three questions, but exactly how the cycles fit into the picture is hard to determine. Except for the Kyoho period, which seems to have ushered in a new level of contentious behavior, the cycles seem to have risen from a background level of considerable conflict, to which level conflict receded after the cycles ended. It is highly unlikely—particularly in light of the frequency with which conflict leaders cited precedent—that the cultural bell of contention could be un-rung after each cycle, but the data at hand do not provide an answer.

The final residue of conflict cycles, according to Tarrow, is the possibility of political reform. In this instance, his model does seem to be borne out: three of the four Tokugawa-era cycles were followed immediately by periods of reform, two of which were explicitly focused on the causes of contention. As noted, the causes of the Keio reform were more complex, but popular conflict was certainly not irrelevant. By far the most important political residue was a major, if tacit, transformation of state policy (a transformation that Tarrow's relatively short-term perspective would miss): by the late eighteenth century it was clear that the government was unwilling to court widespread popular unrest by further raising the basic source of revenue, the rice tax. This failure of will, which became apparent after the Kyoho period, had two consequences: first, it resulted in stagnant government revenues, which eventuated in decaying state capabilities across the board; and second, it led to a search for new revenue sources. Some of these were politically "safe," such as forced loans from merchants and cuts in the stipends paid to the lords' samurai retainers. Others, however, like taxes on newly developing protoindustrial activities, were counterproductive in that they too generated popular grievances and raised society's potential for contention.

In conclusion I add three observations—one about repertoires, one about cycles, and one about history and social science. We have used three definitions of repertoire here; which one is the "best?" The answer, of course, depends on one's goal; mine has been to illuminate the nature of cycles of contention in particular and the evolution of contention in general. Defining repertoires in terms of violence makes cycles stand out the most, although it is questionable how much repertorial intensity adds to simple measures of magnitude of conflict. The sociopolitical composition of contention also brings out cycles clearly, but it also reflects broader processes of economic development and of state development in ways which I find more interesting. Our last definition, in terms of specific types of behavior, also reflects socioeconomic change; it could in principle bring out cycles of contention, but in the case of early modern Japan it does not. Thus as a general prescription I recommend the latter two definitions, with repertorial composition as a superior tool for understanding both short-term cycles and long-term trends in the early modern Japanese state and society.

As for cycles, again one might ask which of the four cycles seen here is "best." That is, which does the most of the things that Tarrow suggests we seek in the analysis of conflict cycles? I suggest that it is the least prepossessing of the four: the Kyoho cycle of the 1720s and 1730s. The Temmei and Keio/Meiji cycles are outstanding both qualitatively and quantitatively, but neither left much behind. The Tempo cycle is quantitatively spectacular, but it had few long-term consequences, and the Tempo reforms were ineffective. The Kyoho cycle, however, while quantitatively least imposing, seems to have initiated a major transformation in the culture of contention in Tokugawa Japan. It raised the annual magnitude of conflict decisively (albeit not irreversibly) above 40 (see Figure 1), and it raised the social component of contention above 40% once and for all (see Figure 6). It also witnessed (a) clear, and not soon to be reversed, drops in the salience of end run appeals and insurrections; (b) an equally sharp rise in coercive appeals; and (c) the emergence of the riot as part of the popular repertoire of contention (see Table 5). Popular contention in the second half of the eighteenth century and government's extractive posture were far different from what they were in 1700. Further investigation of the Kyoho period is very much in order.[10]

My final observation concerns history: looking at long periods (Tong 1991; Goldstone 1991; Tilly 1986), multiple cycles, and ages and cultures far different from our own is helpful in furthering our understanding of cycles and repertoires of popular contention. At several points I have noted that historical stages and levels of economic and state development constitute daunting obstacles to the generation of cross-temporally valid concepts and hypotheses.

Paradoxically, this underscores the need for a historical perspective in theory building in the social sciences.

NOTES

1 That is, the period of the Tokugawa shogunate, 1600–1868, plus 10 years at either end. The data set is drawn from Aoki K. 1981; this source and the characteristics of the data are discussed in White 1989. One might add here only that the Aoki data are, of course, based on written records, and documentation of all types of social, economic, and political phenomena improved as the Tokugawa era progressed. Nevertheless, as noted in White 1989, it is the consensus of Japanese historians that, except for village conflicts, these data are essentially complete and the increase over time is not simply an artifact of documentation. Moreover, occurrences of contention were supposed to be kept secret from the people, and insofar as possible, the feudal domains tried also to keep them from the shogunate. This did *not* mean that the domains themselves did not record such information; officials from the village on up were required to report in detail everything occurring in the course of their duties, and the result (added to the reports of those dispatched to investigate, suppress, or prosecute; the diaries of observers; the confessions of arrestees; etc.) is an "unexpectedly rich" record (Aoki M. 1981: 309–51) for historians, if not for the common people of the time.

2 One might argue that such an exploration is inappropriate—that one should not expect early modern apples and advanced industrial oranges to be theoretically analogous. My argument is that this is an open question, and it is for precisely this reason that an exercise such as this is a better test of the versatility and transitivity of the concepts than another application to another advanced industrial democracy.

3 See, inter alia, Aoki M. 1981; Kokusho 1971; Fukaya 1979; and Hayashi 1976. English sources include Bix 1986; Kelly 1985; Vlastos 1986; and Walthall 1986. The data in Figure 1 are from Iwahashi 1981 (rice prices); Arakawa 1964 (natural disasters); and Umemura 1961 (wages). Kyoto was a single city, but it was located in the Kinai, which was the heart of the national economy and thus reflective of national trends and conditions.

4 For a discussion of these types of contention, see White 1989 or 1992.

5 Table 2 excludes, as "cycle years," the Kyoho years 1715–35, since data for builders' wages are missing for this period.

6 Aggressive behavior includes, inter alia, theft, seizure (of land or property), or coercive "borrowing;" obstruction of or resistance to someone else's actions; forcible entry or occupation of buildings; and rioting. Destruction includes, inter alia, that of shops, offices, houses, or buildings; of records of debt or land titles; and/or of dikes, fields, crops, or irrigation facilities. Each event was coded 0 (no actions of any of these three types), 1 (one or two such actions), or 2 (three or more such actions).

7 My working hypothesis—as yet not thoroughly tested—is that political protest was far more likely to elicit immediate official repression and later punishment than was conflict among the commoners, and the people were

therefore far more circumspect, even when in a challenging mode, when dealing with the authorities.

8 The low proportion of total contention accounted for by these five behavioral types is related, I think, to era-long trends also: the proportion of total conflict accounted for by diffuse grumbling and unrest (*fuon*) and pacific, quite often legal appeals (*shuso*) was 19% in the seventeenth century, fell to 10–13% during the mid-eighteenth and early nineteenth centuries, and rose to 41% in 1873–77. At the same time that insurrection described a similar parabola—smooth and almost unaffected by cycles—these data suggest that for the most part the people tended to play it cool rather than get their brains beaten in during periods of intense regime interest in social control.

9 This does not mean that such contenders are responding uncritically to sudden deprivation rather than calculating their behavior in light of their interests and resources. My assumption is that conflict participation in all situations is the result of conscious balancing of three factors: what people want either to get or to get rid of (interests), what resources under their control they can bring to bear in pursuing these interests (resources), and what the odds are that the objective political, economic, and social status quo will give them a chance to achieve their interests (opportunities). In Tarrow's case the third factor seems key; in mine, the first. But the process is the same.

This in turn does not mean that Tokugawa commoners were rational utility maximizers in the orthodox sense. They were enmeshed in networks of institutions, roles, and values that powerfully mediated the effect of, for example, natural disaster and equally powerfully influenced the repertoires of action chosen. See White 1988a; Little 1989; and March and Olsen 1989.

10 Such an investigation, of course, must be far more than a presumptively unicausal analysis of contentious behavior. The eighteenth century also saw, for example, a sea change in the philosophical climate of Japan wherein the legitimacy of aristocratic rule began to be called into question and the need for the people to rely on themselves for the remedy of their problems began to be advocated (Hall 1991: chap. 12). But this change itself was in part a response to systemic failures of which popular contention was a barometer. Thus a comprehensive examination of the culture of contention must also consider not only prior contention but a multiplicity of institutional (White 1988b) and intellectual (Yasumaru 1975) factors and sequences beyond the scope of this exercise.

REFERENCES

Aoki K. (1981) Hyakusho Ikki Sogo Nempyo. Tokyo: Sanichi.
Aoki M. (1981) Ikki, vol. 5. Tokyo: Tokyo University Press.
Arakawa H. (1964) Saigai no Rekishi. Tokyo: Chibundo.
Bix, H. (1986) Peasant Protest in Japan, 1590–1884. New Haven, CT: Yale University Press.
Borton, H. (1938) "Peasant uprisings in Japan of the Tokugawa period." Transactions of the Asiatic Society of Japan 16: 1.

170   JAMES W. WHITE

Fukaya K. (1979) Hyakusho Ikki no Rekishiteki Kenkyu. Tokyo: Azekura.
Goldstone, J. (1991) Revolution and Rebellion in the Early Modern World. Berkeley: University of California Press.
Hall, J., ed. (1991) The Cambridge History of Japan, vol. 4. Cambridge: Cambridge University Press.
Hayashi M. (1976) Zoku Hyakusho Ikki no Kenkyu. Tokyo: Shinhyoron.
Inglehart, R. (1977) The Silent Revolution. Princeton, NJ: Princeton University Press.
———— (1990) Culture Shift. Princeton, NJ: Princeton University Press.
Iwahashi M. (1981) Kinsei Nihon Bukka Shi no Kenkyu. Tokyo: Ohara Shinseisha.
Jansen, M., ed. (1989) The Cambridge History of Japan, vol. 5. Cambridge: Cambridge University Press.
Kelly, W. (1985) Deference and Defiance in Nineteenth-Century Japan. Princeton, NJ: Princeton University Press.
Kokusho I. (1971) Hyakusho Ikki no Kenkyu, Zokuhen. Tokyo: Dohosha.
Little, D. (1989) Understanding Peasant China. New Haven, CT: Yale University Press.
March, J., and J. Olsen (1989) Rediscovering Institutions. New York: Free Press.
Sasaki J. (1973) Murakata Sodo to Yonaoshi, vol. 1. Tokyo: Aoki.
Sugimoto, Y. (1978) "Peasant rebellion and ruling class adaptation at the time of the Meiji restoration in Japan." Prepared for the World Congress of Sociology, Uppsala, August 1978.
Tarrow, S. (1981) "Cycles of protest and cycles of reform." Proposal to the National Science Foundation, March.
———— (1989) Democracy and Disorder. Oxford: Oxford University Press.
———— (1990) "Political opportunities, cycles of protest, and collective action: Theoretical perspectives." Prepared for the Conference on Social Movements, Cornell University, Ithaca, NY, October 1990.
Tilly, C. (1978) Collective Violence in European Perspective. Ann Arbor: Center for Research on Social Organization.
———— (1986) The Contentious French. Cambridge, MA: Harvard University Press.
Tilly, Charles, Tilly, Louise, and Tilly, Richard (1975) The Rebellious Century. Cambridge, MA: Harvard University Press.
Tong, J. (1991) Disorder under Heaven. Stanford, CA: Stanford University Press.
Totman, C. (1980) The Collapse of the Tokugawa Bakufu, 1862–1868. Honolulu: University of Hawaii Press.
Umemura M. (1961) "Kenchikugyo rodosha no jisshitsu chingin 1726–1958." Keizai Kenkyu 12: 172.
Vlastos, S. (1986) Peasant Protests and Uprisings in Tokugawa Japan. Berkeley: University of California Press.
Walthall, A. (1986) Social Protest and Popular Culture in Eighteenth-Century Japan. Tucson: University of Arizona Press.
White, J. (1988a) "The rational rioters: leaders, followers, and popular protest in early modern japan." Politics and Society 16: 35.
———— (1988b) "State growth and popular protest in tokugawa japan." Journal of Japanese Studies 14: 1.

——— (1989) "Economic development and sociopolitical unrest in nineteenth-century japan." Economic Development and Cultural Change 37: 231.

——— (1992) The Demography of Sociopolitical Conflict in Japan, 1721–1846. Berkeley, CA: Institute of East Asian Studies.

Yasumaru Y. (1975) Nihon no Kindaika to Minshu Shiso. Tokyo: Aoki.

Yokoyama T. (1977) Hyakusho Ikki to Gimin Densho. Tokyo: Kyoikusha.

"New Social Movements" of the Early Nineteenth Century

CRAIG CALHOUN

SOMETIME AFTER 1968, analysts and participants began to speak of "new social movements" that worked outside formal institutional channels and emphasized lifestyle, ethical, or "identity" concerns rather than narrowly economic goals. A variety of examples informed the conceptualization. Alberto Melucci (1988: 247), for instance, cited feminism, the ecology movement or "greens," the peace movement, and the youth movement. Others added the gay movement, the animal rights movement, and the antiabortion and prochoice movements. These movements were allegedly new in issues, tactics, and constituencies. Above all, they were new by contrast to the labor movement, which was the paradigmatic "old" social movement, and to Marxism and socialism, which asserted that class was the central issue in politics and that a single political economic transformation would solve the whole range of social ills. They were new even by comparison with conventional liberalism with its assumption of fixed individual

Craig Calhoun is Professor of Sociology and History at the University of North Carolina at Chapel Hill. Earlier versions of this paper were presented in 1991 to the Social Science History Association, the Department of Sociology at the University of Oslo, and the Program in Comparative Study of Social Transformations at the University of Michigan. The author is grateful for comments from members of each audience and also for research assistance from Cindy Hahamovitch.

identities and interests. The new social movements thus challenged the conventional division of politics into left and right and broadened the definition of politics to include issues that had been considered outside the domain of political action (Scott 1990).

These new social movements (NSMs) grew partly from the New Left and related student movements of the 1960s. The conceptualization of their novelty was part of the movements themselves as well as of the academic analyses that (primarily in Europe) took debate on these movements as an occasion to reform or reject Marxist theory and social democratic politics. The emphasis on novelty was extended to claims of epochal change when the NSMs were taken as signs of postindustrial or postmodern society. In this paper, however, I argue that the historical claim implicit in the idea of *new* social movements (as in the ideas of *post*modernism and *post*industrialism) is specious. I explore the major distinguishing characteristics attributed to NSMs in the recent literature and show that these fit very well the many movements that flourished in the late eighteenth and especially early nineteenth centuries. My point is not just negative, however; I do not suggest that we abandon the notion that NSMs are distinctive to the late twentieth century.

Abandoning the false historical claim enables us to understand better the whole modern history of social movements. This is so in three senses. First, as Tarrow (1989) has suggested, many of the characteristics described in the flourishing movements of the 1960s and after may stem from the newness of each movement rather than from novel features of the whole wave of movements. In other words, all movements in their nascent period—including the labor movement and social democracy—tend to fit certain aspects of the NSM model. Second, we are better prepared to analyze all social movements if we pay attention to the inherent plurality of their forms, contents, social bases, and meaning to participants and do not attempt to grasp them in terms of a single model defined by labor or revolutionary movements, or a single set of instrumental questions about mobilization. Within any historical period, at least in the modern era, we can identify a whole field of social movements shaped by their relationships to each other and appealing to different, though overlapping, potential participants. Of the various movements in such a field, we can fruitfully ask the kinds of questions pioneered by new social movement theory—

about identity politics, the possibility of thinking of movements as ends in themselves, and so forth—and not just those of resource mobilization or Marxism. Third, if we abandon both the developmentalism that treats early nineteenth-century movements as either precursors to the later consolidation of labor and socialism or else as historical sidetracks, and the opposite refusal to look for macrohistorical patterns, we can begin to explore what factors determine whether (in specific settings) periods are characterized by proliferation or consolidation or expansion or contraction in the social movement field as a whole.

Social movement fields include many different kinds of movements; this diversity and the interrelationships among different movements are obscured by overly narrow definitions of social movements. Tilly, for example, approaches movements in terms of an analysis of collective action with "five big components: interest, organization, mobilization, opportunity, and collective action itself" (1978: 7); this leaves out self-understanding and emphasizes instrumental pursuits. Similarly, Tarrow, Tilly, and others have built the idea of conflict and opposition to "established authorities" into their approaches to social movements— as part of "protest" in Tarrow's (1988) case and "contention" in Tilly's (1978, 1986).[1] This focuses their attention on movements with strong economic and political agendas and away from more "cultural" ones. Touraine's definition goes nearly to the opposite extreme: social movements are normatively oriented interactions between adversaries with conflicting interpretations and opposed models of a shared cultural field; in his view NSMs contended with other groups in civil society rather than with the state (1981: 31–32).[2] This is a helpful corrective, but we should not prejudge the question of orientation to the state. For one thing, this is a two-way street. States are institutionally organized in ways that provide recognition for some identities and arenas for some conflicts and freeze others out. States themselves thus shape the orientations of NSMs as well as the field of social movements more generally.

The key point is that it is misleading to compartmentalize religious movements, for example, apart from more stereotypically social or political ones. Religious movements may have political and economic agendas—particularly when politics is not seen as exclusively a matter of relations to the state. More basically, as E. P. Thompson (1968) showed clearly, religious and labor movements can influence each other, compete for adherents, and complement each other in the lives of some participants; in short, they can be part of the same social movement field.[3] Part of the problem is that much of the traditional analysis of social movements (and collective action more generally) has ignored or explicitly set aside questions of culture or the interpretation of meaning. This tends to deflect attention away from those movements concerned largely with values, norms, language, identities, and collective understandings—including those of movement participants themselves—and toward those that focus instrumentally on changing political or economic institutions. Social movement analysts have also often avoided addressing emotions, perhaps for fear of association with discredited accounts of mass psychology. For present purposes, it is better to see social movements as including all attempts to influence patterns of culture, social action, and relationships in ways that depend on the participation of large numbers of people in concerted and self-organized (as distinct from state-directed or institutionally mandated) collective action.

Both the wide range of recent social movements and the literature labeling them NSMs encourage such a broader view. Rather than dismissing NSM theory because of its historical misrepresentation, we should see the importance of the issues it raises for understanding social movements generally. "Identity politics" and similar concerns were never quite so much absent from the field of social movement activity—even in the heydays of liberal party politics or organized trade union struggle—as they were obscured from conventional academic observation. Particularly after 1848, just as socialism became more "scientific," so social scientists lost sight of the traditions of direct action, fluid and shifting collective identities, and communitarian and other attempts to overcome the means/ends division of more instrumental movement organization (Calhoun 1989). The secularism of academics particularly and post-Enlightenment intellectuals generally may have made collective action based on religious and other more spiritual orientations appear of a different order from the "real" social movement of trade-union-based socialism or from liberal democracy. Nationalism was often treated as a regressive deviation rather than a modern form of social movement and identity formation. Early feminism attracted relatively little scholarly attention until later feminism prompted its rediscovery.

In short, one kind of movement—formally organized, instrumental action aimed at economic or institutionally political goals—was relatively new and ascendant through much of the late nineteenth and the twentieth centuries and has often been misidentified as simply a progressive tendency, the rational future of politics, or even insurgent politics. This pattern was particularly pronounced in Europe during the ascendancy of labor and social democracy, and it is what made America look exceptional. But nowhere were movement politics ever limited to this form. While America had relatively weak trade unions and socialist politics, it nurtured a relatively strong and open proliferation of the other sort of social movement, new social movements. This has been true throughout American history, and it is very marked in the early nineteenth-century period on which this paper focuses. The flowering of movements in this period was, however, international (as I will illustrate with brief examples from France and Britain). Indeed, the social movement field of the early nineteenth century was inherently international, linking participants in different countries not only by communications but by a pattern of migration in which people literally moved from one country to another without leaving their movement contexts. Remember Marx's ties to German radicals in London and his writing for their newspaper in New York and recall the émigré intellectual ferment of Paris between 1830 and 1848 (Kramer 1988). Migration to America—to join a socialist commune or to establish a religious community, for example—was a prominent feature of the era and often tied to movement participation. We have only to recall the travels of Tom Paine, however, to remind ourselves that the Atlantic crossing could be reversed.

THE IDEA OF NEW SOCIAL MOVEMENTS

The idea of new social movements has been brought into academic currency by several authors with various conceptual frameworks.[4] In all cases, the concept is defined through a crucial counterexample: the nineteenth- and early twentieth-century working-class or labor movement. This is understood primarily in the singular (while new social movements are plural). The backdrop to the idea of NSMs, thus, is the notion that labor struggles had an implicit telos and were potentially transformative for the whole society.

This was conceptualized sometimes in largely economic terms as the transcendence of capitalism and other times in more political terms as the social democratic transformation of modern states. In either case, a single movement protagonist was generally assumed to have posed *the* social question. At one time, thus, it was common to speak of *the* social movement that would bring about *the* course of social change. NSM theorists hold that this is no longer plausible, if it ever was. In varying degrees they emphasize post-industrial society (Touraine 1971), the options opened by relative affluence and a growing middle class (Offe 1985), the turn to individually defined needs after the common denominator of material sustenance had been satisfied (Melucci 1989; Inglehart 1990), and expansion of the welfare state (Offe 1985). Their positive examples come from the wide range of movements that began to engage people in the 1960s and 1970s after the apparent conservative quiescence of the 1950s. For Touraine (1988), a key question is whether these new movements could ever coalesce in order to embody some of the decisive potential for social transformation once attributed to the labor movement and socialism. Habermas (1984) suggests not, theorizing NSMs in terms of a broader post-Marxist account of why movements can no longer hold the potential for fundamental social transformation in a society where the lifeworld is colonized by economic and administrative systems and large-scale state and capitalist structures are inescapable. He sees the movements as part of the resistance of lifeworld to system. Similarly, Cohen and Arato (1992) and Touraine (1985) treat NSMs as part of the struggle for civil society to maintain autonomy from state and economy and as a source of reform and the introduction of new concerns into political agendas. For Melucci (1981, 1989), NSMs must be seen simply as ends in themselves.

Melucci (1989) also employs the common postmodernist trope of arguing against the "metanarrative" of socialist liberation (Lyotard 1984). With others, he sees the labor movement's claim to be the main or exclusive source of progressive change or representative for those disadvantaged by the established order as intrinsically repressive, not just historically obsolete. In order to mount their challenge to that "old" social movement, however, these NSM theorists have exaggerated the extent to which it ever was a unified historical actor with a single narrative and a disciplining institutional structure. They have reified and hypostatized the labor movement, setting up the most simplistic Marxist accounts as their straw men. In fact, the nineteenth- and early twentieth-century working-class movement (if it even can be described more than tendentiously as a single movement) was multidimensional, only provisionally and partially unified, and not univocal (Katznelson and Zolberg 1987). It did not constitute just one collective actor in a single social drama. There was mobilization over wages, to be sure, but also over women and children working, community life, the status of immigrants, education, access to public services, and so forth. Movement activity constantly overflowed the bounds of the label *labor*. Similarly, the categories of class and class struggle have been used far from the Marxian ideal type of wage laborers in industrial capitalist factories. Artisans and agricultural workers, white collar and service employees, and even small proprietors (not to mention spouses and children of all these) have joined in the struggles or been grouped in the category of the working class. Throughout the history of labor and class movements, there has been contention over who should be included in them and how both common and different identities should be established. Indeed, ironically, by leading to research on the protests of women, people of color, and other marginalized people, the recent growth of NSMs has helped to explode the myth that the narrowly white, male labor movement, against which NSMs were defined, was completely predominant.

Other NSM theorists not only exaggerate labor's one-time hegemony over the social movement field; they tie it to a metanarrative of their own. Inglehart thus treats a move from "materialist" or economistic orientations to "postmaterialism" as a simple linear development based on achievement of higher material standards of living and greater economic security. He explicitly claims that "in the takeoff phase of industrial revolution, economic growth was the central problem. Postmaterialists have become increasingly numerous in recent decades and they place less emphasis on economic growth and more emphasis on the noneconomic quality of life" (1990: 373). Inglehart offers no evidence, however, for the assumption that economic orientations predominated during the early years of industrialization or that nonmaterialism appears only late in the story. The following pages show that the beginning years of industrialization were particularly fertile for the proliferation of nonmaterialist movements; if these were ever really in abeyance for long, it was in the more industrialized later nineteenth and early to mid-twentieth centuries.

DEFINING CHARACTERISTICS OF
NEW SOCIAL MOVEMENTS

Throughout the early nineteenth century, communitarianism, temperance, and various dietary and lifestyle movements attracted hundreds of thousands of adherents in both Europe and America. Religious awakening, revitalization, and proliferation were major themes, as were anticlericalism and freethinking. Antislavery or abolitionist movements were often closely linked to religion but were autonomous from any particular religious organizations. Popular education was the object of struggle, with early success in America. Even after mid-century, the divergence between Europe and America should not be exaggerated. The nationalist discourse of the (northern) Union before and after the Civil War—including even "manifest destiny"—was not altogether different from the nationalist discourse of Giuseppe Mazzini and Young Europe or of Giuseppe Garibaldi. Nativism was recurrent throughout the nineteenth century, from the Know-Nothings through populism, and the racial, ethnic, and religious hostilities taken to an extreme by the Ku Klux Klan were not altogether different from the xenophobic side of nationalism. Ethnic and nationalist movements, moreover, were never as fully suppressed by class as Melucci (1989: 89–92) suggests but have ebbed and flowed throughout modernity. Women's and temperance movements renewed mobilizations dating from the eighteenth century.

The early nineteenth century was fertile ground for social movements as perhaps no other period was until the 1960s.[5] Indeed, direct ancestors of several of the movements that sparked the new social movement conceptualization in the 1960s and 1970s were part of the early nineteenth-century efflorescence. In the early nineteenth century too, the labor movement itself was a new social movement and not clearly first among equals, let alone hegemonic; the idea that a class-based movement might claim to be all encompassing was not widespread. If we ignore the claim that they apply distinctively to the late twentieth century, the core ideas of NSM theory offer a useful lens for looking at early nineteenth-century social movements. Specifically, I turn now to a list of the most widely cited distinguishing features of late twentieth-century NSMs.[6] Relying for the most part on brief examples, I show that each was a prominent concern or feature of early nineteenth-century social movements.

Identity, Autonomy and Self-realization

Compared with the largely instrumental and economistic goals of both the institutionalized labor movement and the European social democratic parties, NSMs have been crucially focused on "identity politics" (Aronowitz 1992). Many of these movements themselves, however, have roots in the late eighteenth and early nineteenth centuries: modern feminist ideology is often traced to Mary Wollstonecraft, and the broader women's movement to the substantial concern with sexual equality and redefinition of gender in Owenite socialism (Taylor 1983) and to the disproportionate participation of women in abolitionist, temperance, and other "moral crusades" of the early nineteenth century.

The tracing of roots, however, is not necessarily the identification of a linear, unidirectional process of development. Claiming an autonomous identity and a moral voice for women often took a different form in the early nineteenth century than in succeeding years. Indeed, Rendall has argued that the very assumptions of twentieth-century feminists about equality make it hard "to understand that the assertion of an 'equality in difference' could mean a radical step forward. . . . Stress on the latent moral superiority of women could bring with it the basis for a new confidence, a new energy, a new assertion of women's potential power" (1985a: 3). This is more easily recognized in the frame of reference established by the NSMs (and much recent poststructuralist and feminist theory) than in that of the classical liberalism or universalism informing the assumptions to which Rendall refers. The words of the Owenite Catherine Barmby, "Woman and man are two in variety and one in equality" (quoted in Rendall 1985b: 308), no longer sound so unfamiliar. Early nineteenth-century women argued from a claim to morally—and publicly—relevant difference not again so clearly formulated until the final quarter of the twentieth century. "As it is the Divine Will that the two sexes *together* shall constitute humanity, so I believe it to be the Divine intention that the influence and exertion of the two sexes *combined* shall be necessary to the complete success of any human institution, or any branch of such institution" (Agnes Davis Pochin 1855, quoted in Rendall 1985: 312). Not only was there a claim that the different qualities of men and women were complementary (as the broader culture also asserted, though with more bias); there was a claim to moral authority grounded within the domestic sphere, which was in the early nineteenth century becoming increasingly separated from the public sphere. "Within that primarily domestic world, women could and did create a culture which was not entirely an imposed one, which contained within it the possibilities of assertion. . . . That assertion could become the assertion of autonomy" (Rendall 1985a: 3). The very claim to distinct and possibly autonomous identity in the domestic sphere ironically became the basis for public claims. As Mary Ryan (1990, 1992) has shown, from 1830 to 1860 there was a rapid increase in the public life of the American citizenry. This was not just a matter of one public growing more active, but of a proliferation of multiple publics. Some of these were autonomously female and constituted themselves in terms of distinct claims to identity not altogether unrelated to those by which the male-dominated public spheres sought to exclude women.

Not only was moral authority claimed for distinctive female identities; gender relations were directly a focus of concern. By no means all of the social movements of the early nineteenth century oriented their action to the public sphere, and still less to organized politics. Withdrawal from mainstream society in order to reconstitute human relations was a central theme of the communitarian movements of the era and of the often millenarian religious movements with which they sometimes overlapped (see below). Robert Owen's communitarian vision may have turned on a Lockean vision of essential human sameness and malleability, but this was certainly not so for Charles Fourier's notion of phalansteries composed of 1,620 individuals in order to represent all possible combinations of the essential and distinctive passions of each sex. Gender relations were also an important concern of the New England transcendentalists, innovatively treated as a social movement by Anne Rose. "Alienated by a culture built of fear," she writes, "the Transcendentalists took steps to establish social relations allowing freedom, growth, justice, and love" (1981: 93). Communitarian experiments like Brook Farm were designed simultaneously to foster individual self-fulfillment and equitable, nurturant social relationships.

In a very different vein, what was the focus of early nineteenth-century nationalism if not identity? "Nations are individualities with particular talents," wrote Fichte (quoted by Meinecke 1970: 89). At least through the "springtime of nations" that collided with the mid-century crisis, nationalism was conceived substantially as a liberal and inclusive doctrine, not as the reactionary, exclusionary one it would in many cases become. This "nationalist internationalism" (Walicki 1982) of figures like Mazzini maintained that all true nationalities had rights to autonomous self-expression and indeed cast itself as the defender of liberty against empire (a theme that has never entirely disappeared). Not unlike more recent movements that focused on the legitimation of identities, nationalism grew in part because of the rise of the modern state and the ideology of rights that became a crucial part of its legitimation apparatus and a continual opening for new claims. Nationality, despite nationalism's own ideology, was never simply a given identity, inherited unproblematically from the past, but always a construction and a claim within a field of identities. Not only did nationalist movements claim autonomy for specific peoples against others (for example, for Hungarians against the Austrian-dominated empire, or briefly for Texans against both Mexico and the United States) they also claimed a primacy for national identity over class, region, dialect, gender, and other subsidiary identities.

Last but not least in this connection, we need to recognize how profoundly early workers' movements were engaged in a politics of identity. Marx and numerous activists offered the claim that the common identity of *worker* should take primacy over a diversity of craft, region, ethnic, and other identities. Yet this strong version of the claim to working-class identity was seldom if ever realized, and certainly not in the early nineteenth century. What were achieved were more mediated versions of working-class solidarity in which primary identification with a craft or local group became the means of forging a discourse or movement based on national (or international) class identities. This mediated understanding of class membership is quite different from the categorical Marxist notion of individuals equivalently constituted as members of the working class. Yet it is the fluidity of possible workers' identities that stands out in the historiography of the early nineteenth century.[7]

Defense Rather Than Offense

The "old social movement" was utopian and sought to remake the whole of society through overcoming existing relations of domination and exploitation, theorists claim. NSMs, in contrast, defend specific spheres of life; their demands are more limited in scope but are also less negotiable. Here NSM theory points valuably to the importance of the defense of specific lifeworlds and its link to nonnegotiable demands, but through a sharply misleading historical opposition.

The underlying idea is that socialism was a comprehensive utopian project. This is what some of Marxism's poststructuralist detractors decry in attacking the domination implicit in any claim to order the whole of society (or critical thought). It is also implicit in Habermas's (1984, 1988) account of how conflicts moved outside the range of distributive issues that welfare states were developed to manage. In this view, the state embodied the utopian drive of labor and social democratic movements but faced crises as the systems of money and power grew to dominate so much of social life that cultural reproduction could no longer provide people with the motivation for either ordinary participation or transformative rebellion.[8] New social movements arose out of this "exhaustion of utopian energies" and embodied a too-often neoconservative focus on defense of endangered ways of life (Habermas 1990: chap. 2). But this seems exactly backward. The labor movement has been as defensive in much of its struggle as any NSM and has hardly always been committed to a thorough restructuring of society. For most of its history the traditional left was normally suspicious of utopian energies, though these occasionally erupted anyway. The "traditional left," indeed, was formed in the consolidation and institutionalization of a "post-utopian" movement in the late nineteenth century; this replaced the earlier efflorescence of more utopian movements and earned the appellation *traditional* by resisting the challenge of new movements not just in the 1960s but in the early twentieth century and recurrently. Indeed, much of the new left (like the NSMs more generally) can be understood as an attempt to recover the utopian energies of the early nineteenth century.[9] Rooted in the attachments of everyday life and specific communities, these movements were often radical and even utopian in what they sought.

What else, for example, could the perfectionism of the Second Great Awakening mean, if not that people must impose extreme and nonnegotiable demands on themselves and their societies? This might have been the "shopkeepers' millenium" (Johnson 1978), not Marx's, but it was certainly utopian. At the same time, it was fueled in part by local community resistance to the impact of centralizing politics and economics. Thus Habermas's idea that NSMs form largely to defend lifeworld spaces against the "colonization" of large-scale political and economic systems grasps important aspects of crucial nineteenth-century social movements, but this cannot be opposed to utopianism. A similar perfectionism made the utopian socialists utopian, in Marx's and Engels's contemptuous view. Think, for example, of Engels's complaint that St. Simon, Fourier, and Owen claimed to emancipate "all humanity at once," rather than "a particular class to begin with" (1978 [1892]: 701). Indeed, it is crucial to the very radicalism of some early nineteenth-century social movements (as of many others) that they mounted an unyielding and nonnegotiable defense of traditional ways of life that were threatened by social change (including especially capitalist change). Artisans defending traditional crafts and communities against capitalist industrialization could not settle for better wages, working conditions, or health care. It was this defense of their lifeworlds, however, that made their demands radically incompatible with the expansion of capitalism and that set them apart from most industrial workers who, however violent their anger at any point in time, could potentially be pacified by meliorative measures (Calhoun 1982, 1983a, 1983b).

A different kind of defensive orientation was involved in the withdrawal of various religious groups from intercourse with a corrupting worldly society. This was, indeed, one of the goals of many of the German religious migrants to the United States, from the Amish to the Bruderhoff (Hostetler 1980; Kanter 1972; Zablocki 1970). As Marty (1984: 191) writes of the religious colonists, "most believed in natural human innocence and thought that new social arrangements would end corruption." A defensive orientation was more common among the earlier pietists than it was among the new wave of communities of the 1840s. The transcendentalists at Brook Farm certainly aspired to reach a broader public with their example and their written message, and their program was explicitly forward looking. Similarly, the members of the Hopedale community in Milford, Massachusetts, were regular participants in a variety of extracommunal social movements, conceiving of their community as a base for such broader reforming activities (Walters 1978: 49–51).

Just as the common saying suggests that "the best defense is a good offense," so it is hard to distinguish defensive from offensive moments in the nineteenth-century communal movement. Indeed, these often appear as two sides of the same utopian ideology. Utopian visions were often rooted in (or derived part of their appeal from) religious traditions and/or images of the recently vanished golden age of craftsmen and small farmers. At the same time, they stood in tension or confrontation with many of the tendencies and characteristics of contemporary society. The line was not sharply drawn between withdrawing from this world to prepare for the next or to protect a purer life, and withdrawing in order to constitute an example that might transform social relations more generally. It is important to see the ways in which early nineteenth-century social movements were rooted in problems and attachments of everyday life and the defense of valued ways of life; it is crucial not to imagine that this made them intrinsically conservative or deprived them of utopian energies. Roots made many movements radical, even when they did not offer comprehensive plans for societal restructuring.

Politicization of Everyday Life

Central to the importance of identity politics and defensive orientations is the argument that NSMs are distinctive in politicizing everyday life rather than focusing on the large-scale systems of state and economy. Where the postwar consensus consecrated overall economic growth, distributive gains, and various forms of legal protections as the basic social issues that the political process was to address (Offe 1985: 824), the NSMs brought forward a variety of other issues grounded in aspects of personal or everyday life: sexuality, abuse of women, student rights, protection of the environment.

These were not just new issues of familiar kinds, but a challenge to the extant division between public and private spheres, state and civil society. The collapsing of divisions between state and economy paved the way (Galbraith 1967; Habermas 1962, 1967). Giant corporations assumed statelike functions in the putatively private economic sphere, while the welfare state was called to defend a growing variety of civil rights and to intervene regularly in the economy. Several explanations for why this gave rise to NSMs contend that a hierarchy of needs notion suggests that affluence made it feasible to stop worrying about the old economic issues and take up these new concerns (Melucci 1989; Inglehart 1990). A political opportunity argument says that the transformed state created new opportunities for the pursuit of grievances (Tarrow 1989). Habermas's (1988) notion of the colonization of the lifeworld proposes that the erosion of the boundaries between lifeworld and economic and political system was itself experienced as threatening.

Compared with the postwar consensus, a politicization of everyday life certainly began in the 1960s, but this was not a reversal of long-standing consensus about the proper boundaries of the political. On the contrary, the modern era is shaped by a certain oscillation between politicization and depoliticization of everyday life. In the late nineteenth and early twentieth centuries, as well as in the early nineteenth century, social movements brought a range of new phenomena into the public (if not always the political) realm. Indeed, the early labor movements themselves aimed crucially to politicize aspects of everyday life formerly (and by their opponents) not considered properly political. Temperance, abolitionism, campaigns for popular education, and perhaps above all early women's movements sought public recognition or action with regard to grievances their detractors considered clearly outside the realm of legitimate state action (Evans and Boyte 1986: chap. 3). They were moral crusades in almost exactly the same way as the NSMs are in Klaus Eder's (1985) description. For parts of the women's movement this was sometimes a source of contradiction: women had to protest in public and thereby politicize the issue of protecting the female sphere of the private household (Rendall 1985a; see also Ryan 1992). The contradictions have reappeared in the current period, as, for example, when Phyllis Schlafley simultaneously maintained that a woman's proper (and ideally protected) place is in the home but suggested that she herself ought to be appointed to the Supreme Court. In the case of women's movements, the struggle to politicize aspects of everyday life—and the contradictions around it—continued right through the nineteenth and early twentieth centuries. It recurred also in the temperance/prohibition and civil rights movements. The latter, indeed, is almost a quintessential case, with the proprietors of segregated restaurants, for example, arguing that their decisions about whom to serve were purely private matters, beyond the legitimate reach of the state.

Though there was often great political turmoil—over socialism, for example, and over female suffrage—a fairly consistent set of issues was the center of contention during the second half of the nineteenth and the first half of the twentieth centuries. The main legitimate questions of domestic politics focused on electoral democracy (the full extension of the franchise, the efficacy of political parties, and the prevention of corruption among elected officials) and political economy (the proper role of the state in providing for those individuals capitalism harmed or failed to help, in mediating struggles between workers and employers, or in regulating the flow of workers into labor markets).[10] Populism was a step outside the political norms in some respects (for example, in largely defensive use of direct action, as in attempts by farmers to eliminate middlemen by some combination of new cooperative institutions and intimidation; see Goodwyn 1976) but it stuck for the most part to manifestly political and economic issues. When other issues were raised, they commonly had a very hard time attracting serious attention in the public sphere; the voices of authority consistently outweighed those of dissent. The one great victory of women in this period, thus, was on the issue of suffrage, not on any of the other gender concerns that women voiced.[11]

Non-Class or Middle-Class Mobilization

A central link between NSM theory and the notion of a postindustrial or postmodern society is the idea that political economic identities have lost their salience and are being replaced by a mixture of ascriptive identities (like race or gender) and personally chosen or expressive identities (like sexual orientation or identification with various lifestyle communities). NSMs, accordingly, neither appeal to nor mobilize predominantly on class lines.

Offe (1985) suggests that members of the new middle class and "decommodified" persons—that is, those with no stable labor market position or identity—are disproportionately involved in NSMs. Though Offe approaches these groups in economic terms, they are in fact hard to assimilate into schemes of class analysis. The decommodified are obviously outside class categories to the extent that these depend on stable positions in the relations of production. The new middle class is usually defined in terms of high levels of education and technical skill combined with employee status rather than ownership of capital. This too is anomalous.[12] More generally, middle-class affluence may facilitate movement activity, but class membership is not the identity that determines choice of NSM. If Offe is right about the new middle class and the decommodified, however, this is a reason to anticipate growth in NSMs: these are both growing segments of the population. Offe even remarks that this makes NSMs similar to the early labor movement, when the numbers of industrial workers were still growing.[13]

Offe is perceptive to note the similarity to the early labor movement, with its internal diversity and only gradually stabilizing conception of a common labor-market position and class identity. Of course, the labor movement remained internally diverse—rent, for example, by divisions between skilled craftsmen and laborers—and nowhere more so than in America (with, for example, the epic struggles between the American Federation of Labor and the Congress of Industrial Organizations coming close for a time to resembling a civil war within the putatively unitary movement). Where class was offered as a part of political ideology, it did not appeal solely to workers. Socialist parties, unlike trade unions, have mobilized throughout their history across class lines.

If class bases were ever central determinants of mobilization patterns, it was in late nineteenth- and early twentieth-century Europe. Before that, class was seldom the self-applied label or the basis even of workers' mobilization. Was Chartism strictly a class movement? Though its ideology increasingly focused on class, its demands included issues with appeal to most of the range of people excluded from suffrage and effective citizenship rights in early nineteenth-century Britain (D. Thompson 1986; Jones 1984). Indeed, its admixture of members of the industrial working class with artisans, outworkers, and others presaged the fault lines of its eventual demise. Similarly, it has been shown fairly conclusively that class-based analyses fail to explain who manned and who attacked barricades in Paris in 1848 (Traugott 1985). Even more basically, it has been argued that republicanism was the central ideological focus of the early nineteenth-century struggles in France and that class bases mattered mainly as the underpinnings of different visions of the republic (Aminzade forthcoming). The point is not that class was irrelevant but that the early nineteenth-century struggles most often taken as paradigmatic of class-based political movements—Chartism, the revolution of 1848—were political movements internally differentiated by the appeal of their ideology to different groups of workers, shopkeepers, and others.

In America, too, republicanism was a central rhetoric of political and even economic struggle. In his study of Cincinnati workers, Ross (1985) sees an effort to forge and preserve a "republican world" only giving way to an alternative, more economically and class based form of struggles in the 1840s. This was only partly because Cincinnati was more egalitarian and socially integrated than East Coast cities. Wilentz's study of New York also shows the centrality of republican visions into the 1820s. Even after the crucial shifts of 1828–29, the Working Men's movement involved an attempt to push Jacksonian democracy further than the well-connected attorney's and party functionaries of Tammany Hall. The new radicals were shaped by old Adamsite political visions and by new social movements like Owenite socialism and a mixture of feminism, deism, and Jacobinism brought forward by Frances Wright (Wilentz 1984: chap. 5). These radicals were journeyman artisans and small master mechanics but also disaffected elites; their appeals were as apt to be agrarian as focused on the transformation of urban classes. In the words of Thomas Skidmore, the program was to end social oppression and political force "till there shall be no lenders, no borrowers; no landlords, no tenants; no masters, no journeymen; no Wealth, no Want" (quoted in ibid.: 187). This was a vision that would appeal less, no doubt, to elites than to those they oppressed or exploited, but it was not a vision narrowly focused on any specific class (see Evans and Boyte 1986: chap. 4).

The communitarian visions that predominated in the movements of the era generally minimized class divisions. They offered a new kind of social relations—egalitarian and cooperative—to replace the old; they expected the beneficiaries of the old system to resist most, but they argued that the benefit of the new order would flow to everyone. Class variation figured as a source of variable discontent and interest; class-specific patterns of association (working together, living in the same neighborhoods, intermarrying) led to mobilization partly on class lines, but this did not make these class movements. This was, after all, precisely the complaint of Marx and Engels about Owenism; they could praise its communitarianism (particularly where family was concerned) but had to attack its neglect—or denial—of class struggle (see, for example, 1976 [1848]: pt. 3).

If we turn our attention from the self-understanding of movements—or the nature of their ideological appeal—to the class character of their adherents, we find nineteenth-century NSMs in which members of the middle class predominate and others in which workers predominate. Sometimes these are different versions of related movement formations—as, for example, in the different class characteristics of American Protestant denominations and religious mobilizations. The shopkeepers' millennium of the Second Great Awakening may have been predominantly a middle-class affair and extended to workers with an agenda of "taming" them suitably for industrial occupations (as Johnson 1978 suggests), though it is not clear that this is the whole story. The Great Awakening was also in significant part a rural phenomenon, giving birth to circuit-riding ministers and radically populist sects like the Campbellites (later the Disciples of Christ). Transcendentalism was almost entirely middle class (though Brook Farm did admit a large number of working people in 1844), but it was diametrically opposed to the evangelical awakening not only in its theology but in its social vision; it was in many ways an oppositional movement despite the elite status of many of its protagonists (Rose 1981). Abolitionism has long been interpreted as an elite and/or middle-class movement, but recent studies have begun to alter that image, holding that it did indeed mobilize significant pockets of working-class support (Drescher 1987; Fladeland 1984). Class is a significant variable for use in our analyses, but these were not class movements as such.

Self-exemplification

One of the most striking features of the paradigmatic NSMs has been their insistence that the organizational forms and styles of

movement practice must exemplify the values the movement seeks
to promulgate. This means, at the same time, that the movements
are ends in themselves. Relatedly, many NSMs are committed
to direct democracy and a nonhierarchical structure, substantially
lacking in role differentiation, and resistant to involvement of
professional movement staff.

Many versions of the modern women's movement thus eschew
complete identification with instrumental goals—changing legislation, achieving equal job opportunity, and other concerns. They
focus also on constructing the movement itself as a nurturant,
protected space for women. The emphasis on self-exemplification
and noninstrumentality is indeed a contrast to much of the history
of the organized labor movement. Many socialist and especially
communist parties have institutionalized internal hierarchies and
decision-making structures deeply at odds with their professed
pursuit of nonhierarchical, nonoppressive social arrangements.
But what could be a better example of making a "work-object"
(in Melucci's 1989 phrase) of a social movement's own organizational forms than the communal movement(s) of the 1840s?
Charles Lane, influenced by Fourier, was a veteran of several communal experiments from the anarchist Fruitlands to the Shakers;
he praised celibacy and like values in 1843:

> The human beings in whom the Eternal Spirit has ascended
> from low animal delights or mere human affections, to a state
> of spiritual chastity and intuition, are in themselves a divine
> atmosphere, they *are* superior circumstances, and are con-
> stant in endeavoring to create, as well as to modify, all other
> conditions, so that these also shall more and more conduce
> to the like consciousness in others. Hence our perseverance
> in efforts to attain simplicity in diet, plain garments, pure
> bathing, unsullied dwellings, open conduct, gentle behavior,
> kindly sympathies, serene minds. These and several other
> particulars needful to the true end of man's residence on
> earth, may be designated Family Life. . . . The Family, in
> its highest, divinest sense, is therefore our true position, our
> sacred earthly destiny. [quoted by Rose 1981: 201]

End and means are very much the same.

Communal groups were not an isolated aspect of early
nineteenth-century society; they were closely linked to prominent

religious currents, leading philosophies, and the working-class movement. They were, nonetheless, distinctive in the extremes to which they took antihierarchical ideology. Most other movements of the period admitted of clearer leadership structures. Still, direct democracy was a regulative norm for many, including several branches of the workers' movement, radical republicans, and socialists. Marx himself joined in the advocacy of immediate rights of recall over legislators who voted against the wishes of their constituents—a key issue in the relations of the 1848 Paris political clubs to the assembly (Amann 1975)—and proposed limited terms and other measures designed to minimize the development of a leadership too autonomous from the masses.

Unconventional Means

New social movements depart from conventional parliamentary and electoral politics, taking recourse to direct action and novel tactics. As Tarrow (1989) has remarked, however, this description confuses two senses of *new*: the characteristics of all movements when they are new, and the characteristics of a putatively new sort of movement.

It is indeed generally true that any movement of or on behalf of those excluded from conventional politics starts out with a need to attract attention; movement activity is not just an instrumental attempt to achieve movement goals, but a means of recruitment and continuing mobilization of participants. Each new movement may also experiment with new ways to outwit authorities either in getting its message across or in causing enough disruption to extract concessions or gain power. In this way, each movement may add to a repertoire of collective action (in Tilly's 1978 phrase) that is available to subsequent movements.

In another sense, *unconventional* is defined not by novelty per se but by movement outside the normal routines of politics. All forms of direct action thus are unconventional, even when—like barricade fighting in Paris—they have 200 years of tradition behind them. What defines unconventional action in the political realm is mainly the attempt to circumvent the routines of elections and lobbying, whether by marching on Washington, occupying an office, or bombing the prime minister's residence. Unconventional means in this sense are particularly likely in a movement of people who have few resources other than their public actions. One of the key developments of late nineteenth- and early twentieth-century democratic politics in Europe and societies of European settlement was the institutionalization of strong norms of conventional politics, organized primarily through political parties. This drew more than one branch of the socialist movement into the orbit of conventional politics.

Direct action was, by contrast, central to the social movements of the early to mid-nineteenth century. Revolution still seemed to be a possibility in most European countries, which gave an added punch to all forms of public protest and threatened real civil disturbance. In the French revolution of 1848, the predominant radical factions espoused a red republicanism that traced its ancestry to the 1789 revolution and called on the direct action of the people as its main means. Pierre-Joseph Proudhon was the theorist of this politics, and its defeat in 1848 helped to discredit it in academic circles. Though partially sidelined, it hardly ceased to move activists, however, as the subsequent histories of syndicalism and anarchism reveal. With Georges-Eugène Sorel as a bridging theorist, this tradition of direct action also influenced fascism (Calhoun 1988).[14] Without comparably revolutionary aims, a variety of early (and later) labor activists chose direct action both to dramatize and immediately to achieve their ends. The Luddites of early nineteenth-century England are only the most famous. Of course, restrictions on the franchise denied most of them access to the parliamentary system.

If Luddites made a virtue of necessity by direct action, Owenite socialism—and utopian socialists and communitarians generally—rejected conventional politics on principle. E. P. Thompson complains that "Owen simply had a vacant place in his mind where most men have political responses" (1968: 786). This may be, and it is also true that Robert Owen identified with elites and was not shy about approaching those in political power and trying to persuade them of the merits of his social system. Nonetheless, many of his followers had deep convictions against organizing for the pursuit of political power or the disruption of the political system. They attempted to teach by example and exposition and tried to create their own self-organizing sphere of life (Harrison 1969). The recurrent half-aesthetic, half-political romantic movements from Blake and Shelley to Ruskin, Morris, and the arts and crafts movement similarly disdained conventional politics and were determined to carry on their work outside that tawdry sphere. Henry David Thoreau's advocacy of civil disobedience typified the emphasis on purity of conscience. His celebrated essay on the subject stemmed from his individual opposition to the draft, but the theme of direct action by the morally responsible individual tied together Thoreau's retreat to Walden and early effort to teach by striking example and his later more manifestly political and even violent common cause with John Brown (McWilliams 1973: 290–300).

Purity and freedom from corruption were not the only reasons for direct action. At least as important was the sense that organized politics and public discourse were resistant or too slow to respond. Sheer practical expedient led abolitionists to provide material assistance to runaway slaves, for example. While most early protemperance ministers stuck to lectures and essay contests, a direct action wing eventually took to saloon smashing (Rorabaugh 1979). In both cases, tensions between advocates of direct action (who also generally demanded a more complete abolition or abstinence) and adherents of more conventional politics helped to split the movements. In both cases also, the disproportionate and publicly prominent participation of women was in itself an unconventional means of action (as was even more true of women's suffrage campaigns).

Partial and Overlapping Commitments

The claim of old social movements—the labor and socialist movements—was to be able, at least potentially, to handle all the public needs of their constituents. It was not necessary to belong to a variety of special issue groups, for example, if one belonged to a trade union and, either through it or directly, to the labor party. One might struggle within a social democratic party, or within a union, to see that one's specific interests were well attended to, but one made a primary commitment to that organization or at least that movement. The NSMs, by contrast, do not make the same claims on their members or offer the same potential to resolve a range of issues at once.[15] They are not political parties or other organizations that accept the charge of prioritizing the range of issues that compete for public attention. They are affinity groups knit together not by superordinate logic but by a web of overlapping memberships, rather like the crosscutting social circles Georg Simmel (1903) thought essential to modern identity and social organization. One may thus combine feminism with pacifism and not be much moved by environmental concerns, and no organization will divert one's feminist and pacifist dollars or envelope licking to environmentalist uses. This is described sometimes as a consumerist orientation to political involvement, with a variety of movement products to choose from. The various movements are knit together into a field but not a superordinate umbrella organization.[16]

So it was in the early nineteenth century: temperance, nationalism, craft struggle, communitarianism, abolitionism, freethinking, and camp-meeting religion coexisted and sometimes shared adherents without ever joining under a common umbrella. Neither socialism nor liberalism were hegemonic movements before mid-century. Educational reform perhaps came close to being a common denominator in the early American movements (Walters 1978: 210), but it linked others rather than encompassing them.

Though there was no overall umbrella, early nineteenth-century movements nonetheless combined to create a field of activity. Movement activists were joined into networks that crisscrossed specific movements, and the broader public recognized that there were many possible movements to consider. Sometimes these movements demanded near total devotion (as did, for example, most communal settlements, at least while one remained resident in the commune). On the other hand, multiple membership, either simultaneous or serial, was common. It has been argued, for example, that modern feminism was born from the activism of women in abolition and temperance movements. In the former case, the very large number of female activists were marginalized; women like Elizabeth Cady Stanton and Lucretia Mott were denied voting status and were relegated to a curtained balcony at the World Anti-Slavery Convention of 1840. After the Civil War, women made the temperance movement their own and gained experience that would translate crucially into suffrage campaigns (Evans and Boyte 1986: 80–95). Similarly, the Second Great Awakening helped to spark the militant abolitionist movement, transcendentalists were influenced by other communalists (and antagonistic to evangelicals), feminists were drawn to several of the communitarian groups, some Chartists promoted temperance, and Wesleyan preachers found occasions to preach something like what would later be called the social gospel far too often for the comfort of the church hierarchy and sometimes wound up as trade-union leaders.[17] Sometimes the personal networks of movement activists quickly expanded to touch a range of others. Consider Mary Wollstonecraft (the pioneering feminist) and William Godwin (the anarchist political philosopher). Godwin claimed credit for "converting" Robert Owen from factory management to the task of developing his social system; they met on numerous occasions. The daughter of Wollstonecraft and Godwin, Mary, eloped with Percy Bysshe Shelley (a fan of her father's) and, while living with him and Lord Byron, wrote the story of Dr. Frankenstein's monster. Byron of course died during his Romantic flirtation with Greek nationalism. Feminism, Owenite socialism, anarchism, nationalism, and Romanticism were thus linked in an intimate network.

The connections were not just intimate, though, but included public events and opportunities for those less involved to enter the movement field, learn its discourse, and choose among its protagonists. In April 1829, for example, in the midst of the Second Great Awakening, Robert Owen, the genius of New Lanark, journeyed to Cincinnati, Ohio, to debate a prominent evangelical clergyman, Alexander Campbell of Bethany, Virginia. The focus of the debate was on religion, with Owen out to demonstrate the superiority of rational unbelief and Campbell taking equally rationalist grounds to argue the merits of biblical Christianity. Interestingly, Owen was pushed to defend his doctrine of environmental determination against attacks by Campbell, who saw free will as essential to Christianity (a theme that was contradictory to predestination and that would become central to the evangelical upsurge of two years later). Thousands of people attended the eight days of lengthy and abstruse debate, shopping among millennial visions. Both visions were tied to movements; indeed, one of Campbell's challenges to Owen was that if Owen were a self-consistent determinist, he would not bother so much with organizing campaigns and communities but would allow environmental pressures to do their work.[18] In Campbell's view, God's work required the self-conscious struggle of Christians endowed with free agency. Both men agreed, moreover, that their movements were about the radical restructuring of society at large and of personal relations; they were not debating matters of passive belief.

We are accustomed to conceptualizing Owenite socialism as a truly social movement, but it is worth affirming the same of Campbell's revivalist religion. It was Campbell, for example, who raised the issue of gender. Pagan religions had made woman "little else than a slave to the passion and tyranny of man. The Jews rather exile her from the synagogue, as altogether animal in her nature." By contrast, Campbell argued, "wherever Christianity has found its way, the female sex has been emancipated from ignorance, bondage, and obscurity. . . . Christianity has made you not the inferior but the companion and equal of man (Owen and Campbell 1829, 2: 123–24). Likewise, Campbell was clear that his "New Constitution" was no mere "civil religion"; patriotism was not to be confused with Christian virtue (ibid., 2: 117). As to Owen's utilitarian conception of the end of human life as happiness based on material abundance, Campbell all but attacked the Protestant ethic itself, mocking an account in which morality "is just a due regard to *utility*. Bees are *moral* as well as men; and he is the most moral bee which creates the most honey and consumes the least of it" (ibid., 1: 18).

This debate was a major event in its day, attracting widespread attention. A transcript (taken down in stenography by a former resident of New Harmony by then drawn to Christianity) was published with both debaters' approval and sold widely. Yet the event is hardly mentioned in accounts of either Owenite or Campbellite movements (nor in Ross's 1985 history of Cincinnati workers). It is as though later ideas about the relationship between socialism and religion, particularly evangelical protestant religion, have rendered the connection invisible by placing the two movements in separate fields. One figures as a precursor to modern socialism, the other to a mainline protestant sect and less directly to Mormonism. What could be more different? Yet, in the early nineteenth century, especially in America, such new social movements were not only numerous but occupied a vital common space and were often linked.

WHY DID NEW SOCIAL MOVEMENTS
HAVE TO BE REDISCOVERED?

In both early nineteenth- and late twentieth-century America and Europe a lively range of social movements emerged, different in form, content, social bases, and meaning to their participants. These were linked in social movement fields of considerable similarity. The similarities go beyond those noted above through the lens of new social movement theory. They include, for example, a lively involvement with aesthetic production and reception. The 1960s student and kindred movements are all but inconceivable without folk and especially rock music; they also nurtured an aestheticizing of the self and a wide variety of engagements with aesthetic criteria for judging personal activity and social arrangements. Feminism has been distinctive for the extent to which aesthetic production of various sorts—literature, drama, music, graphic arts—has been tied into the movement. Part of the impetus behind the ecology movement is an aesthetic judgment about nature and about appropriate lifestyles that should not be collapsed into an altogether instrumental concern for saving the earth or ourselves from extinction. This reminds us of the Romantic view of nature, and Romanticism was both an aspect of many late eighteenth- and early nineteenth-century social movements and is in a sense one of those movements. A similar use of aesthetic criteria in judgments about the practical affairs of life was important to the communal movement of the early nineteenth century and to the Transcendentalists.

Of course aesthetics entered prominently into the social movement field at various other times—for example, in the era of high modernism. Nonetheless, mention of aesthetics points us toward part of the answer to a crucial question: why have the similarities between the social movement fields of the early nineteenth and late twentieth centuries not been more generally apparent to social theorists? An easy bit of the answer is simply that many social theorists know little history. It is also true that the concerns of both academic social theory and Marxism were shaped by the prominence of labor and socialist movements in the period of their origins. Variants of liberalism and conservatism dominated universities while Marxism became the dominant extra-academic radical theory, eclipsing the various utopian socialists, proponents of direct action, and other alternative social visions of the early nineteenth century. Thus, both in and out of academia, most theoretical orientations offered little insight into and attributed little contemporary significance to religious movements, nationalism, identity politics, gender difference, sexuality, and other concerns.[19] Thus is so largely because they operate with a highly rationalized conception of human life and relatively fixed notion of interests.[20] Thus aesthetic activity and inquiry and the range of issues raised by the NSMs were typically set apart from the "serious" issues that shaped theorists' largely instrumental inquiries into social movements.

Indeed, even socialism itself was given a one-sidedly economistic definition in classical social theory (and most of its successor traditions). If socialism was about the struggle between capital and labor, as Barbara Taylor has noted, what was one to do with Robert Owen and his followers for whom "socialism represented a struggle to achieve 'perfect equality and perfect freedom' at every level of social existence; a struggle which extended beyond the economic and political reforms necessary to create a classless society into the emotional and cultural transformations necessary to construct a sexual democracy?" (Taylor 1983: xiv). Socialism—and political action generally—made sense in classical social theory to the extent that it was instrumentally focused on tangible, material goals. Social movements that were not so oriented were necessarily relegated to the margins of theoretical relevance.

The late nineteenth-century institutionalization of the labor/socialist movements and the response to them crystallized the notion of a division between sorts of movements. There was *the* social movement that was tied into the overall process of industrialization and social change, and there was the variety of false starts and short circuits that expressed human dreams and frustrations but had little to do with the overall course of social change. Rather than treating the different sorts of movements together, late nineteenth- and early twentieth-century social scientists compartmentalized them. The very field of social movement studies shows traces of this. Its roots lie on the one hand in sociopsychological studies of collective behavior (generally interpreted as deviant) and on the other in studies of the labor movement (analyzed broadly in liberal/Weberian or Marxian terms). This contributed to a tendency to conduct argument as though the joint activity of large numbers of people must either be shown to be instrumentally rational or be deemed irrational and explicable on sociopsychological criteria (see, for example, the arguments among Smelser 1962; Smelser 1970; Currie and Skolnick 1970; Berk 1974; and Marx 1970; and the review in McAdam et al. 1988). This pattern was overdetermined by the relative paucity of historical studies among American sociologists; few looked back at major formative movements— all but inescapable to students of American history—which did not fit the prevailing divisions. The Great Awakenings, abolition, temperance—these clearly shaped American history, but they did not fit very neatly the alternatives of liberal or left, instrumental or psychologically deviant.[21]

Social movement research also developed in a surprising disconnection from political analysis. This worked in both directions. Sociologists studying social movements (and even more "collective behavior") tended for many years to focus on movements not manifestly political or to neglect the political dimensions of those they studied (Tarrow 1989: 25). Thus an academic campaign could be launched in the 1970s to "bring the state back in" to the study of social movements and related sociological phenomena (Evans et al. 1985). In this context Charles Tilly (1978, 1982, 1986), in some of the most important and influential work in the field, tied the study of social movements closely to state making and economic issues. An advance on collective behavior psychologism, this produced a kind of mirror image in which only directly political-economic, nationally integrated, and state-oriented movements received full attention.

Conversely, democratic theory long treated movements as exceptions to normal institutional political processes and often mainly as disruptions rather than central dimensions of public discourse and political agenda setting (see discussion in Cohen and Arato 1992: chap. 10). Only parts of the Marxist tradition consistently presented social movements as politically central rather than epiphenomenal. Marxists concentrated, however, not on the role of movements in ordinary democratic politics but rather in the transformation of capitalist society (and bourgeois democracy) into something else that would putatively not require such movements. Even in the wake of the social movements of the last thirty-some years, democratic theory has remained remarkably focused on institutionalized politics (Pateman's 1970 challenge to this still applies). When pluralist thinkers looked to the role of diverse segments of the population, they conceptualized this in terms of interest groups rather than movements (see, for example, Dahl 1956; Dahl 1961; Held 1987). Even when more critical thinkers addressed issues of direct democratic participation, their attention turned to forms of everyday citizen decision-making—that is, to an alternative set of stable, perhaps community-based routines, not to movements (for example, Barber 1984). Seymour Martin Lipset went so far as to assert that "political apathy may reflect the health of a democracy" (1963: 32). Normative democratic theory remains focused on the conceptualization of ideal routines rather than forcefully including a role for movements as continual sources of innovation.

The field of social movement research was transformed by the attempt to comprehend the civil rights movement and the antiwar and student movements of the 1960s (Oberschall 1973; Tilly 1978; Zald and McCarthy 1979; McAdam et al. 1988). The range of movements studied and the perspectives employed were broadened, and emphasis was shifted from micropsychological to macrostructural and/or rational choice accounts. Leading approaches reproduced, however, the basic division between liberal (utilitarian, rational choice, and resource mobilization) and Marxist perspectives. Most theories saw movements either as challengers for state power or as contentious groups pursuing some other set of instrumental objectives. There was little recognition of how "the personal is political" or of how important political (or more generally macrostructural) results may stem from actions that are not explicitly political or instrumental in their self-understanding.[22] Such theories overcame the division of collective behavior from real politics, but they did not bring culture—or any rich understanding of democratic processes and civil society—to the foreground. This was done primarily by NSM theory.

NSM theory not only brought culture to the fore but challenged the sharp division between micro and macro, processual and structural accounts. In Cohen and Arato's words, "Contemporary collective actors see that the creation of identity involves social conflict around the reinterpretation of norms, the creation of new meanings, and a challenge to the social construction of the very boundaries between public, private, and political domains of

action" (1992: 511). It is as important not to prejudge whether
to apply a political process model of instrumentally rational interaction (Tilly 1978; McAdam 1982) as to avoid an assumption that
collective behavior stems from psychological breakdown.

CONCLUSION: MODERNITY
AND SOCIAL MOVEMENTS

For at least 200 years, under one label or another, the public
has been opposed to the private; the economic to the aesthetic;
the rationalist to the romantic; secularization to revival; and institutionalization to nascent movements intent on breaking free.
These tensions lie behind recurrent ebbs and flows in movement
organization, changing forms of movement activity, and recurrent proliferations of movements beyond any single narrative of a
developing labor movement, socialism, or even democracy. This
essay does not trace a longer narrative or attempt to graph the ebbs
and flows of different styles of movement. Its main contributions
are limited to (a) showing how prominent new social movements
were in the early nineteenth century and (b) suggesting that attention should be focused not simply on a supposed transition from
old to new forms of movement, but on the interplay of different
sorts of movements in a social movement field that was and is not
only basic to modernity but internally diverse and international.
By not confounding the variety of movement characteristics with
a presumed unidirectional narrative we can better discern the variables that distinguish movements of varying age in terms of their
extent and forms of organization, their relative emphasis on identity politics, their social bases, and orientations to action. These
are themes to which we should be alert in the study of all social
movements, and we should seek to explain their absence as well
as their presence.

Attuned to the richness of the social movement field in the early
nineteenth and late twentieth centuries, we may see on further
investigation that the late nineteenth and early twentieth centuries
were not so completely dominated by economistic organization as
is commonly thought. Trade unions and social democracy com-
peted with the Salvation Army and xenophobic nationalists nearly
everywhere and with revivalist preachers in America and anti-
Semites in much of Europe. Academic social scientists, however,

failed to grant such other forms of movement attention proportionate to their popular appeal, while tending to expect the labor movement and mainstream party politics to grow ever stronger and more institutionalized.

If, however, it is also true, as I suggest, that the early nineteenth-century social movement field is in certain respects more similar to the late twentieth century than to the intervening years, we are faced with an interesting problem of historical explanation. The standard account of movement cycles proposed by Hirschman (1982) and Tarrow (1989) focuses primarily on shorter term phenomena: the way specific mobilizations exhaust participants' energies within a few months or years. But the mid-century shift in social movement activity was more than this. The struggles of many different varieties of people about the conditions and rewards of their work were increasingly joined in a single labor movement; their diverse ideologies were transformed, at least in part, into a continuum of more or less radical labor values from strong socialism to elitist unionism. Similarly, the so-called utopian socialisms faded in the face of Marxism, Fabianism, and other reform programs and social democracy. As Taylor (1983) has noted, this had striking implications for women, who had been included centrally, if asymmetrically, in Owenism but who found themselves marginalized in Marxist socialism, trade unionism, and social democratic parties. Underlying this specific instance was a general redefinition of private and public life that removed not only women but the concerns most closely identified with women—family, for example—from the public sphere, transforming political questions into merely personal concerns. It was this historically specific change—not some eternal tendency of patriarchy—that feminists later challenged with the slogan "the personal is political."

Phases of state and capitalist development were probably significant in all this (Hirsch 1988; Tarrow 1989). State elites may have become more unified and thus both better able to respond to movements and less likely to split between support and opposition. Certainly states developed better mechanisms for managing discontent (though these were hardly proof against the new, largely middle-class mobilizations of the 1960s). Not least of all, the franchise was extended, and in its wake electoral politics offered the chance to trade votes for various kinds of largely economic distributional benefits. At the same time, the institutional development of states created mechanisms for continual negotiation over some issues—notably labor and welfare concerns. This brought certain movement concerns permanently into the political arena while leaving others out.

The concentration of large parts of the population in industrial work may also have played a role, offering unions a fertile organizing base. Perhaps more basically, workers within capitalist production were in a position (unlike most of their predecessors) to bargain for increased shares of capitalist growth. They were not asking for the protection of old crafts or the communities attached to them. There was, thus, an increasing return to investment in economistic movement organizations once workers were asking for something that capitalists could give in monetary terms. Mature industrial capitalism also posed organizational challenges to the labor movement that pushed it toward large-scale, formally organized, institutional structures. Of course, the labor movement dominated in the movement field because of its success; its dominance was an achievement of struggle, not just an inheritance from background variables. Finally, we should not fail to consider the impact of delimited events as well as trends in underlying factors. The repression of the revolutions of 1848 and the American Civil War most visibly helped to bring the early nineteenth-century burgeoning of social movements to a close. The demographic effects of both—increased migration as well as massive killing—also may have reduced the probability of movement formation and proliferation and increased popular preference for institutionalized rather than riskier forms of collective action.

I will not try to offer even a similar ad hoc list of possible factors worth exploring in the attempt to explain the reopening of the social movement field in the 1960s (or at the turn of the century). Arguments about the shift from mass-production capitalism to smaller scale, more dispersed patterns of work; about the role of new media; and about the role of the state only scratch the surface of contending positions. Perhaps demographics were again crucial; perhaps rapid social change created a sense of new possibilities. Most basically, we need to consider the possibility that proliferation of NSMs is normal to modernity and not in need of special explanation because it violates the oppositions of left and right, cultural and social, public and private, aesthetic and instrumental that organize so much of our thought. The challenge may be to explain the relative paucity of NSMs in some periods or places. While rebellions, reforms, and other kinds of collective actions have certainly occurred throughout history, the modern era is in general distinctively characterized by a rich efflorescence of social movements. This is in part because it provides opportunities and capacities for mobilization lacking in many other epochs and settings. A proneness to various sorts of social movements, indeed, seems to be one of the features that links the distinctive history of Western modernity to the novel modernities being pioneered on the Indian subcontinent, in China, in Africa, and elsewhere.

It is a mistake thus to equate the mid-nineteenth- to mid-twentieth-century pattern simply with modernity. This helps, among other things, to nourish illusions about what it could mean to pass into postmodernity. The relative predominance of a single cluster of movements during this period is not necessarily either more typical than the proliferation of different movements both before and after it; indeed, it may be less so. The seeming dominance of labor and social democracy—whether in European actuality or only in the minds of social scientists—is historically specific and contingent. There never was *the* social movement of modernity. Rather, modernity was internally split and contested from the beginning—or perhaps I should say was "always already" the object of contending movements.

We need to constitute our theoretical notion of modernity not as a master narrative but in a way that reflects both its heterogeneity and contestation and that takes full account of the central place of social movements within it. If we are to discern a postmodernity, a change of tendency, or a trend, we need more clearly to know what we may be moving beyond. State power and capitalism have not been transcended; neither has competitive individualism passed away nor the world of merely instrumental relations become inherently more spiritual. Many of the grievances and dissatisfactions that drove the movements of the early nineteenth century remain. Likewise, the proliferation of new social movements should not be taken too quickly to spell the end of trade union activism or mainstream political and economic concerns as movement themes. The cycle may continue. In any case, modernity remains visible, in part, precisely in the shape of the movements challenging it and asking for more from it.

NOTES

1   Tilly (see also 1982) focuses overwhelmingly on contentious action challenging the growing state. He finds the social movement to be invented
in Britain only with Chartism and the rise of a movement integrated on a
national scale, addressing the state as the central societal actor and voicing
contentious, largely economic demands. He is concerned to distinguish
"proactive," modern movements from "reactive" or defensive ones. This
echoes the way Karl Marx and other late nineteenth-century reformers and
radicals distinguished their mobilizations and programs from those of their
predecessors and more old-fashioned contemporaries. This definition of
what really counts as a serious social movement shaped nearly all subsequent
attention to the matter, including studies of the early nineteenth century.
It is in part from this definition that E. P. Thompson (1968) struggled to
escape (while remaining in the Marxist-radical fold) with his account of
"class as happening" and his inclusive attention to a range of unconventional
movements. At some points, Tilly focuses less on the overall "modernization" process and comes closer to Thompson's position (though he never
fully sorts out his position on culture and "voluntarism"): The "long-run
reshaping of *solidarities*, rather than the immediate production of stress
and strain, constituted the most important impact of structural change on
political conduct" (Tilly et al. 1974: 86).

2   As Cohen and Arato (1992: 510) note, a still more extreme view is Pizzorno's
(1978 and 1985) "pure identity" model.

3   Political sociologists have consistently tended to work with an idea of what
counts as properly political that marginalizes religion, even where it seems
obviously central to the phenomena under study. As Matthews (1969: 26–
27) remarked of Lipset's *The First New Nation*, "What is surprising and
not a little distressing about Lipset's study of a changing and growing new
nation is that he never explained how it got to be so religious."

4   Touraine (1971, 1977, 1981, 1985, and 1988), Melucci (1980, 1981, 1988,
and 1989), Habermas (1984 and 1988), Offe (1985), Eder (1985), Pizzorno
(1978 and 1985), and Cohen (1985; Cohen and Arato 1992) are among the
more prominent. In addition, Hirsch (1988) has adapted a version of neo-
Marxist regulation theory to an account of NSMs; the concept is central to
Laclau and Mouffe's (1985) rethinking of "hegemony and socialist strategy"
and to the broader reconceptualizations of social movements by Tarrow
(1989) and his colleagues (Klandermans et al. 1988). Inglehart (1990) links
NSMs to "postmaterialism" and the "cognitive mobilization" wrought by
higher education levels, greater media involvement, etc.

5   In focusing on the early nineteenth century, I do not wish to argue that
NSMs ceased to be prominent in the second half of the nineteenth century
or the first half of the twentieth. On the contrary, some of the same NSMs
maintained or returned to prominence—as, for example, the Women's
Christian Temperance Union of the 1870s and 1880s succeeded the American Temperance Union of the 1830s and 1840s. The followers of W. K.
Kellogg, promoter of abstinence and cold cereals in the early twentieth cen-

tury, were not so different from those of Sylvester Graham, the "peristaltic persuader" and inventor of the Graham cracker in the 1830s (Nissenbaum 1980). Many manifestations of antimodernism in late nineteenth- and early twentieth-century intellectual circles involve NSM activity (Lears 1981). There is no ready index for assessing when movement activity is greater or lesser, so my impressionistic comparative judgment is open to challenge, though I think there can be little doubt that the early nineteenth century was particularly active.

6   This account is indebted to discussions with George Steinmetz; see also Steinmetz 1990.

7   See, for example, Sean Wilentz's very qualified tracing of the episodic appearance of some form of class consciousness among New York workers involved in a variety of other identities and never quite reducible to proletarians: "Between 1829—the annus mirabilis of New York artisan radicalism—and 1850, both a process and a strain of consciousness emerged in numerous ways from the swirl of popular politics, in which people came at various points to interpret social disorder and the decline of the Republic at least partly in terms of class divisions between capitalist employers and employees" (1984: 16–17). Like E. P. Thompson's *The Making of the English Working Class* (1968), Wilentz's *Chants Democratic* suggests in its subtitle a rise of the American working class that implies a stronger unity than is revealed in its rich account of diversity, particularly between an earlier artisan and Republican politics and a later (but less examined) working-class politics and trade-union organization.

8   "In the past decade or two, conflicts have developed in advanced Western societies that deviate in various ways from the welfare-state pattern of institutionalized conflict over distribution. They no longer flare up in domains of material reproduction; they are no longer channeled through parties and associations; and they can no longer be allayed by compensations. Rather, these new conflicts arise in domains of cultural reproduction, social integration, and socialization; they are carried out in subinstitutional—or at least extraparliamentary—forms of protest; and the underlying deficits reflect a reification of communicatively structured domains of action that will not respond to the media of money and power. The issue is not primarily one of compensations that the welfare state can provide, but of defending and restoring endangered ways of life" (Habermas 1988: 392). See the similar argument in Bell (1982).

9   Part of the confusion comes from failing to distinguish two senses of utopian. The programs of neocorporatist social democratic parties may be all encompassing and in that sense utopian, but they are eminently negotiable and not necessarily radical. Feminist calls for an end to all violence and discrimination against women are in a sense defensive but are also both radical and nonnegotiable, and in that sense utopian. In different ways, each utopian goal may be unreachable in the world as we know it, a shared sense of the term.

10 I focus here mainly on America, but this generalization seems to hold in considerable degree for Britain, France, the low countries, and Scandinavia. There were of course local variations, like the extent to which linguistic

standardization or religious establishment were major political issues. In central, eastern, and southern Europe, the generalization is more problematic, both in timetable and in content. The issue of national unification of course transformed German politics; that of the reorganization and/or breakup of empire was critical in Austria-Hungary and its successor states. Indeed, one can see some consistency between the extent of this domestic normalization of politics and international alliances in this period, but I do not want to push that line very far. It should also be noted that national unification of other sorts was a central theme in American politics of the second half of the nineteenth and first part of the twentieth century. Not just the defining conflict of the Civil War, but the recurrent question of the incorporation of western territories kept the national definition of the Union on the agenda.

11 Despite the opposition of such feminists as there were, in 1873 the United States made distribution of birth control devices or advice illegal, indeed criminal (Gordon 1990: 94). The feminist movement of the 1840s did have successors (like the free-love movement of the 1870s), but these have been obscured until recently from historical writing just as they were repressed (and partly because they were repressed) by contemporary political morality. As Gordon (1990: 24) notes, "Religious and political leaders denounced sexual immorality increasingly after mid-century."

12 In a different, less Marxist class scheme one could look for disproportionate NSM mobilization among the "dominated fraction of the dominant class" and others who have more cultural than economic capital (Bourdieu 1984).

13 He somewhat misleadingly identifies this with the early nineteenth century, when the numbers of industrial workers were certainly growing but (a) remained very small and (b) did not constitute the core of the nascent labor movement that was rooted more in artisans and protoindustrial works like outworkers (see various essays in Katznelson and Zolberg 1987).

14 Tucker (1991) has, however, convincingly addressed French syndicalism as a new social movement, suggesting the limits to any reading of the late nineteenth and early twentieth centuries as unproblematically the era of the "old" labor and social democratic movements.

15 Cohen and Arato (1992: 493) term this "self-limiting radicalism," but they unnecessarily assume that action not focused on the state is not deeply radical in some senses and that its adherents accept existing political and economic arrangements: "Our presupposition is that the contemporary movements are in some significant respects 'new.' What we have in mind, above all, is a self-understanding that abandons revolutionary dreams in favor of radical reform that is not necessarily and primarily oriented to the state. We shall label as 'self-limiting radicalism' projects for the defense and democratization of civil society that accept structural differentiation and acknowledge the integrity of political and economic systems."

16 This does not mean that all potential identities enter such a field with equal chances of becoming the basis of action or commitment. As Cohen and Arato (1992: 511) summarize Touraine's view, "the various *institutional potentials* of the shared cultural field, and not simply the particular identity of a particular group, comprise the stakes of struggle" (original emphasis).

Projects of identity formation become identity politics largely by making demands—for example, at a minimum, for recognition—on the cultural field as such.

17 Individuals and groups could unite many of the widespread themes. Adin Ballou, the founder of the Hopedale community, for example, described it as a "missionary temperance, antislavery, peace, charitable, woman's rights, and educational society" (Walters 1978: 49). While guiding Hopedale, he was a lecturer for temperance and the American Anti-Slavery Society, and president of the pacifist and Christian anarchist New England Non-Resistance Society.

18 Moreover, Campbell asked why Owen's views differed so from those of other men raised under similar circumstances (Owen and Campbell 1829, 1:236).

19 Weber of course made a variety of contributions to the analysis of cultural movements and their relationship to politics and economics, but these are noteworthy partly because of their atypicality. They do not, in any case, overcome his tendency to analyze contemporary phenomena largely in terms of instrumental pursuit of interests—including culturally constituted interests like status. Durkheim and Mauss each thought nationalism important after World War I (which did not take startling perspicacity), but neither wrote a major work on it or, indeed, on social movements generally.

20 This is linked not just to the issues thematized in this paper, but also to the relative neglect of emotions as a theme in social movement analysis (except as part of accounts of psychosocial deviance) and until recently in sociology generally.

21 It is perhaps no accident that one of the few classic social movement studies to break out of these dualisms was Joseph Gusfield's (1963) historical study of the temperance movement (which treats it largely in terms of the "status politics" by which new or upwardly mobile social groups affirmed their distinctive identity and place in the social order).

22 Trying to make sense of the New Left, Alvin Gouldner (1970: vii) contemplated the song "Light My Fire," recorded by Jim Morrison and the Doors. He saw it in two guises: "an ode to urban conflagration" sung during the Detroit riots, and a singing commercial for a Detroit carmaker. The question, in other words, was between political resistance and economic hegemony. What Gouldner missed, apparently, was the centrality of sex to the New Left as to so much of the rest of the new social movement ferment of the era (as of the early nineteenth century).

REFERENCES

Amann, Peter (1975) Revolution and Mass Democracy: The Paris Club Movement in 1848. Princeton: Princeton University Press.

Aminzade, Ronald (forthcoming) Ballots and Barricades. Princeton, NJ: Princeton University Press.

Aronowitz, Stanley (1992) Identity Politics. London: Routledge.

Barber, Benjamin (1984) Strong Democracy: Participatory Politics for a New Age. Berkeley: University of California Press.

Bell, Daniel (1982) The Cultural Contradictions of Capitalism. New York: Basic Books.

Berk, Richard A. (1974) Collective Behavior. Dubuque, IA: W. C. Brown.

Bourdieu, Pierre (1984) Distinction. Cambridge, MA: Harvard University Press.

Calhoun, Craig (1982) The Question of Class Struggle. Chicago: University of Chicago Press.

———— (1983a) "The radicalism of tradition: Community strength or venerable disguise and borrowed language?" American Journal of Sociology 88: 886–914.

———— (1983b) "Industrialization and social radicalism: British and French workers' movements and the mid-nineteenth century crisis." Theory and Society 12: 485–504.

———— (1988) "Populist politics, communications media, and large scale social integration." Sociological Theory 6: 219–41.

———— (1989) "Classical social theory and the French revolution of 1848." Sociological Theory 7: 210–25.

———— (1993) "Postmodernism as pseudohistory." Theory, Culture and Society: 10: 75–96.

Cohen, Jean (1985) "Strategy or identity: New theoretical paradigms and contemporary social movements." Social Research 52: 663–716.

Cohen, Jean, and Andrew Arato (1992) Civil Society and Political Theory. Cambridge, MA: MIT Press.

Currie, Eliott, and Jerome H. Skolnick (1970) "A critical note on conceptions of collective behavior." Annals of the American Academy of Political and Social Science 391: 34–45.

Dahl, Robert A. (1956) A Preface to Democratic Theory. Chicago: University of Chicago Press.

———— (1961) Who Governs? Democracy and Power in an American City. New Haven, CT: Yale University Press.

Drescher, Seymour (1987) Capitalism and Antislavery. New York: Oxford University Press.

Eder, Klaus (1985) "The 'new social movements': Moral crusades, political pressure groups, or social movements?" Social Research 52: 869–901.

Engels, Friedrich (1978 [1892]) "Socialism: Utopian and scientific," in R. C. Tucker (ed.) The Marx-Engels Reader. 2d ed. New York: Norton: 683–717.

Evans, Peter B., Dietrich Rueschemeyer, and Theda Skocpol, eds. (1985) Bringing the State Back In. New York: Cambridge University Press.

Evans, Sara M., and Harry C. Boyte (1986) Free Spaces. Chicago: University of Chicago Press.

Fladeland, Betty (1984) Abolitionists and Working-Class Problems in the Age of Industrialization. Baton Rouge: Louisiana State University Press.

Galbraith, John K. (1967) The New Industrial State. Boston: Houghton-Mifflin.

Goodwyn, Lawrence (1976) Democratic Promise: The Populist Movement in America. New York: Oxford.

Gordon, Linda (1990) Woman's Body, Woman's Right: Birth Control in America. Baltimore: Penguin.

Gouldner, Alvin (1970) The Coming Crisis of Western Sociology. Boston: Beacon.

Gusfield, Joseph (1963) Symbolic Crusade: Status Politics and the American Temperance Movement. Urbana: University of Illinois Press.

Habermas, Jurgen (1962) The Structural Transformation of the Public Sphere. Cambridge, MA: MIT Press.

———— (1967) Legitimation Crisis. Boston: Beacon.

———— (1984) The Theory of Communicative Action. Vol. 1, Reason and the Rationalization of Society. Boston: Beacon.

———— (1988) The Theory of Communicative Action. Vol. 2, Lifeworld and System: A Critique of Functionalist Reason. Boston: Beacon.

———— (1990) The New Conservatism: Cultural Criticism and the Historians' Debate. Cambridge, MA: MIT Press.

Harrison, John F. C. (1969) Quest for the New Moral World: Robert Owen and the Owenites in Britain and America. New York: Scribners.

Held, David (1987) Models of Democracy. Stanford, CA: Stanford University Press.

Hirsch, Joachim (1988) "The crisis of Fordism, transformations of the 'Keynesian' security state, and new social movements." Research in Social Movements, Conflict and Change 10: 43–55.

Hirschman, Albert (1982) Shifting Involvements. Princeton: Princeton University Press.

Hostetler, John A. (1980) Amish Society. 3d ed. Baltimore: Johns Hopkins University Press.

Inglehart, Ronald (1990) Culture Shift in Advanced Industrial Society. Princeton, NJ: Princeton University Press.

Johnson, Richard (1978) A Shopkeepers' Millenium: Society and Revivals in Rochester, New York, 1815–1837. New York: Hill and Wang.

Jones, Gareth Stedman (1984) Languages of Class. Cambridge: Cambridge University Press.

Kanter, Rosabeth Moss (1972) Commitment and Community: Communes and Utopias in Sociological Perspective. Cambridge, MA: Harvard University Press.

Katznelson, Ira, and Ari Zolberg, eds. (1987) Working-Class Formation: Nineteenth-Century Patterns in Western Europe and the United States. Princeton, NJ: Princeton University Press.

Klandermans, B., H. Kriesi, and S. Tarrow, eds. (1988) From Structure to Action: Comparing Movement Participation across Cultures. Greenwich, CT: JAI Press.

Kramer, L. (1988) Threshold of a New World: Intellectuals and the Exile Experience in Paris, 1830–1848. Ithaca, NY: Cornell University Press.

Laclau, Ernesto, and Chantal Mouffe (1985) Hegemony and Socialist Strategy. London: Verso.

Lears, Jackson (1981) No Place of Grace: Antimodernism and the Transformation of American Culture, 1880–1920. New York: Pantheon.

Lipset, Seymour Martin (1963) Political Man. New York: Doubleday.

Lyotard, J.-F. (1984) The Postmodern Condition. Minneapolis: University of Minnesota Press.

McAdam, Doug (1982) Political Process and the Development of Black Insurgency, 1930–1970. Chicago: University of Chicago Press.

McAdam, Doug, John D. McCarthy, and Mayer Zald (1988) "Social movements," in N. J. Smelser (ed.) Handbook of Sociology. Newbury Park, CA: Sage: 695–737.

McWilliams, Wilson Carey (1973) The Idea of Fraternity in America. Berkeley: University of California Press.

Marty, Martin (1984) Pilgrims in Their Own Land. New York: Penguin.

Marx, Gary (1970) "Issueless riots." Annals of the American Academy of Political and Social Science 391: 21–23.

Marx, Karl, and Friedrich Engels (1976 [1848]) Manifesto of the Communist Party, in Karl Marx/Frederick Engels: Collected Works, vol. 6. London: Lawrence and Wishart: 477–519.

Matthews, Donald (1969) "The Second Great Awakening as an Organizing Process, 1780–1830: An Hypothesis," American Quarterly 21: 21–43.

Meinecke, Friedrich (1970) Cosmopolitanism and the National State. Princeton: Princeton University Press, 1970.

Melucci, Alberto (1980) "The new social movements: A theoretical approach." Social Science Information 19: 199–226.

——— (1981) "Ten hypotheses for the analysis of new movements," in D. Pinto (ed.) Contemporary Italian Sociology. New York: Cambridge University Press: 173–94.

——— (1988) "Social movements and the democratization of everyday life," in J. Keane (ed.) Civil Society and the State. London: Verso: 245–60.

——— (1989) Nomads of the Present: Social Movements and Individual Needs in Contemporary Society. Philadelphia: Temple University Press.

Nissenbaum, Stephen (1980) Sex, Diet, and Debility in Jacksonian America. Greenwich, CT: Greenwood.

Oberschall, Anthony (1973) Social Conflict and Social Movements. Englewood Cliffs, NJ: Prentice-Hall.

Offe, Claus (1985) "New social movements: Challenging the boundaries of institutional politics." Social Research 52: 817–68.

——— (1990) "Reflections on the institutional self-transformation of movement politics: A tentative stage model," in R. Dalton and M. Kuchler (eds.) Challenging the Political Order: New Social and Political Movements in Western Democracies. Oxford: Oxford University Press: 232–50.

Owen, Robert, and Alexander Campbell (1829) Debate on the Evidences of Christianity Containing an Examination of the "Social System" and of All the Systems of Scepticism of Ancient and Modern Times. 2 vols. Bethany, VA: Alexander Campbell.

Pateman, Carole (1970) Participation and Democratic Theory. Cambridge: Cambridge University Press.

Pizzorno, Allessandro (1978) "Political exchange and collective identity in industrial conflict," in C. Crouch and A. Pizzorno (eds.) The Resurgence of Class Conflict in Western Europe since 1968, vol. 2. London: Macmillan: 277–98.

——— (1985) "On the rationality of democratic choices." Telos 18 (63): 41–69.

Rendall, Jane (1985a) The Origins of Modern Feminism: Women in Britain,

France and the United States, 1780–1860. Chicago: Lyceum.

———, ed. (1985b) Equal or Different: Women's Politics, 1800–1914. Oxford: Blackwell.

Rorabaugh, W. J. (1979) The Alcoholic Republic: An American Tradition. New York: Oxford University Press.

Rose, Anne (1981) Transcendentalism as a Social Movement, 1830–1850. New Haven, CT: Yale University Press.

Ross, Steven J. (1985) Workers on the Edge: Work, Leisure and Politics in Industrializing Cincinnati, 1788–1890. New York: Columbia University Press.

Ryan, Mary (1990) Women in Public: Between Banners and Ballots. Baltimore: Johns Hopkins University Press.

——— (1992) "Gender and public access: Women's politics in 19th century America," in C. Calhoun (ed.) Habermas and the Public Sphere. Cambridge, MA: MIT Press: 259–88.

Scott, Alan (1990) Ideology and the New Social Movements. London: Unwin Hyman.

Simmel, G. (1903) "The metropolis and mental life," in D. N. Levine (ed.) Georg Simmel on Individuality and Social Forms. Chicago: University of Chicago Press: 324–39.

Smelser, Neil (1962) Theory of Collective Behavior. New York: Free Press.

——— (1970) "Two critics in search of a bias: A response to Currie and Skolnick." Annals of the American Academy of Political and Social Science 391: 46–55.

Steinmetz, George (1990) "Beyond subjectivist and objectivist theories of conflict: Marxism, post-Marxism, and the new social movements." Wilder House Working Paper #2, University of Chicago.

Tarrow, Sidney (1988) "National politics and collective action: Recent theory and research in Western Europe and the United States." Annual Review of Sociology 14: 421–40.

——— (1989) Struggle, Politics and Reform: Collective Action, Social Movements and Cycles of Protest. Ithaca, NY: Cornell University Press (Western Societies Papers no. 21).

Taylor, Barbara (1983) Eve and the New Jerusalem. New York: Pantheon.

Thompson, Dorothy (1986) Chartism. New York: Pantheon.

Thompson, E. P. (1968) The Making of the English Working Class. Rev. ed. Harmondsworth: Penguin.

Tilly, Charles (1978) From Mobilization to Revolution. Reading, MA: Addison-Wesley.

——— (1982) "Britain creates the social movement," in J. E. Cronin and J. Schneer (eds.) Social Conflict and the Political Order in Modern Britain. New Brunswick, NJ: Rutgers University Press: 21–51.

——— (1986) The Contentious French. Cambridge, MA: Harvard University Press.

Tilly, Charles, Richard Tilly, and Louise Tilly (1974) The Rebellious Century. Cambridge, MA: Harvard University Press.

Touraine, A. (1971) Post-Industrial Society. London: Wildwood House.

——— (1977) The Self-Production of Society. Chicago: University of Chicago Press.

―――― (1981) The Voice and the Eye. New York: Cambridge University Press.
―――― (1985) "An introduction to the study of social movements." Social Research 52: 749–88.
―――― (1988) The Return of the Actor. Minneapolis: University of Minnesota Press.

Traugott, Mark (1985) Armies of the Poor: Determinants of Working-Class Participation in the Parisian Insurrection of June 1848. Princeton, NJ: Princeton University Press.

Tucker, Kenneth H. (1991) "How new are the new social movements." Theory, Culture and Society 8: 75–98.

Walicki, Andrzej (1982) Philosophy and Romantic Nationalism: The Case of Poland. Oxford: Clarendon.

Walters, Ronald G. (1978) American Reformers, 1815–1860. New York: Hill and Wang.

Wilentz, Sean (1984) Chants Democratic: New York City and the Rise of the American Working Class, 1788–1850. New York: Oxford.

Zablocki, Benjamin (1970) The Joyful Community. Baltimore: Penguin.

Zald, Mayer N., and John D. McCarthy, eds. (1979) The Dynamics of Social Movements. Cambridge: Winthrop.

"Initiator" and "Spin-off" Movements: Diffusion Processes in Protest Cycles

DOUG MCADAM

OVER THE PAST 20 YEARS the study of social movements and collective action has been something of a growth industry in American social science. Spurred, in part, by the turbulence of the 1960s, scholars in a variety of disciplines—principally sociology and political science—turned their attention to the study of social movements and revolutions. This dramatic increase in research attention was accompanied by something of a paradigm shift in the field, with the new generation of scholars rejecting the then dominant collective behavior approach in favor of the newer resource mobilization and political process perspectives.

Meanwhile in Europe a similar renaissance in social movement studies was initiated in the late 1970s and early 1980s with the appearance of the first writings in the "new social movements" tradition. The emergence of an active community of European movement scholars also fostered international discourse among

Doug McAdam is professor of sociology at the University of Arizona. His work on social movements and revolutions has focused primarily on the intersection of institutionalized politics and movements, network processes in collective action, and the biographical consequences of activism. He would like to thank Jeff Goodwin, Kelly Moore, Ed Amenta, Jim Jasper, and the other members of the New York University Workshop on Politics, Power, and Protest for their extremely insightful comments on an earlier draft of this article. Mark Traugott provided substantive feedback throughout the writing of the piece. Finally, a special thanks to Kevin Dougherty for pointing out the inherent compatibility of the perspective developed here with Rupp and Taylor's work on the continuities that often link different phases of the same movement.

those interested in the dynamics of collective action. These various developments have resulted in a remarkable proliferation of work in the field. Contemporary scholars are now blessed with a profusion of theory and empirical research on social movements, revolutions, and collective action. Reflecting on these materials, I have no doubt but that our knowledge and understanding of collective action dynamics has moved far beyond where it was in the early 1970s.

At the same time, the persistence of certain conceptual and methodological conventions in the field continues, in my view, to obscure several simple truths that have long been obvious to activists. These "truths" include the following four propositions. First, social movements are not discrete entities, akin to organizations. Second, social movements are normally inseparable from the broader, ideologically coherent "movement families" (della Porta and Rucht, 1991) in which they are embedded. Third, as Sidney Tarrow (1983, 1989) has long argued, it is the rise and fall of these "families" or cycles of protest that we should be trying to explain. Fourth, most social movements are caused by other social movements and the tactical, organizational, and ideological tools they afford later struggles.

Again, these propositions might seem obvious, but they do not accord easily with the prevailing conceptual and methodological canons in the field. In particular, the conception of the social movement as the fundamental "unit of analysis," combined with the methodological dominance of the case study approach, has resulted in a highly static view of collective action that privileges structure over process and single movements over cycles of protest. This highly truncated "movement-centric" view of collective action helps explain the excessive attention traditionally accorded the question of movement emergence. If, in fact, movements are discrete phenomena, independent of one another, then the central challenge confronting the researcher is accounting for the unique mix of factors or processes that brought each into being.

If we take seriously the "truths" noted above, our conceptual and methodological approach to the study of collective action would, of necessity, change. First, following Tarrow, we would want to shift our focus of attention from discrete social movements to the broader "movement families" or "cycles of protest" in which they are typically embedded. Second, in emphasizing the relationships between ideologically and temporally proximate movements, we would need to supplement the traditional case study approach with those methods expressly designed to assess the extent and nature of links between social groups. Such methods might include network analysis, diffusion studies, and the comparative case approach. Finally, we would want to reconceptualize the question of movement emergence. Instead of conceiving of all movements as independent entities whose emergence reflects unique internal dynamics, we might want to distinguish between two broad classes of movements whose origins reflect very different social processes. The first category consists of those rare, but exceedingly important, *initiator movements* that signal or otherwise set in motion an identifiable protest cycle. Historical examples of such movements would include Solidarity in Poland and the American civil rights movement. The second and more "populous" category of movements includes those *spin-off movements* that, in varying degrees, draw their impetus and inspiration from the original initiator movement.

Distinguishing between these two classes of movements has important implications for the study of movement emergence. In effect, the single question of movement emergence is replaced by two separate queries: 1) What specific factors and processes account for the emergence of initiator movements? and 2) What are the processes—diffusion, contagion, etc.—by which initiator movements give rise to broader cycles of protest and the specific spin-off struggles that define the cycle?

In this paper I will take up both of these questions. Specifically, I want to briefly sketch a model of initiator movements and draw on the diffusion and network literatures to outline a perspective on the relationship of initiator movements to cycles of protest. Throughout I will seek to illustrate the main tenets of the argument by reference to the American civil rights movement and the myriad spin-off struggles it helped spawn.

THE ORIGIN OF INITIATOR MOVEMENTS

So central to the study of social movements has been the question of emergence that it is fair to say that all of the so-called theories of social movements are really theories of movement emergence. The classic statements of collective behavior (Lang and Lang 1961; Smelser 1962) fit this description. According to this perspective, movements develop as a collective response to the feelings of fear and anxiety that instances of rapid social change tend to engender. The initial formulation of the resource mobilization perspective (McCarthy and Zald 1973, 1977) was framed explicitly as an alternative to the collective behavior account of emergence. McCarthy and Zald rejected the latter's stress on grievances or discontent, arguing instead that it was an increase in the availability of the resources needed to wage collective action that triggered initial mobilization. The term "new social movement theory" has been applied to a disparate set of writings, but, at its core, most of the work in the tradition adheres to a distinctive and shared account of movement emergence (Melucci 1980; Touraine 1981), emphasizing the developing material and ideological contradictions in late capitalist society as the root cause of the "new" movements. Finally, the political process model is also seen by its proponents (McAdam 1982; Tarrow 1983; Tilly 1978) as, first and foremost, an explanation of the rise of a social movement. Specifically, movements are held to emerge in response to the confluence of three factors: expanding political opportunities, established organizations, and the development of certain shared cognitions legitimating and motivating protest activity.

As different as these various accounts of movement emergence are, they do have one thing in common. None of them rests on a view of movements as developmentally dependent on one another. Instead, all of them are framed as universal explanations of social movements. The implication is that all movements arise independently of one another, while at the same time conforming to the general causal sequence embodied in the theory. This dubious set of assumptions is no less true of the political process model that I have long espoused. In proposing my specific version of the theory, I specified no scope conditions for the model's applicability. The suggestion was clear: the emergence of each and every movement—or at least every political movement—was expected to conform to the developmental dynamics specified in the model.

It should be clear from the introduction to this paper that I no longer subscribe to this view. At the same time, it will perhaps come as no surprise that I think the political process model affords the most convincing explanation of the origins of initiator movements. The model has been described in great detail elsewhere

(McAdam 1982), so a highly abbreviated sketch will suffice here. Specifically, the model stresses the confluence of three factors in shaping the chances of movement emergence. The first is the level of organization within the aggrieved population; the second, the collective assessment of the prospects for successful insurgency within that same population; and third, an increase in the vulnerability or receptivity of the broader political system to challenge by the group in question. The first factor can be conceived of as the degree of "organizational readiness" within the community; the second as the level of "insurgent consciousness" among the movement's mass base; and the third as an expansion in the "political opportunities" available to the group.

While all three factors are seen as necessary to the process, it is the last factor—political opportunities—that is clearly the analytic key to understanding movement emergence. Initiator movements are not so much willed into being through effective mobilization as they are born of broad demographic, economic, and political changes that destabilize existing power relations and grant to insurgents increased leverage with which to press their claims. Whether or not this leverage is exercised may depend on the organizational and ideational resources available to insurgents, but, in the absence of "expanding political opportunities" it matters little how resource-rich the aggrieved group is.

In attributing ultimate causal significance to "expanding political opportunities," I am, by extension, also locating the roots of protest cycles and entire "movement families" in the kinds of broad social change processes—migrations, wars, fiscal crises, political realignments, etc.—whose links to collective action have been stressed by a good many researchers (Goldstone 1991; McAdam 1982; Skocpol 1979; Tilly 1978). But here again these processes have been used to explain the rise of a single movement or revolution rather than a protest cycle per se. Therefore the question that must be answered is, What are the specific links between these broad change processes and the protest cycle? How do these broad historical trends serve to set in motion a heightened period of political unrest? They do so through the mediating effects of an initiator movement.

Two different dynamics can be identified in this regard. Expanding political opportunities can facilitate collective action either by seriously undermining the stability of an entire political system or by increasing the political leverage of a single challenging group. Either way, the result is apt to be a generalized protest cycle, but the dynamics by which it unfolds and the ultimate consequences that follow from it are hypothesized to be quite different. Let us take a closer look at each of these separate cases.

Generalized Regime Crises

Though they may disagree on the specific mix of factors that precipitate the crisis, all recent theorists of revolution (Arjomand 1988; Goldstone 1991; Skocpol 1979) attribute the development of a true "revolutionary situation" to the destabilizing effects of precisely the kinds of broad change processes identified earlier. For Skocpol, periods of revolutionary turmoil are typically set in motion by military losses and the fiscal overextension of the state. For Goldstone, the key precipitant is population pressure and the constraints it places on the regime's ability to distribute the material benefits on which its ruling coalition rests.

Whichever theory one subscribes to—and it is not clear that they are necessarily incompatible—the effects are seen by all theorists as the same. The resulting pressures dramatically weaken the regime, thus encouraging collective action by *all* groups sufficiently well organized to contest the structuring of a new political order. Invariably, though, there is a discernible sequence by which the various parties to the revolutionary process mobilize. This raises a more general and important point. Our popular perceptions of revolutions distort two important features of the unfolding conflict. First, revolutions generally are not born as revolutions. Rather, it is the void created by the collapse of the old regime that transforms garden-variety collective action into revolutionary action. Second, use of the term *revolution* obscures the multiple movements that typically constitute a revolutionary coalition. Looking backward at revolutions through the distorting lens of the triumphant new order obscures the complex intermingling of groups within the revolution and the sequence in which these separate movements mobilized. Invariably, though, a close reading of history can identify a specific initiator movement that set the entire process in motion.

The Empowerment of a Single Challenger

The identification of an initiator movement is much easier in the case of those protest cycles that stem not from any fatal weakening of the ruling order but from events or processes that advantage a single challenging group. The reason is simple. The continuing strength and viability of the regime in such cases insures against the development of the kind of revolutionary situation that blurs the boundaries between challenging groups and obscures the specific origins of the crisis. In contrast to the confusion and boundary blurring that necessarily accompany the development of a revolutionary coalition, we know nonrevolutionary protest cycles by the sequential parade of ostensibly separate movements that constitute them.

The American protest cycle of the 1960s and early 1970s is a case in point. Set in motion by the civil rights movement, the cycle gave rise to nominally separate movements on behalf of women, Chicanos, gays, students, Native Americans, and farm workers, to name but a fraction of the struggles we associate with those years.

The differences between a revolutionary and nonrevolutionary cycle, however, are not as great as they might seem. The only real difference concerns the strength of the state and its ability to weather the cycle. But in both cases we see an initiator movement setting the cycle in motion, thereby encouraging subsequent mobilization by any number of other groups. The revolution may blur the distinctions between these groups and our reified conception of social movements may exaggerate them in the case of nonrevolutionary cycles, but the underlying dynamics are essentially the same. The cycle begins with the successful mobilization of a single group and then spreads to others. To understand the dynamics of this spread we need a theory that focuses not on the emergence of a single movement but on the kinds of structural linkages and diffusion processes that encourage mimetic mobilization by other groups.

DIFFUSION AND THE RISE OF
DERIVATIVE MOVEMENTS

The appearance of a highly visible initiator movement significantly changes the dynamics of emergence for all groups who mobilize as part of the broader protest cycle. This includes countermovements no less than the ideologically compatible "family" of movements with which the cycle tends to be identified. The assumption of independence and movement-specific causal factors is simply untenable in the case of spin-off movements. This becomes clear when we seek to account for the rise of such movements on the basis of the three explanatory factors emphasized in the political process model. The most glaring disjuncture between the theory and this class of movements concerns the importance attributed to expanding political opportunities.

Political Opportunities

If political opportunities are crucial to the emergence of initiator movements, they would appear to be largely irrelevant in the rise of spin-off movements. By expanding political opportunities I mean *changes in either the institutional features or informal political alignments of a given political system that significantly reduce the power disparity between a given challenging group and the state*. Given this definition, one would be hard-pressed to document a significant expansion in political opportunities in the case of all—or even most—spin-off movements. There is one general exception to this statement. This concerns the extraordinary expansion in opportunities that accompanies *any* revolutionary cycle. In the case of revolutions, the old regime is so crippled by initiator movements—or what Tarrow (1994) calls "early risers"—as to leave it vulnerable to challenge by all manner of "latecomers."

In the case of reform cycles, however, there is no necessary increase in system vulnerability as regards all subsequent spin-off movements. Take the case of the American reform cycle of the 1960s. Much as those on the Left came to believe that the American state was on the verge of collapse in the late 1960s, a cursory look at various measures of fiscal and political stability would seem to support the opposite conclusion. The state remained strong throughout the period and generally invulnerable to most of the movements that proliferated in those years.

The gay rights movement affords a good example. The so-called Stonewall riot of June 1969 is typically credited with giving birth to the movement (D'Emilio and Freedman 1988). The riot developed when patrons of the Stonewall, a gay bar in Greenwich Village, fought back following a police raid on the premises. The movement developed quickly from that point, spawning a number of gay rights groups, but by the late 1970s had waned as an organized phenomenon.

It is hard to account for the rise of this movement on the basis of expanding political opportunities. It would be difficult to identify any specific change in the institutional features of the system that suddenly advantaged gays. Nor would it appear as if the movement benefited from any major political realignment during this era. In fact, the movement was preceded by a highly significant electoral realignment that can only be seen as disadvantageous to gays. I am referring, of course, to Richard Nixon's ascension to the White House in 1968, marking the end of a long period of liberal Democratic dominance in presidential politics. If anything, then, it would appear that the movement arose in a context of *contracting* political opportunities.

In general, there would seem to be a certain illogic to the argument that a reform cycle improves the bargaining leverage of *all* organized contenders. On the contrary, the demands of the initiator and other early-riser movements would seem to preclude much leverage for the latecomers. Certainly the history of the American protest cycle of the 1960s can be interpreted in this way, with the civil rights and other early-riser movements—principally the student, antiwar, and women's movements—garnering the lion's share of attention and significant victories and the latecomers— gay rights, antinuclear, American Indian movement, etc.—never really able to generate the public attention and leverage necessary for success. I cannot be certain that my interpretation is correct. But it is at least consistent with a more general suspicion that not all spin-off movements are necessarily advantaged by their embedding in a larger reform cycle. Specifically, I think there is good reason to think that those movements that arise fairly late in a reform cycle are disadvantaged by the necessity of having to confront a state that is already preoccupied with the substantive demands and political pressures generated by the early risers.

Finally, in arguing against the idea that protest cycles invariably render the affected political system vulnerable to challenge by *all* participating movements, I have steered clear of that special category of spin-off movements for whom the opportunities argument is clearly untenable. Here I have in mind those spin-off movements that develop in countries other than that of the initiator movement. The point is, despite our descriptive language (e.g., "the Italian protest cycle of the 1960s and 1970s"), protest cycles are not necessarily restricted by national boundaries. The generalized political turbulence that marked much of western Europe in 1847–48 is an obvious and instructive case in point. Most of the scholarly attention granted these years has been lavished on France and the Paris revolt of February 1848. But as Tarrow (1994: 61) notes, "No less French a historian than Halèvy would later assert that 'the revolution of 1848 did not arise from the Parisian barricades but from the Swiss civil war.'" Preliminary findings from an ongoing study of the links between the American and German student New Left of the 1960s support a similar conclusion. The rise of the German student movement would appear to owe as much to events in the U.S. as substantive political shifts within Germany (McAdam and Rucht 1993).

These two examples further undermine the causal primacy previously assigned to expanding political opportunities. In what conceivable way could the rise of the American student New Left have reduced the power disparity between the West German state and German college students? Initiator movements may help to spawn later struggles, but the impetus for this process would appear to be cognitive or cultural rather than narrowly political. That is, at least in the case of reform cycles, initiator movements encourage the rise of latecomers not so much by granting other groups increased leverage with which to press their claims, but by setting in motion complex diffusion processes by which the ideational, tactical, and organizational "lessons" of the early risers are made available to subsequent challengers.

Level of Organization

Spin-off movements are no less dependent on some rudimentary form of organization than are initiator movements. Quite often, however, it is the early risers who supply the crucial organizational context within which later movements develop. The empirical literature is rife with examples of this sort. So the women's rights movement that arose in the United States in the 1840s developed within established abolitionist groups. In similar fashion, Evans

(1980) shows clearly that it was associational networks forged in the southern civil rights movement and the New Left more generally that gave rise to the women's liberation movement. These examples serve merely to underscore the interdependence of movements that cluster in the same "family." Not only are such movements apt to lack any unique set of political opportunities, they are also likely, in the initial stages, to rely heavily on the organizational context and resources of earlier movements. This organizational or associational dependence makes sense in terms of the basic tenets of diffusion theory (Rogers 1983). Two tenets are especially relevant in this regard. First, diffusion tends to spread along the lines of established interpersonal communication. Second, "the higher the degree of social integration of potential adopters, the more likely and the sooner they will become actual adopters" (Pinard 1971: 187). If we begin to think of initiator movements as sources of new cultural items and latecomers as adopters of same, then these tenets help explain why spin-off movements are apt to develop within early risers or in groups with close ties to the early risers. The close ties increase the likelihood of diffusion and the ultimate adoption of early riser ideas and tactics by later movements. This argument is consistent with the conclusion reached in the previous section. The rise of an initiator movement may bear the imprint of expanding political opportunities, but the spread of a reform cycle would seem to owe to cultural, rather than political, processes.

Insurgent Consciousness and Framing Processes

It should be clear by now that I see the fundamental impulse to mobilization in the case of spin-off movements as essentially cognitive/cultural. This makes the third factor stressed in the political process model, namely the level of "insurgent consciousness" present in a given population, especially germane to an understanding of the rise of spin-off movements and the full flowering of a reform cycle. But it is in the development of this consciousness among the latecomers that the imprint of the early risers is most clearly evident.

At the level of cognition and affect, collective action depends on two socially shared and constructed perceptions: that some aspect of life is a) illegitimate, and b) subject to change through group (as opposed to individual) action. In a previous work (McAdam 1982) I used the term "cognitive liberation" to refer to the development of these twin perceptions. Dave Snow and various of his colleagues (Snow et al. 1986; Snow and Benford 1988, 1992) employ the twin concepts of "framing" and "frame alignment processes" to describe the kinds of strategic activities in which organizers engage in order to develop an insurgent consciousness. Movements, note Snow and Benford (1988: 198), are "actively engaged in the production of meaning for participants. . . . They *frame*, or assign meaning to and interpret, relevant events and conditions in ways that are intended to mobilize potential adherents." Finally, Gamson (1992) has sought to extend the framing concept by distinguishing between what he sees as the three principal components of any "collective action frame." Gamson labels these three components a) injustice frames, b) agency frames, and c) identity frames. Injustice frames define some aspect of life not simply as illegitimate but as affectively intolerable. Agency frames offer an account of how the group can effect change in the offending condition(s). And the identity frame offers the group an altered—often dramatically so—collective vision of itself.

The relevance of these conceptual tools for an understanding of spin-off movements and protest cycles comes from recognizing that the presence of a highly visible initiator movement makes the "framing work" of all later struggles much easier. To put the matter succinctly, among the most important impetuses to the development of a protest cycle is the diffusion and creative adaptation by latecomers of the ideas of the early risers. Snow and Benford (1992) advance a highly compatible argument in their work on "master protest frames." Two of their hypotheses are worth noting here. First, they argue that "associated with the emergence of a cycle of protest is the development or construction of an innovative master frame" (1992: 143). Second, they hypothesize that "movements that surface early in a cycle of protest are likely to function as progenitors of master frames that provide the ideational and interpretive anchoring for subsequent movements within the cycle" (1992: 144).

A cursory examination of the empirical literature on various protest cycles suggests that Snow and Benford are correct on both counts. Two examples will serve to illustrate these hypotheses. The first of these examples concerns the revolutions of 1988–91 that marked the end of communist rule throughout Eastern Europe. Animating this revolutionary cycle was what might be termed a "democracy/market economy" master frame. First developed in Poland, this frame stressed the importance of democratic governance, free markets, and the elimination of Party privilege as the keys to national renewal and rebirth.

The U.S. reform cycle of the 1960s and early 1970s also betrays the imprint of a dominant master frame. This was the "civil rights frame" first articulated by black activists during the heyday of the southern civil rights struggle. In short order, however, the frame was adapted by the majority of groups associated with the sixties' protest cycle. This would include students, gays, farm workers, feminists, the handicapped, and Native Americans. Nor did the frame lose all resonance with the end of the protest cycle. On the contrary, its imprint is clearly evident in a good many contemporary movements, including the animal rights crusade and the pro-life movement.

The case of the U.S. reform cycle of the 1960s and early 1970s will also help to illustrate the limits of the latecomers' cultural dependence on the early risers. In arguing that initiator movements have a culturally catalytic effect on later struggles, I am not claiming that the latter are mere adopters of the ideas of the early risers. Instead I want to underscore the role of latecomers as *creative adapters and interpreters of the cultural "lessons" of the early risers*. A cursory reading of the historical literature suggests wide variability in how closely spin-off movements adhere to the ideas of the initiator movement. In some cases latecomers borrow liberally from the broad cultural template associated with the early risers. More often, however, spin-off movements draw only the broadest inspiration from a given initiator movement, over time fashioning ideologies and specific cultural practices distinct from the movement(s) that set them in motion. Among the factors shaping variation in the cultural distinctiveness of latecomers is the extent to which the movement has access to a latent activist tradition or history of struggle that can serve as another "tool kit" into which the new generation of activists can dip for inspiration.

Here the important work of Rupp and Taylor (1987) on the continuities between earlier feminist organizing and the emergence— or reemergence—of the U.S. women's movement in the 1960s is relevant. At first glance, the kind of continuities that Rupp and

Taylor document in their work would seem to undermine the very notion of initiator and spin-off movements. If certain enduring struggles ebb and flow over time, how can later periods of intense activity be characterized as "spin-offs" of other contemporary struggles?

In point of fact, I think the perspective sketched here is highly compatible with the idea of continuities. Consistent with Rupp and Taylor's argument, my view is that enduring movements such as feminism never really die, but rather are characterized by periods of relative activity and inactivity. Moreover, I am increasingly persuaded that movement leaders and organizations are most critical to the struggle not during the peak of a protest cycle, but rather during what Rupp and Taylor term the "doldrums." During the "lean years" career activists and the formal organizations and informal networks they maintain serve a critically important "keeper of the flame" function. That is, they serve to maintain and nourish a tradition of activism, making it available to a new generation of activists during the next protest cycle.

Thus the perspective sketched here in no way diminishes or denies the importance of the kind of continuities noted by Rupp and Taylor. It only argues that these continuities, while safeguarding a tradition of struggle, cannot account for the timing and extent of the next wave of mobilization. So, for example, the emergence of the women's liberation movement cannot be explained on the basis of the continuities detailed by Rupp and Taylor in their book. As Evans (1980) convincingly demonstrates, the development of this specific spin-off movement owed primarily to the kind of network linkages and diffusion dynamics under discussion here. What the continuities did, however, was provide 1960s feminists with a rich history of struggle that ultimately reduced their cultural dependence on the civil rights movement and other early risers in the sixties' reform cycle. While feminists—especially radical feminists—were attuned to the ideological, tactical, and organizational lessons of the New Left, they also soon rediscovered and sought to adapt the sedimented layers of a rich tradition of feminist struggle to the contemporary movement.

Diffusion, Network Ties, and the
Attribution of Similarity

My attempt to apply the political process model to spin-off movements tells us much about their dependence on an initiator movement. Specifically, spin-off movements often develop within the formal organizations or associational networks of an earlier movement, while also appropriating and adapting elements of its collective action frame. But this tells us little about the *process* by which these borrowings take place. I turn to these dynamics of process in this section, emphasizing three concepts in turn: diffusion, network proximity, and the attribution of similarity.

1. Diffusion The relevance of the diffusion literature to the study of protest cycles would seem to be obvious. At one level initiator movements are nothing more than clusters of new cultural items— new cognitive frames, behavioral routines, organizational forms, tactical repertoires, etc.—subject to the same diffusion dynamics as other innovations. Yet the movement literature has been distinguished by the virtual absence of any explicit application of diffusion theory.

To be sure, early theorizing emphasized the role of "contagion" in the spread of collective behavior (Tarde 1903). Later work in the collective behavior tradition proposed various mechanisms, including suggestibility, circular reasoning, and simple imitation, to account for the mimetic quality of much collective action. All of these approaches, however, betray a psychologistic bias and are guilty of ascribing to social movements (and all other forms of collective behavior) the status of a unique behavioral phenomenon governed by sociological processes distinct from "normal" behavior.

Diffusion theory makes no such assumption, nor does it depend upon any implicit notion of the irrationality of the crowd to account for the spread of collective action. Instead, the diffusion of the ideational and material elements of a given movement are thought to reflect normal learning and influence processes as mediated by the network structures of everyday social life.

2. Network Ties Despite the lack of explicit attention to the diffusion literature, much of the recent work on the emergence and spread of collective action can be readily interpreted in terms of diffusion theory. The oft-noted role of existing organizations or associational networks in the emergence of collective action is entirely consistent with the stress in the diffusion literature on the importance of strong, established networks of communication as a precondition for diffusion (Freeman 1973; Kriesi 1988; McAdam 1982; Morris 1984; Oberschall 1973; Zurcher and Kirkpatrick 1976). Empirical accounts of the growth of various movements also fit with the importance attributed to "weak bridging ties" in the diffusion literature. Numerous studies have shown that movements typically spread by means of diffuse networks of weak bridging ties or die for lack of such ties (Jackson et al. 1960; McAdam 1988; Oppenheimer 1989).

In short, there is a marked convergence in the empirical literatures on diffusion and the emergence and spread of collective action. Indeed, these two literatures tell the same story: the likelihood and extent of both diffusion and collective action is conditioned by the network properties of the subject population. The chances of either occurring would seem to be greatest in communities having both a dense network of internal ties as well as an extensive system of weak bridging ties to other social and/ or geographic units. This confluence of strong internal ties and weak bridging ties is, thus, one of the conditions that facilitates the development of a protest cycle. Groups with direct links to the initiating movement are especially likely to be early risers in the cycle and then to provide additional points of network contact for other groups who, in turn, provide access for still more groups. This pattern helps explain the accelerating speed at which protest cycles tend to develop. As more groups mobilize, more and more of the overall population is exposed to the behavioral, ideational, and material innovations associated with the cycle. As a result, ever more diverse population segments are likely to be drawn into the cycle.

3. *Attribution of Similarity* To this point, I have merely applied the basic tenets of diffusion theory to the phenomenon of the protest cycle. Spin-off movements are conceived of as adopters or, more accurately, adapters of some subset of the innovations associated with the early risers. Moreover, following diffusion theory, we can expect the likelihood and timing of adoption to be mediated by the strength of the ties linking a potential adopter to an early riser.

But while network proximity may dispose a group to mobilize, it hardly guarantees that they will do so. What we lack to this point is any sense of the social psychological processes that trigger the adoption process. Here I draw upon the recent work of David Strang and John Meyer (1992) on cross-national diffusion of policy innovations. Strang and Meyer argue that in such cases diffusion is keyed by a process of social construction in which the adopters define both themselves and the situation they face as essentially similar to that of the innovators. In turn, this fundamental "attribution of similarity" makes the actions and ideas of the innovator relevant to the adopter. Thus in identifying themselves ("identity frame") and the problem at hand ("injustice frame") with that of the initiator movement, latecomers set the stage for a more general diffusion process by which any number of cultural elements may be borrowed from the original movement.

The American protest cycle of the 1960s and 1970s affords numerous examples of this fundamental identification of latecomers with the movement that triggered the cycle: the civil rights struggle. Indeed, it would be fair to say that the oppression of blacks came to serve as the standard and model by which other groups sought to understand their own situations. For some groups the analogy was straightforward. In particular, other nonwhite minorities such as Hispanics and Native Americans found it relatively easy to map their plights and demands onto those offered by black activists. For other groups, the analogy demanded more in the way of creative framing. Drawing upon their experiences as civil rights workers, early radical feminists tentatively voiced comparisons between their situation and that of southern blacks. The first to do so were Casey Hayden and Mary King, two field secretaries for the Student Non-violent Coordinating Committee. Writing in 1966, Hayden and King argued that, just like blacks, women

> seem to be caught up in a common-law caste system that operates, sometimes subtly, forcing them to work around or outside hierarchical structures of power which exclude them. Women seem to be placed in the same position of assumed subordination in personal situations too. (Hayden and King, 1966: 36)

In later years the comparison of women to blacks was starkly captured in the movement saying "Women are the niggers of the world" and has remained a staple of American feminist thought to the present.

Perhaps the most surprising and consequential effort to appropriate the model of black oppression was that made by student activists of the period. Most observers date the beginnings of the student movement to the Free Speech Movement at Berkeley in the fall of 1964. What has never been fully appreciated is the extent to which the Berkeley movement was fueled by a strong identification of the students with southern blacks. At the height of the movement its acknowledged leader, Mario Savio, gave explicit voice to this identification.

> Last summer I went to Mississippi to join the struggle there for civil rights. This fall I am engaged in another phase of the *same* struggle, this time at Berkeley. The two battlefields may seem quite different to some observers, but this is not the case. The *same* rights are at stake in both places—the right to participate as citizens in democratic society and the right to due process of law. Further, it is a struggle against the *same* enemy. In Mississippi an autocratic and powerful minority rules, through organized violence, to suppress the vast, virtually powerless majority. In California, the privileged minority manipulates the University bureaucracy to suppress the student's political expression. (Quoted in McAdam 1988: 168–69; emphasis added)

These last two cases—women's liberation and the student movement—are important not merely as illustrations of the close identification of spin-off with initiator movements but also for the important function they ascribe to bridging ties in helping to cement this identification. A disproportionate number of the pioneering activists in both movements had been active in the civil rights struggle. These links insured that the pioneers were aware of movement ideas and that they had also been exposed to a process of socialization in which longtime civil rights workers encouraged them to see the connections between the plight of blacks and "the sources of oppression in [their] own lives."

Direct ties are important, then, for the role they play in helping to encourage the kind of fundamental identification of latecomers with early risers that is necessary for diffusion to take place. This does not mean that identification is impossible in the absence of direct ties. Especially in the later stages of a cycle, groups lacking any real connection to an established movement may well mobilize. By that point the general model or template for organizing is so generally available that the process of adoption often takes on a more diffuse character. Early in a cycle, however, direct ties would appear to be highly correlated with the timing and extent of mobilization.

PROTEST CYCLES AND THE DIFFUSION
OF ACTION REPERTOIRES

The perspective sketched here on diffusion and the rise of spin-off movements is relevant not only to an understanding of protest cycles but also to the emergence and spread of what Tilly has called "repertoires of contention." Repertoires are the learned forms of collective action by which actors seek to press or resist claims by other actors. In short, they are the tactics groups employ in their struggles with one another. Moreover, as Tilly notes in his piece for this volume, these tactical forms tend to be fairly restricted at any given moment within a particular society. He writes:

> Repertoires are learned cultural creations, but they do not descend from abstract philosophy or take shape as a result of political propaganda; they emerge from struggle. People learn to break windows in protest, attack pilloried prisoners, tear down dishonored houses, stage public marches, petition, hold formal meetings, organize special-interest associations. At any particular point in history, however, they learn only a rather small number of alternative ways to act collectively. (p. 25)

Drawing on the perspective sketched here, Tilly's remarks can be extended in two important ways. The pace of the "cultural creation" he speaks of tends to be most rapid during cycles of protest. Indeed, we often know a protest cycle by the innovative tactical forms to which it gives rise. Second, the learning of these repertoires tends to conform to the diffusion dynamics sketched above. Let me elaborate on each of these points, beginning with the second.

As noted above, the identification of a latecomer with an early riser tends to key a more thoroughgoing diffusion process in which the latecomer is receptive to all manner of innovations associated with the initiator movement. These may include new organizational forms, collective action frames, material cultural items, and, most important from our point of view, innovative tactical forms. From the point of view of the latecomer, the adoption of these repertoires is entirely consistent with their generalized identification with the early riser. Having defined themselves and their situation as essentially similar to that of another movement, the decision to make use of the other's tactics makes both expressive and instrumental sense.

The instrumental logic underlying the adoption should be clear. If the latecomers see themselves as confronting the same underlying problem as the early risers, it only makes sense that they would employ the same means for remedying the problem as the initiator movement, especially if the latter's use of the repertoire(s) has been defined as successful.

The expressive function of the adoption of tactical forms has rarely, if ever, been acknowledged, but is no less important in helping to account for the rapid spread and signature quality of novel repertoires during a protest cycle. Especially during the early stages of a cycle, the tactical choices made by challenging groups express their identification with the earliest of risers and signal a more inclusive and broader definition of the emerging struggle. In retrospect, scholars may see a cycle—especially a reform cycle—as a cluster of $6, 7, 8 \ldots n$ discrete movements, but this view almost invariably distorts the perspective shared by participants at the time. In their view, they are but a part of a broad and rapidly expanding political-cultural community fighting the same fight on a number of related fronts. And a significant part of what links and defines these various groups as a coherent community is their reliance on the same tactical forms.

This mix of expressive and instrumental motives largely accounts for the close association of certain repertoires with particular cycles. So, for example, we know the European revolts of 1847–48 by the widespread use of the barricade; the American protest cycle of the 1960s by its signature tactic, the sit-in; and the Velvet Revolutions of 1988–89 by the rapid spread of mass demonstrations in countries that previously had lacked even the semblance of a public. Repertoires, then, are properly viewed as among the key cultural innovations whose diffusion gives the protest cycle its characteristic shape and momentum. In this sense they are also indispensable to our understanding of the rise of spin-off movements.

CONCLUSION

I am now in a position to translate these various ideas into a fairly simple model of reform cycles. First and foremost, a reform cycle depends on the emergence and subsequent development of a highly prominent and apparently successful initiator movement. The presence of such a movement sets up the minimum condition necessary for diffusion. Whether or not diffusion takes place, however, depends more on the strength of the structural ties linking the movement to other groups in society than to the prominence or success it attains. To the extent that the movement remains isolated from other population segments, it is not apt to encourage the rise of the spin-off movements that constitute a reform cycle. On the other hand, should the movement succeed in forging ties to other groups, we can expect some subset of these groups to mobilize and, in turn, to encourage another round of mimetic mobilization by still more groups.

The importance of these ties is only partly informational. Obviously, such ties make available to potential adopters the various innovations—collective action frames, new organizational forms, new tactics, etc.—emanating from the movement. However, access to new ideas or other innovations means little if one attaches no salience or relevance to them. The real significance of these ties, then, stems from the role they play in encouraging the fundamental "attribution of similarity" so crucial to the diffusion process. Direct contact with the initiator movement helps to cement a basic identification that keys a thoroughgoing process of diffusion by which the ideational, organizational, and, most relevant for us, *tactical* "lessons" of the "borning struggle" are adapted for use by subsequent movements.

REFERENCES

Arjomand, Said Amir (1988) The Turban for the Crown: The Islamic Revolution in Iran. New York: Oxford University Press.
della Porta, Donatella, and Dieter Rucht (1991) "Left-libertarian movements in context: A comparison of Italy and West Germany, 1965–1990." Discussion paper FS III, Wissenschaftszentrum Berlin.
D'Emilio, John, and Estelle Freedman (1988) Intimate Matters: A History of Sexuality in America. New York: Harper and Row.
Evans, Sara (1980) Personal Politics. New York: Vintage Books.

Freeman, Jo (1973) "The origins of the women's liberation movement." American Journal of Sociology 78: 792–811.

Gamson, William (1992) Talking Politics. New York: Oxford University Press.

Goldstone, Jack (1991) Revolution and Rebellion in the Early Modern World. Berkeley: University of California Press.

Hayden, Casey, and Mary King (1966) "Sex and caste: A kind of memo." Liberation 10 (April): 35–36.

Jackson, Maurice, Eleanora Petersen, James Bull, Sverre Monsen, and Patricia Richmond (1960) "The failure of an incipient social movement." Pacific Sociological Review 3: 35–40.

Kriesi, Hanspeter (1988) "Local mobilization for the people's petition of the Dutch peace movement," in Bert Klandermans, Hanspeter Kriesi, and Sidney Tarrow (eds.) From Structure to Action: Comparing Social Movement Research across Cultures. Greenwich, CT: JAI Press: 41–81.

Lang, Kurt, and Gladys Engel Lang (1961) Collective Dynamics. New York: Thomas Crowell.

McAdam, Doug (1982) Political Process and the Development of Black Insurgency, 1930–1970. Chicago: University of Chicago Press.

——— (1988) Freedom Summer. New York: Oxford University Press.

McAdam, Doug, and Dieter Rucht (1993) "The cross-national diffusion of movement ideas." Annals 528: 56–74.

McCarthy, John D., and Mayer N. Zald (1973) The Trend of Social Movements in America: Professionalization and Resource Mobilization. Morristown, NJ: General Learning Press.

——— (1977) "Resource mobilization and social movements: A partial theory." American Journal of Sociology 82: 1212–41.

Melucci, Alberto (1980) "The new social movements: A theoretical approach." Social Science Information 19: 199–226.

Morris, Aldon (1984) The Origins of the Civil Rights Movement: Black Communities Organizing for Change. New York: Free Press.

Oberschall, Anthony (1973) Social Conflict and Social Movements. Englewood Cliffs, NJ: Prentice-Hall.

Oppenheimer, Martin (1989) The Sit-in Movement of 1960. Brooklyn, NY: Carlson Publishing, Inc.

Pinard, Maurice (1971) The Rise of a Third Party: A Study in Crisis Politics. Englewood Cliffs, NJ: Prentice-Hall.

Rogers, Everett M. (1983) Diffusion of Innovations. 3d ed. New York: Free Press.

Rupp, Leila, and Verta Taylor (1987) Survival in the Doldrums: The American Women's Rights Movement. New York: Oxford University Press.

Skocpol, Theda (1979) States and Social Revolutions. New York: Cambridge University Press.

Smelser, Neil (1962) Theory of Collective Behavior. New York: Free Press.

Snow, David A., and Robert D. Benford (1988) "Ideology, frame resonance, and participant mobilization," in Bert Klandermans, Hanspeter Kriesi, and Sidney Tarrow (eds.) From Structure to Action: Comparing Social Movement Research across Cultures. Greenwich, CT: JAI Press: 197–219.

——— (1992) "Master frames and cycles of protest," in Aldon D. Morris and

Carol McClurg Mueller (eds.) Frontiers in Social Movement Theory. New Haven: Yale University Press: 133–55.

Snow, David A., E. Burke Rochford, Jr., Steven K. Worden, and Robert D. Benford (1986) "Frame alignment processes, micromobilization, and movement participation." American Sociological Review 51: 464–81.

Strang, David, and John W. Meyer (1991) "Institutional conditions for diffusion." Paper delivered at the Workshop on New Institutional Theory, Ithaca, New York, November 1991.

Tarde, Gabriel (1903) The Laws of Imitation. New York: Holt, Rinehart & Winston.

Tarrow, Sidney (1983) Struggling to Reform: Social Movements and Policy Change During Cycles of Protest. Cornell University, Western Societies Paper #15.

———— (1989) Democracy and Disorder: Protest and Politics in Italy, 1965–1975. New York: Oxford University Press.

———— (1994) Power in Movement: Social Movements, Collective Action, and Mass Politics in the Modern State. New York: Cambridge University Press.

Tilly, Charles (1977) "Getting together in Burgundy." Theory and Society 4: 479–504.

———— (1978) From Mobilization to Revolution. Reading, MA: Addison-Wesley.

Touraine, Alain (1981) The Voice and the Eye: An Analysis of Social Movements. Cambridge: Cambridge University Press.

Turner, Ralph, and Lewis Killian (1987) Collective Behavior. 3d ed. Englewood Cliffs, NJ: Prentice-Hall.

Zurcher, Louis A., and R. George Kirkpatrick (1976) Citizens for Decency: Antipornography Crusades as Status Defense. Austin: University of Texas Press.

Index

Repertoires
  action/instrumental, 5–6, 75–78
  changes in, 33–37
  of collective action, 2–3, 26,
    27–29, 43–46
  of contention, 26–30
  definitions of, 26, 59, 91–92,
    97, 166–67, 235
  diffusion and, 235–36
  discursive/expressive, 59–61,
    65, 68–75, 77–78
  innovation in, 27–28, 156, 165
  interaction, importance of, 4,
    12, 27, 30, 60
  magnitude/intensity of action,
    152–53, 159–60
  and modernization theory,
    28–29
  and political protest, 154, 157,
    158
  Tilly on, 3, 43–46
  Traugott on, 4
  types of, 145
Repression/popular-protest para-
    dox, 7–8, 117–19
  Central American reality,
    124–30
  political cycle explanation,
    130–34
  rational individualist explana-
    tion, 119–24
Republicanism, American, 190
Resource mobilization perspec-
    tive, 220
Revel, Jacques, 3–4
*Revolution and Rebellion in the
    Early Modern World*
    (Goldstone), 53
Revolutions
  differences between revolution-
    ary and nonrevolutionary
    cycles, 223
  initiator movements and, 222

Ricardo, David, 58
Rice, Japanese reforms and price
    of, 147–59
Roehl, W., 118
Romanticism, 197, 199
Rose, Anne, 182
Ross, Steven J., 190
Rudé, George, 9, 28, 93
Rupp, Leila, 229–30
Ryan, Mary, 182

St. Matthew's Bethnal Green
    parish, 61
Savio, Mario, 234
Schlafley, Phyllis, 187–88
Seize, the 48
"Self-reduction" campaigns (*auto-
    riduzione*), 7, 107–8,
    109
Sewell, William H., Jr., 4, 46–47,
    52, 53
Shelley, Mary, 197
Shelley, Percy Bysshe, 197
Shorter, Edward
  concept of the protest cycle and,
    93
  data on rate of violence and
    collective action in France,
    92–93
Silk weavers, and Spitalfields,
    5–6, 57–59, 61–65
Simmel, Georg, 196
Sinclair, George, 20
*The Sixties: Years of Hope, Days of
    Rage* (Gitlin), 96
Skidmore, Thomas, 190
Skocpol, Theda, 222
Smith, Adam, 73, 74
Snow, David A., 228
Social conflict, repertoires of
    contention and, 153, 157,
    158